SECOND EDITION

Intentional Interviewing and Counseling
Facilitating Client Development

SECOND EDITION

Intentional Interviewing and Counseling
Facilitating Client Development

Allen E. Ivey

University of Massachusetts

Illustrated by Zig Kapelis

Brooks/Cole Publishing Company
Pacific Grove, California

Brooks/Cole Publishing Company
A Division of Wadsworth, Inc.

Printed in the United States of America

10 9 8 7 6 5

Library of Congress Cataloging-in-Publication Data
Ivey, Allen E.
    Intentional interviewing and counseling.

    Includes bibliographies and indexes.
    1. Interviewing.   2. Counseling.   I. Title.
BF637.I5I93   1987   158'.3   87-12076
ISBN 0-534-08796-5 (pbk.)

Sponsoring Editor: *Claire Verduin*
Editorial Associate: *Linda Ruth Wright*
Production Editor: *Phyllis Larimore*
Production Associate: *Dorothy Bell*
Manuscript Editor: *Pamela Evans*
Permissions Editor: *Carline Haga*
Interior Design: *Sharon L. Kinghan*
Cover Design and Illustration: *David Aguero*
Art Coordinator: *Lisa Torri*
Interior Illustration: *Patricia Little*
Typesetting: *Omegatype Typography, Inc., Champaign, Illinois*
Cover Printing: *The Lehigh Press Company, Pennsauken, New Jersey*
Printing and Binding: *Malloy Lithographing, Inc., Ann Arbor, Michigan*

CREDITS

To Dwight W. Allen

originator of the microteaching framework,
personal inspiration, tuba player, and dear friend.

Preface

This is a practical book committed to a detailed examination of what makes the interview work. It presents skills, concepts, and methods that are designed to help the reader develop concrete competencies. Once equipped with the necessary skills developed in the first half of the book, interviewers, counselors, and therapists can then examine their own interviewing styles. Finally the text shows how personal style and interviewing competencies may be related to four major approaches of helping: person-centered, decisional, assertiveness training, and psychoeducational skills training.

By the time the reader successfully completes this book, he or she will be able to:

1. Identify and demonstrate basic listening and influencing skills necessary in an interview
2. Conduct an interview using only listening skills
3. Engage in basic decisional counseling and assertiveness training
4. Conduct an interview that facilitates client development and measure client developmental change both during and after the interview
5. Utilize attending and listening skills as part of an educational treatment program for clients

Intentional Interviewing and Counseling: Facilitating Client Development is designed for introductory courses in interviewing skills, counseling theory and practice, and for practica. It provides a system for planning the interview, analyzing counselor behavior, and determining developmental impact on the client.

With its new developmental focus, the second edition of *Intentional Interviewing* should also be useful to advanced students and professionals who wish to examine the integration of developmental theory into the counseling and therapeutic interview.

▲ Features New to the Second Edition

The microtraining hierarchy of skills and concepts is basic to this book. Experience and practice with the model has led to some new organizational features in the second edition. An increased emphasis on the basic listening sequence and the five-stage interactional model of the interview are perhaps the most significant among them.

Skill units are grouped more clearly in this edition. Research evidence indicates that students will learn skills and retain them better if they are grouped into meaningful categories. I have found that students express considerable satisfaction about their ability to engage in a well-structured interview with a real or role-played client when they are only halfway through the book. This provides a solid foundation for mastering the more complex skills that follow.

Perhaps the most innovative change in the second edition is my expansion of the material on confrontation, which is now found in Chapter 8. This material is complex and some instructors may prefer to cover this chapter later in the course or to go over it quickly and then return to it later in more depth. In my experience, confrontation is so important that interviewers need to practice it again and again. Exercises in later chapters of the book now provide this opportunity.

Equally important in these reorganized chapters is a new emphasis on integrating developmental assessment and theory into the interview. Development may be described as the aim of counseling and therapy. The developmental therapy and counseling fields provide very specific ways to integrate developmental theory into the helping process. Consequently, it is now possible to use intervention to facilitate *developmental change* in clients.

The work of the Swiss developmental psychologist Jean Piaget is particularly important to the integration of counseling and development. In my recent book, *Developmental Therapy* (San Francisco: Jossey-Bass, 1986), I point out how developmental concepts may be integrated into the interviewing process. The developmental concepts presented here are derived from that discussion of Piaget's developmental concepts and their applications in therapy.

The *Confrontation Impact Scale* (a shortened, less complex version of a similar scale used in *Developmental Therapy*) is also new, and it will help students think through and determine how well the client has responded to their interventions.

Another concept behind the second edition is that teaching skills via the psychoeducational model is, in itself, a helpful intervention. A variety of exercises show students how to integrate the teaching of skills, particularly listening skills, into their own interviewing practice. Experience reveals that clients who lack social skills benefit particularly from learning listening skills. Parent education, management workshops, peer counseling training, self-help groups, and telephone hot-line volunteers are only a sample of the settings in which the skills and concepts of this book can be used.

I have also found this book to be effective in advanced graduate courses when paired with another book that emphasizes human developmental processes. Another approach is to pair it with *Counseling and Psychotherapy* (Ivey, Ivey, and Simek-Downing, Englewood Cliffs, N.J.: Prentice-Hall, 1987), or any other basic theory text, thus integrating practice with theory.

▲ Teaching Aids

An instructor's manual with teaching suggestions and multiple-choice questions is available from Brooks/Cole. Overhead transparency masters for use in workshops or classes are available as well. In addition, videotapes illustrating the several microskills discussed in the book are available from Microtraining Associates, Box 641, North Amherst, Massachusetts, 01059. The *Microtraining Newsletter*, a yearly publication, is also available at the same address.

▲ Acknowledgments

Robert Marx and Joseph Litterer, my colleagues and friends at the University of Massachusetts School of Management, have been central to the development of this book for ten years. Discussions with Otto Payton and Viktor Frankl have clarified the important concepts of reflection of meaning. William Matthews has been especially helpful in my formulation of the five-stage model of the interview. Conversations with Mary Bradford Ivey, Terry Anderson, Ursula Delworth, Lois Grady, and Kenneth Blanchard were important in establishing the spherical developmental model presented here. Lia and Zig Kapelis of Flinders University and Adelaide University are thanked for their support and participation while I served as Senior Fulbright Scholar in South Australia.

The interview transcripts in the book were generated in cooperation with Robert Marx and Mary Bradford Ivey. All interviews are role-plays and have been edited to clarify certain points, but are essentially close to the originals.

Reviewers who offered suggestions for improvement and criticisms of the manuscript were Terry Anderson, Fraser Valley College; Margaret Armitage, Howard Community College; George Armstrong, Bucks County Community College; Harold Engen, University of Iowa; Carol Gross, Southern Illinois University; Linda O'Daniel, Pan American University; Richard Percy, Peabody College of Vanderbilt University; and Fred Stickle, Western Kentucky University.

The skills and concepts of this book rely on the work of many different individuals over the past 22 years, notably Eugene Oetting, Dean Miller, Cheryl Normington, Richard Haase, Max Uhlemann, and Weston Morrill at Colorado State University, who were there at the inception of the microtraining framework. The following have been especially important personally and professionally in the growth of microcounseling and microtraining over the years: Norma Gluckstern, Jeanne Phillips, John Moreland, Jerry Authier, David Evans, Margaret Hearn, Lynn Simek-Downing, Dwight Allen, Paul and Anne Pedersen, Lanette Shizuru, Derald Sue, Steve Rollin, Bruce Oldershaw, Machiko Fukuhara, and Bertil Bratt. I feel rich and lucky in their support. John Ivey was central to this process from the beginning, contributing consultation, editing, and many suggestions for revision. Many of my "585" students at the University also contributed in important ways through their reactions, questions, and suggestions.

Finally, it is always a pleasure to work with the group at Brooks/Cole, notably with Claire Verduin, Linda Wright, Phyllis Larimore, Sharon Kinghan, and Lisa Torri.

I thank all of the above. We all build on the past and on our relations with significant people.

Allen E. Ivey

Contents

Before You Start

▲ What Does This Book Offer for Your Development?

My first courses in counseling were fascinating. I enjoyed the theoretical ideas and the information about testing and vocations, but what I enjoyed most was the course on theories of counseling. To me, this was what the whole process was about.

But then came the second semester and my first real opportunity to work with clients. I found myself overwhelmed by the amount of information brought to me by troubled and concerned people. The theories in the books on interviewing didn't apply easily and directly to the immediate problems of the interview. How was I to survive and help people? Somehow I survived, but to this day I am not sure if some of those early clients benefited much from my work with them.

This book is about clarifying the interviewing process so you can enter the interview with specific skills, competencies, and concepts that give you a place to start. If you can take the ideas you learn from this book and use them in your interviewing practice with specific effects, the book will have provided you with a base on which to build your own natural style of helping. While many concepts and ideas may be found in this book, the following objectives are important in that they call for specific results that you can anticipate. By working through the reading and practice sessions of this book you may expect to be able to do the following:

1. Engage in many basic skills of the interview: listening, influencing, and structuring an effective session.
2. Conduct a full interview using only listening skills.
3. Analyze with considerable precision your own natural style of helping and its impact on clients.
4. Master a basic structure of the interview that can be applied to many different theories. Specifically, you may expect to be able to engage in a decisional interview, a person-centered interview, and a behavioral assertiveness-training session.
5. Learn a new developmentally oriented theory and practice of interviewing and counseling that can be used to assess the immediate effectiveness of your interventions with a client.

Before you begin reading, let's review together the central concepts and features of this book.

Natural Style

I used to think there was a "right way" to help another person. I no longer believe that. I have found again and again that my natural approach and style works for me, though not always for someone else. This has led me to encourage beginning counselors and interviewers to look to themselves and their natural styles and strengths. "Natural style" may be described as your original and "natural" way of helping people *before* you undertake formal training in interviewing and counseling. The ideas in this book can increase your competence and possibilities for effective interviewing, but you should select those ideas that appeal most to *you*.

At the same time, you will eventually find out that your natural style doesn't work with everyone you talk to. If you wish to reach more people, you may want to try an alternative approach to supplement your own approach. But again, add only what fits naturally.

Audiotapes, Videorecordings, and Practice

This book is oriented toward a *practical* approach to counseling and interviewing. Each concept and communication skill must be practiced if it is to be truly useful.

My first recommendation is that you purchase an inexpensive audiotape recorder. This is one of the necessary tools of the trade. You'll need frequent practice and audiotape feedback if you are to master the skills at the highest level and become an effective interviewer.

Videotape is an even better tool. It is increasingly available in many homes, colleges, schools, and community settings. Try to see yourself as others see you at least once during the time you work with this book.

Each chapter includes a variety of practice exercises. To really learn something from this book, you should practice these concepts in small groups and use them in your daily life.

Mastering the Concepts of Basic Intentional Interviewing

The practice exercises in each chapter provide specific ways you can master the concepts of the chapter, use them in the interview, and, finally, teach them to others.

Four levels of mastery are identified in each chapter, and you'll have to decide which level of competence you want to reach with each skill or concept.

▲ *Level 1: Identification.* The most elementary mastery of the skills requires the ability to identify and classify interviewing behavior. Most often this will be done by observing others' behavior in a practice session or through an examination.

▲ *Level 2: Basic mastery*. This involves being able to perform the skills in an interview—for example, demonstrating that you can use both open and closed questioning, even though you may not use the skills at a high level.

▲ *Level 3: Active mastery*. Intentional interviewing demands that you have a variety of skills that you can use for specific purposes. For example, attending behavior skills should increase client talk-time in the interview, while the lack of them usually reduces client talk. Active mastery means that you can produce specific client results from your interviewing leads and behavior.

▲ *Level 4: Teaching mastery*. One way to achieve deeper mastery of a skill is to teach that skill to someone else. Other people who wish to learn about the interview can profit from your teaching them specific skills. In addition, many clients can gain from being taught skills of interviewing, which are simply effective communication skills.

As you move through this book, you will assess your level of mastery of the concepts. Full mastery occurs when you can recognize skills, use them in the interview with specific client impact, and also teach them to others. This book is designed for beginning helpers who wish only a brief introduction to helping skills, as well as for experienced counselors and therapists who may wish to advance their expertise to new levels of mastery.

If you are just beginning work in the study of helping, aim to master Levels 1 and 2. In most courses, students are expected to be able to write about and discuss the concepts—and this is most often assessed via an examination. Mastery Level 1—identification—requires the reader to identify and understand the more than 100 basic concepts of the interview presented in this book. However, you will find Level 2—basic mastery—equally or more important than identification and understanding. To demonstrate basic mastery, you will want to practice the interview in role-play sessions. The goal of this book is to provide you with usable and useful skills central to the helping process.

For those of you who are more experienced helpers, and as you develop further in the helping profession, you will want to seek to develop Level 3—active mastery. At this level, you will demonstrate your ability to produce predictable results in your clients. Active mastery requires the ability to anticipate clients' needs and responses and to use a variety of skills and concepts to facilitate client development and growth. Undoubtedly, you will develop active mastery of some concepts and ideas in this book. But few people, even those with considerable experience, are able to demonstrate active mastery of all the concepts presented here. Thus, it is suggested that you use this book as a long-term frame of reference to which you can return, whatever your level of expertise.

Experienced helpers will also want to focus on active mastery and the teaching of skills to clients. You will find that many of the concepts of this book are useful to clients. The skills of counseling and interviewing are basically skills of effective communication; most clients can profit from learning how to talk more effectively with others. For example, some clients are poor listeners—these can benefit from your teaching them listening skills such as questioning or paraphrasing. Other clients lack assertiveness and may benefit from learning about focusing or the skilled use of feedback.

As you mature in the helping professions, you may want to teach groups of parents, community workers, or helping volunteers (for example, Scout leaders, church workers, telephone hot-line workers) some of the skills in this book. The Appendix provides guidelines and suggestions for teaching individuals and groups the basic skills of communication and interviewing.

▲ The Structure of the Book

You will find this book divided into four major sections. The first (Chapters 1 and 2) introduces key constructs, the next (Chapters 3 through 7) focuses on basic listening skills, the third (Chapters 8 through 11) introduces the advanced skills, and the fourth (Chapters 12 and 13) addresses skill integration. Most individual chapters focus on one specific skill or skill area of the interview. Chapter 1 presents the basic concepts of the book. Chapters 2 through 6, which develop the solid foundation of listening skills, are organized as follows:

▲ *Introduction.* The skill is introduced and defined briefly. An exercise designed to make the skill personally meaningful to you is presented.
▲ *Transcript.* An example interview demonstrates the skill in action.
▲ *Instructional reading.* The single skill or skill area is elaborated with more applications and details.
▲ *Key points of the chapter.* The major points of the chapter are summarized. Included here are the functions of the skill in the interview, what the skill is, how it may be used effectively, and with whom.
▲ *Practice exercises and self-assessment.* The all-important practice follows that will enable you to identify, use, and teach the skill. This feature includes the following:

1. *Individual practice.* Can you identify the presence or absence of the skill? A short series of practice-and-observation exercises will provide the opportunity to test your ability to understand the central aspects of behavior.
2. *Systematic group practice.* Practice by yourself is a good beginning, but you will need to work with someone else in a role-play interview if you are to obtain precise feedback on your attending skills. (If no group is available, adapt the systematic practice exercises for practice with a friend or family member.) Each chapter includes a *feedback form* you can use to observe the behavior of others (or yourself) in the interview.
3. *Self-assessment and follow-up.* At the conclusion of the chapter you'll find a self-assessment form where you can evaluate your performance on this skill and assess its value to you.

Chapter 7 provides you with an especially important exercise. You will be expected to conduct a complete interview using listening skills only. After mastering this basic understanding and ability, you will be able to encounter and understand more advanced concepts presented in the final sections of the book. Furthermore, demonstrating that you can conduct a successful interview using only listening skills reflects what is perhaps the most important guideline of this book: when in doubt about what to do with a client, *listen*.

The more complex skills of confrontation and assessing a client's developmental level are presented in Chapter 8. The ideas in this chapter are perhaps the most difficult of the book. It is suggested that you focus first on understanding the concept of confrontation and second on using listening skills to confront the client. The developmental concepts and the advanced use of confrontation will take more time. A general understanding of developmental processes is what you may wish to aim for in the early stages of your study. Integrating developmental theory in this specific way is new to counseling and therapy; thus, more experienced counselors may want to give this material considerable attention.

Focusing, reflection of meaning, and influencing skills are presented in Chapters 9 through 11. All these skills will help you enrich your understanding and potential for helping clients to change.

Chapter 12 presents a detailed analysis of a single interview. It is suggested that you audiotape an interview of your own and use the format of this chapter as a means of evaluating your own interviewing style. Finally, Chapter 13 returns to the issue of natural style, providing specific suggestions for examining yourself and your goals. It suggests ways in which you may use person-centered, decisional, and behavioral theory to expand your alternatives for action.

A Final Word

This book discusses both concepts related to, and specifics of, effective interviewing that are derived from years of research and experience. The ideas presented here work and can make a difference to the impact you have on clients.

While I am committed to skill training and analyzing the interview as a critical ingredient of helping, skills exist only in unique individuals. Your special challenge is to maintain a focus on yourself and your practice in the interview. Read the book from your own point of view. Study each idea and determine whether it feels comfortable to you, appears correct, and sounds as if it will be helpful to you and your clients. Only those concepts and skills that fit with your experience should be added to your natural style. Even if the concept doesn't feel right at first, try it on and see if it fits, as you would try on a new jacket. What seems awkward at first may be a favored method later in your interviewing practice.

To provide a baseline for examining your natural style or present style, I suggest you audiorecord an interview as soon as possible. An early recording will help you note your changes and additions as you move through the book. And, so that your natural style doesn't get lost in the proliferation of ideas and theories, in the final portions of the book you are asked to step back, look at the skills concepts, and integrate them in your own way.

I hope that this book helps you identify and put into practice your own definition of how you want to help others. Your attitude of caring and respect toward yourself and clients will always be fundamental in successful helping, counseling, and psychotherapy; recognizing and respecting your natural uniqueness makes it easier to recognize and respect the individual before you.

Allen E. Ivey

SECTION

I

Introduction

Underlying effective helping, whether interviewing, counseling, or psychotherapy, is the central concept of intentionality, the focus of Chapter 1. A simple but useful summary of that concept is that lack of intentionality results in immobility—the inability to change ineffective behavior or thinking patterns—while positive intentionality opens one to change and development, to movement, and to pursuing alternatives for action. Although Chapter 1 focuses primarily on intentionality as the central concept underlying this book, it also outlines other key ideas and research critical to the approach of this book.

Attending behavior, the focus of Chapter 2, is a foundation skill of counseling, perhaps the most important and basic skill of all. We must attend or listen to the client if we are to be of help. Many beginning helpers inappropriately strive to solve the client's problems in the first 5 minutes of the interview by giving premature advice and suggestions. Perhaps you may want to set one early goal for yourself as you start working with this book: allow your clients to talk. It may have taken your clients several years to develop the problems they consult you about. It is useful to listen to them carefully and hear them out *before* you undertake problem solving.

Later portions of this book emphasize more advanced skills of helping such as confrontation, interpretation, and directives, the action skills. However, virtually all who work in interviewing, counseling, and psychotherapy consider the ability to listen to and to enter into the world of the client the most important part of effective helping.

1   Toward Intentional Interviewing and Counseling

You can make a difference in the lives of others in your work as an interviewer or counselor. This difference can be for the better . . . or for the worse. Through the individual interview you can enrich others or hinder their growth.

Development is the aim of counseling and interviewing. Humanity appears to have an infinite capacity for growth. Yet you will find many clients seated before you who are stuck, immobilized, and unable to meet developmental challenges. This book is about the *how* of interviewing and counseling: how can you facilitate another person's developmental growth?

You undoubtedly have experienced an interview in which you weren't heard and your point of view wasn't seen, one that perhaps left you feeling less in touch with yourself. And you very likely have encountered other helping relationships that have brightened your outlook, provided an experience of warmth and good feeling, and engendered ideas that enabled you to attack your life issues more confidently. In the effective interview you probably felt listened to and heard—with the aid of the effective helper, your own personal development was enhanced.

Throughout this book, you will be examining intentional interviewing. You will learn specific skills that will enable you to help others develop and grow. Through step-by-step study and practice, you will encounter and master specific interviewing skills that will do the following:

▲ Enable you to define what you and others are doing in the interview to achieve specific results.
▲ Expand your skills repertoire so you will be able to generate an almost infinite number of responses to any client statement with a predicted result in client behavior.
▲ Illustrate how interviewing skills may be adapted for use in a variety of settings ranging from interviewing and counseling to nursing, business management, social work, and other fields.

▲ Counseling versus Interviewing

The terms *counseling* and *interviewing* are often used interchangeably in this book. Though the overlap is considerable, interviewing may be considered the most basic process used for information gathering, problem solving, and information and advice giving. Interviewers may be guidance and counseling staff, medical personnel, business people, or members of a wide variety of other helping professions. Counseling is a more intensive and personal process. It is generally concerned with helping normal people cope with normal problems and opportunities. Though many people who interview may also counsel, counseling is most often associated with the professional fields of social work, guidance, psychology, pastoral counseling, and, to a limited extent, psychiatry.

We can clarify this difference with some examples. A personnel manager may interview a candidate for a job, but in the next hour counsel an employee who is deciding whether or not to take a new post in a distant town. A school guidance counselor may interview each class member for 10 minutes during a term to check on course selection, but also may counsel some of them when problems arise. A psychologist may interview a person to obtain research data, and the next hour be found counseling a client concerned about an impending divorce. Even in the course of a single contact, a social worker may interview a client to obtain financial data and then move on to counseling about personal relationships.

Many people who interview at some time find themselves counseling as well. Most counselors at some time find themselves interviewing. Both interviewing and counseling may be distinguished from psychotherapy, which is a more intense process, focusing on deep-seated personality or behavioral difficulties. But most therapists at some time find themselves functioning as both interviewers and counselors. The skills and concepts of intentional interviewing are equally important for the successful conduct of psychotherapy.

▲ Intentionality as a Goal for Interviewing and Counseling

Imagine that you are a helper working with a client. What would you say in response to the following?

Client: (talking about a conflict on the job) I just don't know what to do about Bob. It seems he's always on me, blaming me even when I do a good job. He's new on the job, I know. Perhaps he doesn't have much experience as a supervisor. But he's got me all jumpy. I'm so nervous I can't sleep at night, and yesterday I even lost my lunch. My family isn't doing well, either. Sandy doesn't seem to understand what's going on and is upset. Even the kids aren't doing well in school. What do you suggest I do?

How would you respond? Write it below.

_____

_____

_____

_____

_____

_____

What you say and how you formulate the central issues of the problem presented may say as much about you and your style as they say about the client or interviewee. One of the goals of this book is to help you look at yourself and your typical response style. Your present way of conceptualizing the world of the other person is a valuable natural tool. At the same time, if you compare what you wrote with others, you'll find that they probably responded differently. A key question is *Who made the correct response in this case?*

The answer, of course, is that there are many possibly useful responses in an interviewing situation. At times an open question ("Could you tell me more?") may be most facilitative. At other times it may be more useful to reflect feelings ("Looks like you feel terribly anxious and upset over the situation with Bob.") And again, there are times when self-disclosure and direct advice are what is needed ("My experience with Bob is . . . , and I suggest you try . . . ").

Beginning interviewers are often eager to find the "right" answer for the client. In fact they are so eager that they often give quick patch-up advice that is inappropriate. For example, it is possible that broad cultural factors such as ethnicity, race, sex, lifestyle, or religious orientation may determine your response and interview plan for the client above. How ideal it would be to find the perfect empathic response that would unlock the door to the client's world and free the individual for more creative living! However, the tendencies to search for a single "right" response and to move too quickly can be damaging.

Intentional interviewing is concerned not with which single response is correct, but with how many potential responses may be helpful. Intentionality is a core goal of effective interviewing. We can define it as follows:

Intentionality is acting with a sense of capability and deciding from a range of alternative actions. The intentional individual has more than one action, thought, or behavior to choose from in responding to changing life situations. The intentional individual can generate alternatives in a given situation and approach a problem from different vantage points, using a variety of skills and personal qualities, *adapting styles to suit different cultural groups.*

The culturally intentional interviewer remembers a basic rule of helping: if something you try doesn't work, don't try more of the same . . . try something different!

▲ Cultural Intentionality and Development

Cultural Differences

One of the critical issues in interviewing is the fact that the same skills may have different effects on people with different individual and cultural backgrounds. Intentional interviewing requires an awareness that cultural groups each have different patterns of communication. Eye contact patterns differ, for example. In our culture, middle-class patterns call for rather direct eye contact, but in some cultural groups direct eye contact is considered rude and intrusive. Some groups find the rapid-fire questioning techniques of many North Americans offensive.

Many Spanish-speaking groups have more varying vocal tone and sometimes a more rapid speech rate than do English-speaking people.

It is also important to remember that the word *culture* can be defined in many ways. Religion, ethnic background (for example, Irish American and Black American), sex, and lifestyle differences as well as the degree of a client's developmental or physical handicap also represent cultural differences. There is also a youth culture, a culture of those facing imminent death through AIDS or cancer, and a culture of the aging. In effect, any group that differs from the mainstream of society can be considered a subculture. All of us at times are thus part of many cultures that require a unique awareness of the group experience.

Thus it is incorrect to assume that the communication patterns emphasized in this book work with everyone, regardless of cultural background. Effective helpers will be flexible enough to switch approaches when things seem to be going wrong. If, for example, you find that questions are ineffective, don't use more questions. Perhaps you need to slow down and try another skill, such as self-disclosure or even advice giving.

Furthermore, individuals differ as much as or more than do cultures. You will want to attune your responses to the unique human being before you. Lack of intentionality shows in the interview when the helper persists in using only one skill, one definition of the problem, and one theory of interviewing, even when that theory isn't working.

Development

Development has been described as the aim of interviewing and counseling. Clients come to us to solve problems, to find answers, to discover reasons for patterns of behavior, but always to *develop their own unique potential*. Development and the assessment of developmental level is a particularly central concept of counseling, which will be examined in detail in Chapter 8. There you will be encouraged to look for and examine clients' discrepancies and incongruities and then to use confrontation and other skills to facilitate their development. Interviewing and counseling that work and are helpful will be evidenced by how your client develops and changes through the interview. Thus Chapter 8 may be described as the lynchpin of this book, but one that is meaningless without a mastery of basic listening skills and the observance of cultural intentionality.

In sum, this book is about one's own and others' development, about the goal of generating an increased array of alternatives to help others through interviewing and counseling. This goal will be achieved through the careful delineation and practice of the *microskill* units of the interview.

▲ The Microskills Approach

Microskills are communication skill units of the interview that will help you develop the ability to interact more intentionally with a client. They will provide specific alternatives for you to use with different types of clients. Microskills form the foundation of intentional interviewing.

The microskills hierarchy (see Figure 1-1) summarizes the successive steps of intentional interviewing. The skills of the interview rest on a foundation of culturally and individually appropriate *attending behavior*, which includes patterns of eye contact, body language, vocal qualities, and verbal tracking. Attending behavior is the first microskill unit discussed in this text. In your study and practice sessions you will have the opportunity to define this skill further, see attending demonstrated in an interview, read about further implications of this skill, and finally, practice attending yourself.

Once you have mastered attending behavior, you will move up the microskills pyramid to learn client observation, questioning, paraphrasing, and other basic listening skills. It is important to remember that the foundation for effective interviewing and eventual skill integration is the ability to listen to and understand the client.

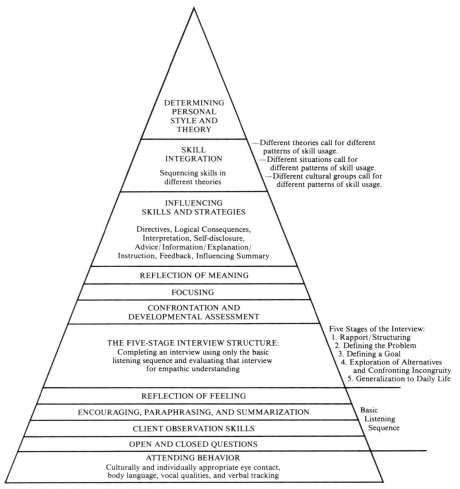

Figure 1-1. The microskills hierarchy

With a solid background in these introductory skills, you will then learn how to structure a "well-formed interview." It is possible to conduct a complete interview with a verbal client using only listening skills. You will later find that the structure of the interview presented here can be adapted and shaped to help you understand and master several alternative methods and theories of counseling.

You will then encounter the advanced skills of interviewing and counseling. The first of these is confrontation, which is considered basic to the developmental and change process. You will learn how to assess the developmental level of your client and to choose appropriate skill sequences and confrontation statements.

The microskills of focusing, reflection of meaning, and interpersonal influence come next in the hierarchy. In Chapters 9 through 11, which deal with those skills, you'll have the opportunity to study and master directives (telling a client to engage in specific actions), interpretation (providing the client with an alternative frame of reference for viewing a concern), and other skills, such as giving feedback and pointing out logical consequences.

Box 1-1.   Focusing on the Social Context

Include broader client concerns	Focusing is an important advanced skill of interviewing. You will find that your clients present what at first glance appear to be individual problems. However, as is well documented by social workers, community-oriented helpers, and family therapists, our clients live in a social context. At times, an awareness of clients' environment and surrounding social context may be as important as the individual before us.
	Thus, for full understanding of any client problem, you will most likely find it extremely helpful to consider the contextual framework of the individual client talking with you. You will want to examine factors such as his or her family, school, and neighborhood, and the impact of broader social issues such as unemployment, poor housing, racism, and ageism.
	In your first attempts at practicing interviewing skills, aim to focus your conversation on the client before you, but as you develop increased understanding and skill in the interview, you will want to add broader environmental dimensions to your consideration and planning as well.

With a mastery of listening, the ability to conduct an interview using only listening skills, and a command of the advanced skills, you are prepared to consider alternative theories and modes of helping. You will find that these microskills can be organized into different patterns utilized by different theories. As one route toward your own integration of skills, examine Table 1-1, which presents examples of microskill usage in different theoretical orientations to counseling and in different situations, such as vocational planning, medical diagnostic interviewing, and business problem solving. Many different theories and fields use the same basic microskills of communication. For example, the business problem-solving interview involves the same microskills in roughly the same proportion as might be found in a group working on vocational planning. The context and content of the interviews might be very different, but the skills are similar. On the other hand, the microskills usage of a psychodynamic therapist differs quite markedly from a modern Rogerian counselor. Although the microskills are basic to communication in many different settings and styles, individual and group usage of skills varies widely.

Table 1-1. Examples of microskill leads used by interviewers of differing theoretical orientations

	MICROSKILL LEAD	Nondirective	Modern Rogerian person-centered	Behavioral	Psychodynamic	Gestalt	Trait-and-factor	Tavistock group	Decisional vocational	Business problem solving	Medical diagnostic interview	Correctional interrogation	Traditional teaching	Student-centered teaching	Eclectic
ATTENDING SKILLS	Open question	○	○	◐	◐	●	●	○	◐	◐	◐	●	◐	●	◐
	Closed question	○	○	●	○	◐	◐	○	◐	◐	◐	●	●	◐	◐
	Encourage	◐	◐	◐	○	◐	◐	○	◐	◐	◐	◐	○	◐	◐
	Paraphrase	●	●	◐	◐	○	◐	○	◐	◐	◐	◐	○	●	◐
	Reflection of feeling	●	●	○	◐	○	◐	○	◐	◐	◐	◐	○	●	◐
	Reflection of meaning	◐	●	○	◐	○	○	◐	○	○	○	○	○	◐	◐
	Summarization	◐	◐	◐	○	○	◐	○	◐	◐	◐	◐	○	●	◐
INFLUENCING SKILLS	Feedback	○	●	○	○	◐	○	○	◐	◐	○	○	○	●	◐
	Advice/information/ instruction/other	○	○	◐	○	○	●	○	●	●	◐	◐	●	◐	◐
	Self-disclosure	○	●	○	○	○	○	○	◐	◐	○	○	○	◐	◐
	Interpretation	○	○	○	●	●	○	●	◐	◐	◐	◐	○	◐	◐
	Logical consequences	○	○	◐	○	○	◐	○	◐	●	◐	●	◐	◐	◐
	Directive	○	○	●	○	●	◐	○	◐	●	●	●	●	◐	◐
	Influencing summary	○	○	◐	○	○	◐	○	●	●	◐	○	◐	◐	◐
	CONFRONTATION (Combined Skill)	◐	◐	◐	◐	●	◐	●	◐	◐	◐	●	◐	◐	◐
FOCUS	Client	●	●	●	●	●	●	○	◐	◐	◐	◐	○	●	◐
	Counselor, interviewer	○	◐	○	○	○	○	○	◐	○	○	○	○	◐	◐
	Mutual/group/"we"	○	◐	○	○	○	○	●	◐	○	○	○	○	◐	◐
	Other people	○	○	◐	◐	◐	◐	○	◐	○	○	◐	○	◐	◐
	Topic or problem	○	○	◐	◐	○	●	○	●	●	●	●	●	●	◐
	Cultural/ environmental context	○	○	◐	○	○	◐	○	◐	◐	○	○	○	◐	◐
	ISSUE OF MEANING (Topics, key words likely to be attended to and reinforced)	Feelings	Relationship	Behavior problem solving	Unconscious motivation	Here and now behavior	Problem solving	Authority, responsibility	Future plans	Problem solving	Diagnosis of illness	Information about crime	Information/ facts	Student ideas/ info./facts	Varies
	AMOUNT OF INTERVIEWER TALK-TIME	Low	Medium	High	Low	High	High	Low	High	High	High	Medium	High	Medium	Varies

Legend

● Frequent use of skill
◐ Common use of skill
○ May use skill occasionally

As you can see from a glance at the apex of the microskills hierarchy, "determining personal style and theory," however, it isn't enough just to master skills and theories. You will eventually have to determine your own theory and practice of counseling and interviewing. Interviewers, counselors, and therapists are an independent lot; the vast majority of helpers prefer to develop their own style, and through eclecticism move toward their own blend of skills and theories. The final chapter of this text will present several alternative theories in brief form, but you will be encouraged to generate your own style and personal theoretical commitment.

Once you have mastered the entire microskills hierarchy you will be able to use those skills and concepts in a variety of settings, and will find that you can master the complex theories of counseling more easily.

▲ Alternative Settings and Microskills

Microskills training began with an emphasis on human services settings, such as school counseling and community mental-health clinics. Very shortly, however, it was discovered that the basic skills of interviewing were equally valid in the business setting. The basic listening skills sequence is an example.

In defining the nature of a client's problem in a mental-health clinic, the interviewer often begins the session with an open question—for instance, "Could you tell me what's on your mind today?" This question is coupled with appropriate attending behavior, encouraging, and effective nonverbal communication. Later the interviewer may paraphrase the client's ideas to ensure clarity of understanding: "Let me see if I have heard you correctly. You've been saying so far that your problem is. . . . Am I hearing your views accurately?" Then the counselor will most likely reflect feelings—"You seem to be feeling angry/happy/discouraged over the situation"—and may ask some closed questions such as "Did you try . . . ? Who did what?" to check on and define the client's problem. Finally, at the close of the problem-definition phase of the interview, the counselor often summarizes the problem as the client has described it: "In other words, the problem seems to be that. . . . "

The situation of counseling and management are different, but the patterning of skill usage is almost identical. A manager whose subordinate has a problem on the production line uses a similar sequence of skills. "Can you tell me what's the matter on the production line?" may be coupled with appropriate attending, nonverbal behavior, and encouraging, followed by closed questions to define the issue. The effective manager paraphrases, in a form quite similar to the counselor's, to check on the accuracy of his listening. Reflection of feeling as a skill does not figure as prominently in management, but it does often show itself briefly—for instance, "You feel pretty uptight about the production snag." Finally, before moving to problem resolution and action via influencing skills, the manager often summarizes the problem to ensure clarity.

In a similar fashion, the physician or nurse diagnosing a headache works through the basic listening sequence, as does the police officer obtaining information by interviewing a victim about a crime. Helping professionals and non-professionals in many settings use similar basic communication skills.

▲ A Model for Learning and Teaching Microskills

Teaching workshops and courses on communication skills and interviewing is an increasingly important responsibility of professionals in the helping fields. Microskills are well adapted for teaching beginning interviewers, whether they are in community volunteer groups, police departments, management, teaching, or any of a myriad of settings.

Perhaps even more important, particularly in the early stages of helping, is to teach clients communication skills. You'll find teaching microskills in your interviews a useful counseling adjunct. Many clients and families benefit by learning attending behavior and listening skills.

The Appendix of this book shows how to teach interviewing skills to others and provides suggestions for you to generate your own teaching plan. The microskills method of teaching is based on over 20 years of research and clinical experience. The model of this book and that suggested for your own teaching of skills to others follows a basic sequence: (1) warm-up and introduction to the skill, (2) example of the skill in action, (3) reading, (4) practice leading to mastery of the skill, and (5) self-assessment and generalization.

▲ Research Validation of the Microskills Approach

Over 250 data-based studies have been completed on the microtraining model (Kasdorf & Gustafson, 1978; Daniels, 1985). To these studies should be added more than 20 years of clinical testing with trainees in counseling, business, and many other settings. The basic finding of the research data has been the classic "more research is needed." However, the following practical points may be made with some assurance:

1. The skills of the microskills hierarchy have been shown again and again to be clear, replicable in the interview, and teachable.
2. Students who are trained via the model used in this book are able to recognize and classify interviewing skills with accuracy.
3. Students are able to demonstrate their mastery of these skills on audiotape or videotape following completion of their training.
4. Students who practice the skills do change and improve their pattern of microskill usage as a result of this training. Personal involvement makes a difference in whether or not learning "takes."
5. The use of the complete training package of introductory exercises, video or audio model, reading, and experiential practice appears to be most effective. Practice with the single skills to mastery levels appears to be particularly important to the development of competence.
6. Not only does the training seem to affect trainees, but their clients also seem to change behavior. Clients of students who have gone through the microskills training appear to change their verbal patterns and to demonstrate more complex patterns of thinking.
7. Different counseling theories do indeed appear to have differing patterns of microskill usage. The microtraining framework may be used to teach complex interviewing behavior according to alternative theoretical perspectives on the interview.

For those who are interested, the two major reviews of microtraining research previously mentioned are strongly recommended. The microtraining framework's feasibility and effectiveness have now been established over a considerable time, and thousands of students have experienced the framework in one form or another. The concepts have been translated into numerous languages and adapted to many cultures including Japanese, Malaysian, Swedish, Native American, and Canadian groups. Examine the framework and determine what it has to offer you for improving your understanding and skills in the interview.

▲ You and the Microtraining Process: A Suggested Exercise

When the concept of cultural intentionality was introduced earlier in this chapter, you were asked to give your own response to an interviewee experiencing a conflict on the job. Microtraining seeks to give you additional alternatives for intentional responding to the client. However, these responses must be genuinely your own. If you adopt a response simply because it is recommended, it is likely to be ineffective for both you and your client. Not all parts of the microtraining framework are appropriate for everyone. You have a natural style of communicating, and it is that natural style these concepts should add to—not change.

You are about to engage in a systematic study of the interviewing process. By the end of the book you will have been given many ideas for analyzing your interviewing style and skill usage. Along the way, you will find it helpful to have nearby a record of where you were before you started this training. Your present natural style is a baseline you will want to keep in touch with and honor. Identifying who you are and what you do before beginning systematic training can be invaluable.

It would be useful for you now to audiorecord yourself in a natural interview. Without further training and analysis, find someone who is willing to role-play a client with a concern, problem, opportunity, or issue. Interview that client for at least 15 minutes using your own natural communication style.

Since you are going to audiorecord that interview, be sure to ask the role-played client the critical closed question, "May I record this interview?" Also inform the client that, if he or she wishes, the tape recorder may be turned off at any time. Common sense demands ethical practice and respect for the client.

You can select almost any topic for the interview. If you work in a business setting, a friend discussing a business problem may be appropriate. If you are in human services, perhaps a colleague can role-play a client he or she has had in the past, and you can test your natural skills. A useful topic is interpersonal conflict—for example, concerns over family tensions or decisions about a new job opportunity.

Save the audiotape until a later time. At that point you will want to listen to it again, perhaps even make a transcript of what you and your client say, and analyze your behavior, noting its impact on your client. After you have finished this book you may want to record another interview, noting the similarities and the differences in your style. Comparing your behavior before and after you have had some training will help you evaluate the microskills training. After all, it is *you* who will ultimately determine the worth of this program.

Box 1-2.   Key Points

Cultural intentionality	Achieving cultural intentionality is the major goal of this book and a major goal of the interviewing process itself. Intentionality is acting with a sense of capability and deciding from a range of alternative actions. The intentional individual has more than one action, thought, or behavior to choose from in responding to life situations. The culturally intentional individual can generate alternatives from different vantage points, using a variety of skills and personal qualities within a culturally appropriate framework.
Development	The aim of interviewing and counseling is development. Through the use of the listening, confrontation, and influencing skills of this book, it is possible to assess the developmental level of a client and to facilitate movement and growth to reach fuller potential.
Microskills	Microskills are the single communication skill units (for example, questions, interpretation) of the interview. They are taught one at a time to ensure mastery of basic interviewing competencies.
Microskills hierarchy	The hierarchy organizes microskills into a systematic framework for the eventual integration of skills into the interview in a natural fashion. The microskills rest on a foundation of attending (listening) skills followed by focusing and influencing skills, confrontation, and eventual skill integration.
Use of skills with different situations and theories	Different counseling and interviewing theories have varying patterns of skill usage; however, they all use the communication skill units. Basic skills of interviewing and counseling appear in many situations, such as medicine, management, and social work, although the content of the interview may vary.
Basic listening sequence	A sequence of attending skills (questioning, encouraging, paraphrasing, reflecting of feelings, summarization) is basic to problem definition and is used in many different settings. Discussed in detail in Section II, the basic listening sequence is basic to all skills and theories taught in this book.
Teaching model	The microskill teaching model includes (1) warm-up and introduction to the skill, (2) examples of the skill in operation, (3) reading, (4) practice, and (5) self-assessment and generalization. Most of the chapters of this book follow the same model.
Research validation	The microskills model has been validated by over 250 data-based studies and 20 years of clinical practice. The skills can be learned, and they do have an impact upon clients, but they must be practiced constantly or they may disappear.
You and microskills and the interview	Microskills are only useful if they harmonize with your own natural style in the interview. Before you proceed further with this book, audiorecord an interview with a friend or a classmate, make a transcript of this interview, and later—as you learn more about interview analysis—analyze your behavior in that interview. You'll want to compare it with your performance in an interview some months from now.

▲ References and Recommended Supplementary Reading

Advanced Development Division (1980). *Tuning in: Intentional attending.* Ottawa: Occupational and Career Analysis and Development Branch, Employment and Immigration Canada. This manual describes the use of basic attending skills in the work of the Canadian Employment Service.

Daniels, T. (1985). *Microcounseling training in skills of therapeutic communication with R.N. diploma-program nursing students.* Unpublished doctoral dissertation, Dalhousie University, Halifax, N.S. Updates research review of microcounseling studies and provides data illustrating the effectiveness of the microtraining concepts with nursing.

Evans, D., Hearn, M., Uhlemann, M., & Ivey, A. (in press). *Essential interviewing: A programmed approach to effective communication* (3rd ed.). Monterey, Calif.: Brooks/Cole. A programmed text covering most of the basic microskills discussed in this book.

Hall, E. (1959). *The silent language.* New York: Fawcett. Despite its age, this slim paperback volume still provides one of the best summaries of issues in cross-cultural communication.

Ivey, A. (1986). *Developmental therapy: Theory into practice.* San Francisco: Jossey-Bass. The developmental constructs emphasized in this book are outlined in detail with many specific theoretical and practical applications.

Ivey, A. (1981). Counseling and psychotherapy: Toward a new perspective. In T. Marsella & P. Pedersen (Eds.), *Cross-cultural counseling and psychotherapy.* New York: Pergamon Press. Cross-cultural implications of counseling and therapy are considered in some detail. A new theoretical perspective on microskills is presented.

Ivey, A. (1971). *Microcounseling: Innovations in interviewing training.* Springfield, Ill.: Charles C Thomas. The original microcounseling text, which first outlined the microtraining paradigm in depth. Translation available in Dutch.

Ivey, A., & Authier, J. (1978). *Microcounseling: Innovations in interviewing, counseling, psychotherapy, and psychoeducation.* Springfield, Ill.: Charles C Thomas. An updated version of the 1971 text, approximately doubled in size. Research data, instruments for evaluation of the interview, new theoretical material, and transcripts are included. Translation available in Japanese.

Ivey, A., Gluckstern, N., & Ivey, M. (1982 and 1983). *Basic attending skills* and *basic influencing skills* [Manuals and videotapes]. North Amherst, Mass.: Microtraining. Training manuals and videotapes illustrating skills and concepts of intentional interviewing and counseling. Translations and videotapes available in French, Japanese, Swedish, and Malaysian.

Ivey, A., Ivey, M., & Simek-Downing, L. (1987). *Counseling and psychotherapy: Integrating skills and theory in practice.* Englewood Cliffs, N.J.: Prentice-Hall. An introductory text in counseling and psychotherapy that illustrates how microskills and the basic interviewing structure may be used in alternative theoretical orientations.

Ivey, A., & Litterer, J. (1979). *Face to face: Communication skills in business* [Training manual and videotapes]. North Amherst, Mass.: Amherst Consulting Group. A business version for management training utilizing concepts of microtraining. Available in German, Swedish, and British-English adaptations.

Ivey, A., Normington, C., Miller, C., Morrill, W., & Haase, R. (1968). Microcounseling and attending behavior: An approach to pre-practicum counselor training [Monograph]. *Journal of Counseling Psychology, 15,* Part II, 1–12. The original publication on microcounseling, outlining three basic research studies on the efficacy of the model.

Ivey, A., & Shizuru, L. (1981). *Issues in cross-cultural counseling* [Videotape and workbook]. North Amherst, Mass.: Microtraining. Videotape and workbook illustrating cultural differences in microskills.

Jessop, A. (1979). *Nurse-patient communication: A skills approach* [Training manual and videotapes]. North Amherst, Mass.: Microtraining. Microskills applied to the nursing context. Translation available in Swedish.

Kasdorf, J., & Gustafson, K. (1978). Research related to microtraining. In A. Ivey & J. Authier (Eds.), *Microcounseling: Innovations in interviewing, counseling psychotherapy, and psychoeducation.* Springfield, Ill.: Charles C Thomas. Detailed analysis of the 150 data-based studies on microtraining completed as of that date.

2 Attending Behavior: Basic to Communication

How can attending behavior be used to help your clients?

Major function

Attending behavior encourages client talk. You will want to use attending behavior to help a client talk more freely and openly, and to reduce interviewer talk. Conversely, the lack of attending behavior can also serve a useful function. Through inattention, you can help other people talk less about topics that are destructive or nonproductive.

Secondary functions

Knowledge and skill in attending result in the following:

▲ Communicating to the client that you are interested in what is being said.
▲ Increasing your awareness of the client's pattern of attending.
▲ Modifying your patterns of attending to establish rapport with each individual. Different people and different cultural groups often have different patterns of attending.
▲ Having some recourse when you are lost or confused in the interview. Even the most advanced professional doesn't always know what is happening. When you don't know what to do, attend!

▲ Introduction

Foremost in any interview or counseling situation is the ability to make contact with another human being. We make this contact through listening and talking as well as by nonverbal means. *Listening* to other people is most critical, as it enables them to continue to talk and explore. Effective attending behavior may be considered the foundation skill of this program.

How can we define effective listening more precisely? A simple warm-up exercise may help. It is best if you work with someone else, but you can do it in your imagination, especially if you recall parallel experiences in your own life.

One of the best ways to understand quality listening is to experience the opposite: poor listening. Find a partner to role-play an interview, and together think of the incorrect things that an ineffective listener or interviewer does. If no partner is available, think back on some bad interviews you have gone through. Spend about 3 minutes role-playing the poor interview (or recalling the many aspects of the ineffective session). The emphasis here is on what went wrong; you should feel free to exaggerate in order to underline the many things that can cause a session to go poorly.

List below some behaviors, traits, and qualities that are characteristic of the effective interviewer or counselor who fails to listen.

_____

_____

_____

_____

_____

This exercise is often humorous. We recall with laughter the bored interviewer, the uninterested counselor, or the ineffective therapist. Yet as you recall your own experience of not being heard, your strongest memory may be of a feeling of emptiness when you needed help. Or perhaps you recall your anger at the insensitivity of the interviewer. Lists of ineffective interviewing behaviors sometimes run to 30 items or more. If you are to be effective and competent, the obvious course is to do the opposite of the ineffective counselor.

Obviously you can't learn all the qualities and skills immediately. Rather, it is best to learn them step-by-step. The first step, the foundation skill of attending behavior, consists of four dimensions and is critical to all other skills. To communicate that you are indeed listening or attending to someone else, you need the following:

1. *Eye contact.* If you are going to talk to people, look at them.
2. *Attentive body language.* Clients know you are interested if you face them squarely and lean slightly forward, have an expressive face, and use facilitative, encouraging gestures.
3. *Vocal qualities.* Your vocal tone and speech rate also indicate clearly how you feel about another person. Think of how many ways you can say "I am really interested in what you have to say" just by altering your vocal tone and speech rate.
4. *Verbal tracking.* The client has come to you with a topic of concern; don't change the subject. Keep to the topic indicated by the client.

The four dimensions of attending all have one goal in common: to reduce interviewer talk-time and provide the client with an opportunity to talk and examine issues concretely and in more detail. You can't learn about the client if you are doing the talking!

▲ Example Interviews

The first interview presented, part of a job interview, is deliberately designed to be a particularly ineffective example, to provide a contrast to the second interview. Note how patterns of eye contact, body language, vocal qualities, and failure to maintain verbal tracking can disrupt a session.

Negative Example

Al: The next thing on my questionnaire is your past job history. Tell me a little bit about it, will ya? (The vocal tone is casual, almost uninterested. Eye contact is on the form, not on the client. He slouches in his chair.)

Hank: Well, I guess the job that, uh . . .

Al: Hold it! That's the doorbell. I'll be back in a minute. (long pause) Uh, okay, okay, where were we? (impatiently)

Hank: The job that really comes to mind is my work as a camp counselor during my senior year of high school . . .

Al: (interrupts) Oh, yeah, I did a camp counselor job myself. I did it at Camp Eagle in Minnesota. Jeez, I had a really good time doing that. I'm glad to hear that. Yeah, that was really great fun. What else have you been doing?

Hank: Ah . . . well, I . . . ah . . . wanted to tell you a little bit more about this counseling job; I . . .

Al: (interrupts) I got that down, so tell me about something else. Did you ever work on a farm?

Hank: Ah . . . no, I didn't. (looks puzzled and confused)

Al: I liked working on a farm a lot.

Hank: I lived in St. Louis, it was . . .

Al: (interrupts) I don't like that town much.

Hank: I was miles from the closest farm. I mean I don't see how I could have worked on a farm. (defensive vocal tone) I did work at my dad's grocery store when I was in grade school and high school. I would come down Saturday morning and . . . (Note that Al has taken control of the topic from Hank, and Hank is talking about what Al wants to talk about rather than determining his own direction. Attending behavior demands that we listen to the client and go the way he or she wishes. This interview may seem far-fetched, but in fact many interviews are not as different from this as we would wish.)

Al: Yeah, that sounds like something I ought to write down. (pauses and looks at his form for a period of time) . . . What did you do for him?

Hank: Well, uh, it was a grocery store and I sold . . .

Al: (interrupts) Do you like to eat?

Hank: Yeah . . . ah . . . (looks confused) . . . I like to cook too.

Al: You? Interested in cooking? (scornful look)

Hank: (angrily) Yes, and I'm good at it, too! What . . .

Al: That's a weird thing to do!

Comment: This interview is extreme, but it does illustrate the many different ineffective responses the insensitive interviewer can direct to a client. Almost every time Al spoke, he changed the topic. His body language was disrespectful, his gestures were uninterested or scornful, and his vocal qualities were harsh.

Positive Example

Al: Well, Hank, the next thing on this form, uh, is something about your job . . . jobs you've had in the past. Could you tell me a little bit about some of the jobs you've had? (Al uses the client's name and structures this part of the interview briefly. He then asks an open question to obtain information from Hank's perspective. He sits squarely facing the client, leans slightly forward, maintains good eye contact, and his vocal tone and facial expression indicate interest.)

Hank: Sure. The job that comes to mind is the one I had in my senior year in high school and during my college years as a camp counselor for the YMCA. (Hank's vocal tone is confident and relaxed. He seems eager to explore this new area.)

Al: Yeah? Tell me more.

Hank: Well, I was . . . it was a point where I was really looking for a profession to engage in when I got older, and I realized while I was working at this camp with these kids, taking responsibility for them and helping them learn things, that I have always really wanted to work with people. And, uh . . .

Al: Uh-huh. (lets Hank know he is listening)

Hank: . . . I think I began to realize that psychology was a major that I was interested in.

Al: I see. So working in a camp with people was one of the things that you liked. Could you give me an example of one of the things that happened in that camp that you particularly liked? (helps Hank be specific and concrete)

Hank: Well, I seemed to be able to get the kids in the group to work well together. It was an overnight camp, and there were kids from lots of different racial groups, from different socioeconomic classes, and I seemed to be able to organize them in a way that really built on the strengths of everybody. And we resolved a lot of their conflicts. I think I made them feel . . . helped them feel pretty good about themselves.

Al: So, you resolved a lot of conflicts, and you helped them feel pretty good. How did that make you feel?

Hank: Oh, I was delighted. I felt like my cabin was the most cohesive group in the camp sometimes. I felt real increased self-esteem because I had helped, you know, us become a pretty good unit together, and we also had lots of fun, you know. I learned to play the ukelele and we had some singing sessions. I really couldn't believe I was getting paid to be up in that beautiful country up in northern Michigan every summer, and be with these kids, and I thought, "Gee, you know, this could be a profession for me, that would be great. If I can just do something like this all year round."

Al: So, this leads you to think that you might like to continue this type of work where you could work with people and do it, like you say, all year round.

Hank: Right.

Al: What are some things along that line that you've thought of that you might want to do?

Hank: Well, as I was saying, I thought I might . . . at that time I thought I might become a therapist to help people who, you know, had real personal problems. I thought I even might become a camp director at some point. That was another possibility. I knew that I really wanted to work with people rather than with things, and I knew that I really had an attachment to the outdoors. I wanted to live someplace where I could experience being away from some of the hustle and bustle and noise of the city. So, that particular job was one, I think, that made the greatest impression on me.

Al: So, of all the jobs you've had, that really made the deepest impression—the chance to work with people and be with them and so forth. Just by way of contrast, could you share, maybe, a job where you didn't have those feelings, maybe that you disliked? (clarifies interests via contrasts)

Hank: Oh, I had a job as a paper route . . . as a paper boy, and I found that to be rather tedious. I went around, you know, every day delivering these papers, and it was in Chicago and there were a lot of tenement buildings in this area where I grew up . . .

Al: Uh-huh.

Hank: Sometimes the papers were so thick, I couldn't throw them up to the upper floors, and I had to walk them all the way up. It was bitter cold in the winter, and the pay wasn't very good. But I was determined not to quit, you know, I didn't want to be seen as a quitter . . .

Al: Ah-hah.

Hank: And some of my friends had the same kind of job.

Al: You said you were determined not to quit . . .

Hank: Right.

Al: Could you go a little further with that?

Hank: Well, I had a couple of friends who would deliver these papers and they delivered from, you know, August to October, and as soon as it got cold out, they'd quit and just live off their allowance that their parents gave them. I decided that I was going to tough it out through the winter, and the guy who was the boss down there, he told me in May when I finally quit 'cause school was out, he said, "Hank, you're a good kid, you know, you stuck through the winter." Somehow, that meant a lot to me.

Al: So, to sort of wind up here at this particular part, because you sort of talked about a job you liked and a job you didn't, can you put anything together about what that guy told you? Your sticking through the winter, that may even tie in with some of the stuff you talked about at first . . . the job in the camp. And, it seems to me, you can put those two together in terms of a pattern. (Al invites Hank to take an active part and put his own interpretations forward to help understand the patterns.)

Hank: Well, I guess . . . in the job I didn't like so much, the paper route, because it was so tedious and repetitive, I did appreciate getting that reward in the end, that I wasn't a quitter. But it didn't really help me learn that much about myself, except that one thing, that I could really tough it out if I had to. In the other job, really, I felt a lot of challenge. I felt like I could use some of my natural talents. I could learn to, you know, help people get along with one another. I could teach them in a way that didn't scare them, and I began to feel a lot better about myself as a person. I was a little insecure as a teenager, and all of a sudden I was watching myself do something really well. And I think that just made much more of an impression on my life.

Al: So, Hank, one thing that seems to be common to the two jobs is that you like to feel good about yourself, it's important to do a good job. Is that correct?

Hank: That's right. I never thought of that.

Comment: Throughout this interview, Al maintains individually and culturally appropriate eye contact, body language, verbal tracking, and vocal qualities. Hank, in turn, responds with the same. There are very few, if any, topic jumps on Al's part. His task appears to be bringing out Hank's ideas and opinions. When he does change the topic, Al relates something from earlier in the interview to what is being discussed. Through this experience of simple attending, Hank comes to a new understanding of one of his major factors underlying vocational choice—that is, wanting to feel good about himself through a job well done. Here we note the relationship of personal issues to the world of work.

The particular technique Al used in the positive example may be called *contrast interviewing.* A positive experience is identified and discussed in some depth. Then a negative experience is similarly identified and discussed. As the two are contrasted and compared, clients often reveal much of themselves and what is important to them in life and work. The identification of positive experience is particularly important in interviewing and counseling. Many clients will grow faster through an emphasis on their strengths rather than on weaknesses and problems.

▲ Instructional Reading

Nonverbal dimensions of attending demonstrate to clients that they are truly heard. They lead to that central goal of attending—giving the client talk-time—and provide you with useful behaviors to help others talk more freely. The following points detail some critical refinements of eye contact, body language, vocal qualities, and verbal tracking. Additionally, you'll learn why and when nonattention may have a positive value.

Eye Contact

When an issue is interesting to clients, you will find that their pupils tend to dilate. On the other hand, when the topic is uncomfortable or boring, their pupils may contract. If you have a chance to observe your face carefully on

videotape, you'll note that you as a counselor or interviewer indicate to your clients your degree of interest in the same fashion.

You'll also want to notice breaks in eye contact. Clients often tend to look away when discussing topics that particularly depress them. You may find yourself avoiding eye contact while discussing certain topics. There are counselors who say their clients talk about "nothing but sex" and others who say their clients never bring up the topic—through pupil dilation and eye-contact breaks, both types of counselors indicate to their clients whether the topic is appropriate.

Cultural differences in eye contact abound. Direct eye contact is considered a sign of interest in White middle-class culture. However, even in that culture a person often maintains more eye contact while listening and less while talking. Furthermore, when a client is uncomfortable talking about a topic, it may at times be better to avoid eye contact. Research indicates, moreover, that some Blacks in the United States may have reverse patterns; that is, they may look more when talking and slightly less when listening. Among some Native American groups, eye contact by the young is a sign of disrespect. Imagine the problems this may cause the teacher or counselor who says to a youth, "Look at me!" when this directly contradicts basic cultural values. Some cultural groups (for instance, certain Native American, Eskimo, or aboriginal Australian groups) generally avoid eye contact, especially when talking about serious subjects.

Body Language

The anthropologist Edward Hall once examined film clips of Indians of the Southwest and of Whites and found over 20 different behaviors in the way they walked. Just as cultural differences in eye contact exist, body language patterns differ.

A comfortable conversational distance for North Americans is slightly more than arm's length, and the British prefer even greater distances. Many Hispanic people often prefer half that distance, and those from the Middle East may talk practically eyeball to eyeball. As a result, the slightly forward leaning we recommend for attending behavior is not going to be appropriate all the time. A natural, relaxed body style that is your own is most likely to be effective, but be prepared to adapt and flex according to the individual with whom you are talking.

Just as shifts in eye contact tell us about potentially uncomfortable issues for clients, so do changes in body language. A person may move forward when interested and away when bored or frightened. As you talk, notice people's movements in relation to you. How do you affect them? Note yourself in the interview. When do you change body posture markedly? Are there patterns of which you need to be aware?

Vocal Qualities

Your voice is an instrument that communicates much of the feeling you have toward another person or situation. Changes in its pitch, volume, or speech rate convey the same things that changes in eye contact or body language do.

Keep in mind that different people are likely to respond to your voice differently. Try this exercise with a group of three or more people.[1]

Ask all members of the group to close their eyes while you talk to them. Talk in your normal tone of voice on any subject of interest to you. As you talk to the group, ask them to notice your vocal qualities. How do they react to your tone, your volume, your speech rate, perhaps even your regional or ethnic accent? Continue talking for 2 or 3 minutes. Then ask them to give you feedback on your voice. Summarize what you learn below.

_____

_____

_____

_____

This exercise often reveals a point that is central to the entire concept of attending. *People differ in their reactions to the same stimulus.* Some people find one voice interesting, whereas others find that same voice boring; still others may consider it warm and caring. This exercise and others like it reveal again and again that people differ, and that what is successful with one person or client may not work with another.

Verbal underlining is another useful concept. As you examine your own behavior, you will find yourself giving louder volume and increased vocal emphasis to certain words and short phrases. Clients of course do the same. The key words a person underlines via volume and emphasis are often concepts of particular importance.

Awareness of your voice and of the changes in others' vocal qualities will enhance your skill in attending. Again, note the timing of vocal changes, as they may indicate comfort or discomfort depending on the cultural affiliation of a client. Speech hesitations and breaks are another signal, often indicating confusion or stress.

Verbal Tracking

Staying with your client's topic is critical in verbal tracking. Just as they make sudden shifts in nonverbal communication, people change topics when they aren't comfortable. And cultural differences may appear as well. In middle-class U.S. communication direct tracking is most appropriate, but in some Asian cultures the direct verbal follow-up we use may be considered rude and intrusive.

Selective attention is a type of verbal tracking that counselors and interviewers need to be especially aware of. We tend to listen to some things and ignore others. Over time we have developed patterns of listening that enable us to hear some topics more clearly than others. For example, take the following statement, in which the client presents several issues.

---

[1]This exercise was developed by Robert Marx, School of Management, University of Massachusetts.

Client: I'm so fouled up right now. I just got notice that the plant is closing and I'll lose my job. I don't even know whether I'm eligible for unemployment. On the way home someone hit my car. I forgot to get her license number. And finally, when I got home, the kids had left the apartment in a mess, and there was a letter from my parents that really upset me.

There are obviously several different directions in which the interview could go. You can't talk about everything at once. List those several directions below. To which one(s) would you selectively attend?

_____

_____

_____

_____

There are no correct answers. In such a situation different interviewers would place emphasis on different issues. Some interviewers consistently listen attentively to only a few key topics while ignoring other possibilities. Be alert to your own potential patterning of responses. It is important that no issue get lost, but it is equally important not to attack everything at once, as confusion will result.

The concept of verbal tracking may be most helpful to the beginning interviewer or to the experienced interviewer who is lost or puzzled about what to say next in response to a client. *Relax,* take whatever the client has said in the immediate or near past and direct attention to that through a question or brief comment. You don't need to introduce a new topic. Build on the client's topics, and you will come to know the client very well over time.

The Value of Nonattention

There are times when it is inappropriate to attend to client statements. For example, a client may talk insistently about the same topic over and over again. A depressed client may want to give the most complete description of how and why the world is wrong. Many clients only want to talk about negative things. In such cases, intentional nonattending may be useful. Through failure to maintain eye contact, subtle shifts in body posture, vocal tone, and deliberate jumps to more positive topics, you can facilitate the interview process.

The most skilled counselors and interviewers use attending skills to open and close client talk, thus making the most effective use of limited time in the interview.

Silence

Counseling and interviewing are *talking* professions. But, sometimes the most useful thing you can do as a helper is to support your client silently. As a counselor, particularly as a beginner, it may be hard to sit and wait for clients to think through what they want to say. Or, your client may be in tears and you may want to give support through your words. At times, however, the best support is simply being with the person and not saying a word.

Supportive silence at the right time may be your most powerful and useful form of attending behavior. Silence may say more than words in the most important moments.

With other clients, silence can be useful in helping them talk. Some of us have a longer period of time between our thoughts than others. Notice your client's talk patterns and use silence so that you do not interrupt too soon.

Finally, remember the obvious: that a client can't talk while you do.

▲ Summary

There is no need to talk about yourself or give long answers when you attend to someone else. Give the client ownership of "air-time." Your main responsibility as a helper is to assist others in finding their own answers. You'll be surprised how able they are to do this if you are willing to attend.

Respect yourself and the other person. Ask questions and make comments on things that interest you and seem relevant to you. If you are truly interested in what is being said, attending behavior follows automatically. But keep in mind that, as you become more interested, you may be tempted to overinvolve yourself and intervene too much. The goal of attending is to listen to the other person. Your patterns of eye contact, body language, vocal qualities, and verbal tracking are the skills that enable you to help clients express themselves. See Box 2-1 for a summary of this chapter's major ideas, then start on the practice exercises that follow.

Box 2-1.   Key Points

Why?	The four attending behaviors all have one goal in common: to reduce interviewer talk-time while providing the client with an opportunity to talk and examine issues. You can't learn about the other person or the problem while you are doing the talking! Lack of attending may also be used to stop needless client talk at any time during the interview.
What?	Attending behavior consists of four simple but critical dimensions: 1. *Eye contact.* If you are going to talk to people, look at them. 2. *Attentive body language.* In general, clients know you are interested in them if you face them squarely and lean slightly forward, have an expressive face, and use facilitative, encouraging gestures. 3. *Vocal qualities.* Your vocal tone and speech rate indicate much of how you feel about another person. Think of how you feel about another person. Think of how many ways you can say "I am really interested in what you have to say" just by your vocal tone and speech rate. 4. *Verbal tracking.* The client has come to you with a topic of interest; don't change the subject. Keep to the topic initiated by the client. If you change the topic, be aware that you have and realize the purpose of your change.
How?	Attending is easiest if you focus your attention on the client rather than on yourself. Note what the client is talking about, ask questions, and make comments that relate to your client's topics. For example:

(continued)

Box 2-1 (continued)

Client:	I'm so confused. I can't decide between a major in chemistry, psychology, or language.
Interviewer:	(nonattending) Tell me about your hobbies. What do you like to do? *or* What are your grades?
Interviewer:	(attending) Tell me more. *or* You feel confused? *or* Could you tell me a little about how each subject interests you? *or* Opportunities in chemistry are promising now. Could you explore that field a bit more? *or* How would you like to go about making your decision?

Note that all attending responses follow the client's verbal statement. Each might lead the client in a very different direction. Interviewers need to be aware of their patterns of selective attention and how they may unconsciously direct the interview. Finally, nonattending responses may be helpful to discourage certain client talk and focus the interview.

With whom? — Attending is vital in all human interactions, be they counseling, a medical interview, or a business decision meeting. It is important to note that different cultural groups may have different patterns of attending. Some may maintain distinctly different patterns of eye contact, for example, and consider the direct gaze rude and intrusive. The effective interviewer is constantly aware of group, cultural, and individual differences in attending patterns.

And? — A simple but often helpful rule for interviewing is to *attend* when you become lost or confused about what to do. Simply ask the client to comment further on something just said or mentioned earlier in the interview.

▲ Practice Exercises and Self-Assessment

Attending behavior is a simple set of skills. Yet it is the awareness of and competence in those skills that form the foundation of effective interviewing, counseling, or therapy. You can never stop bettering your skill in attending; there is always room for improvement.

The following steps and the subsequent chapter sections to which they refer have proven most helpful as a systematic framework for mastering attending behavior.

1. *Individual practice.* Can you identify the presence or absence of attending? A short series of practice and observation exercises will provide an opportunity to test your ability to understand the central aspects of attending behavior.
2. *Systematic group practice.* Practice by yourself is a good beginning, but you will need to work with someone else in a role-play interview if you are to obtain precise feedback on your use of attending behavior. If no group is available, adapt the systematic practice exercise for practice with a friend or family member.

3. *Self-assessment and follow-up.* At the conclusion of this chapter you'll find a self-assessment form with which to evaluate your performance of this skill and assess its value to you.

Individual Practice

Exercise 1. Generating alternative attending and nonattending statements

A client comes to you stating the following:

I just got fired. It wasn't my fault. It just wasn't fair. The boss gave me a bad time. I wasn't late very often, and I did a good job. I'd like to fix him. But . . . I need a job. What ideas do you have for me?

Write below three things you might say, each of which could lead the client in a different direction, yet all of which would be attending responses.

1. _____

2. _____

3. _____

The most important gift you can give a client is attending. At the same time, it is important to be aware of the impact of nonattending; at times it can be useful. Write below one potentially effective and one potentially ineffective nonattending statement.

Potentially effective _____

Potentially ineffective _____

Exercise 2. Behavior tallies

Observe an interview. This could be a role-played counseling session, a television talk show, or simply an interaction between friends or family. Use the following form to count problem behaviors.

_____ Number of eye contact breaks
_____ Number of distracting nonverbal gestures
_____ Number of distracting vocal hesitations/changes
_____ Number of topic jumps

The same dimensions may be counted in a positive way. Observe another interview and complete the following form.

_____ Approximate percentage of time appropriate eye contact is maintained
_____ Number of facilitative nonverbal gestures
_____ Number of helpful vocal changes, emphasis, underlining
_____ Number of times person stayed on the same topic

Both experiences provide useful data. What did you discover from this experience?

_____

_____

_____

_____

_____

_____

Exercise 3. Deliberate attending

During a conversation with a friend or acquaintance, deliberately attend and listen more carefully than usual. Maintain eye contact and an open, attentive posture, and stay on that person's topic. Note the reaction of the other person. What happens to his or her body posture? To his or her language patterns?

You may wish to contrast deliberate attending with nonattending. What happens when your eye contact wanders, your body posture becomes more rigid, or you change the topic?

Note your reactions to this exercise below.

_____

_____

_____

_____

_____

_____

_____

_____

_____

_____

_____

Systematic Group Practice

The instructions below are designed for groups of four, but may be adapted for use with pairs, trios, and groups up to five or six in number. Ideally, each group has access to video- or audiorecorders. However, careful observers using the feedback sheets provided can still offer enough structure for a successful practice session without the benefit of equipment.

Step 1. Divide into practice groups.   Get acquainted with each other informally before you go further.

Step 2. Select a group leader.   The leader's task is to ensure that the group follows the specific steps of the practice session. It often proves helpful if the least experienced group member serves as leader first.

Step 3. Assign roles for the first practice session.

▲ Role-played client. The role-played client will be cooperative, talk freely about the topic, and not give the interviewer a difficult time.
▲ Interviewer. The interviewer will demonstrate a natural style of attending behavior with the client and practice the basic skills.
▲ Observer 1. The first observer will fill out the feedback form detailing some aspects of the interviewer's attending behavior.
▲ Observer 2. The second observer will time the session, start and stop any equipment, and fill out a second observation sheet as time permits.

Step 4. Planning.[2]   The interviewer should state his or her goals clearly, and the members of the group should take time to plan the role-play. The interviewer should plan to open and to facilitate client talk. An increased percentage of client talk-time on a single topic will indicate a successful session. The interviewer may also plan to close off client talk and then open it again. It may help to keep conversation going if he or she elicits both positive and negative comments: this also results in a deeper understanding of the client. The more concrete the plan, the more likelihood of success.

The suggested topic for the attending practice session is "Why I want to be a counselor or interviewer." The client talks about his or her desire to do such work while the interviewer demonstrates attending skills. Other possible topics for the session include the following:

▲ A job I had in the past that I liked, and one I didn't like
▲ Attitudes and experiences in school
▲ Thoughts about current political or social situations
▲ Favorite books or hobbies

The topics and role-plays are most effective if you talk about something meaningful to you. You will also find it helpful if everyone in the group works on the same topic as roles are rotated. In that way you can compare styles and learn from one another more easily.

While the interviewer and the interviewee plan, the two observers preview the feedback sheets and plan their own practice sessions to follow.

---

[2]The importance of planning as part of microskills practice was brought to my attention by Kevin Heath, Health Commission of South Australia. Heath suggests that it is essential to think through what we will do *before* we do it. Then, after having attempted the task, we must evaluate and review whether we did what we said we would do (see Step 6.)

Step 5. Conduct a 3-minute practice session using attending skills. The interviewer practices the skills of attending, the client talks about the current work setting or other selected topic, and the two observers fill out the feedback sheets. Do not go beyond 3 minutes. If possible, record the interview.

Step 6. Review the practice session and provide feedback to the interviewer for 12 minutes. As a first step in feedback, the role-played client will often want to give her or his impressions of the session. This may be followed by interviewer self-assessment and comments by the two observers. As part of the review, ask yourselves the key question, "Did the interviewer achieve his or her own planning objective?" This is critical for assessing the level of mastery obtained.

On the feedback sheet, note both verbal and nonverbal behaviors and the different effects they had on the client and observers. Giving useful, *specific* feedback is particularly critical. Note the suggestions for feedback in Box 2-2.

Finally, as you review the audio- or videotapes of the interview, *start and stop the tape periodically.* Replay key interactions. Only in this way can you fully profit from the recording media.

Box 2-2. Guidelines for Effective Feedback

To see ourselves as others see us.
To hear how others hear us.
And to be touched as we touch others . . .
These are the goals of effective feedback.

Feedback

Feedback is one of the skill units of the basic attending and influencing skills developed in this book; it is discussed in more detail in Chapter 11. However, if you are to help others grow and develop in this program, you must provide feedback to them now on their use of skills in practice sessions.

Here are some guidelines for effective feedback:

Guidelines

▲ *The person receiving the feedback should be in charge.* Let the interviewer in the practice sessions determine how much or little feedback is wanted.

▲ *Feedback should focus on strengths,* particularly in the early phases of the program. If negative feedback is requested by the interviewer, add positive dimensions as well. People grow from strength, not from weakness. Feedback should be helpful, not harmful.

▲ *Feedback should be concrete and specific.* Not "Your attending skills were good" but "You maintained eye contact throughout except for breaking it once when the client seemed uncomfortable." Make your feedback factual, specific, and observable.

▲ *Feedback should be relatively nonjudgmental.* Feedback often turns into evaluation. Stick to the facts and specifics. Though the word *relatively* recognizes that judgment inevitably will appear in many different types of feedback, the non-judgmental attitude often expressed by vocal qualities should appear in the other skills of interviewing as well. Avoid the words "good" and "bad" and their variations.

(continued)

Box 2-2 (continued)

▲ *Feedback should be lean and precise.* It does little good to suggest that a person change 15 things. Select one to three things the interviewer actually might be able to change in a short time. You'll have opportunities to make other suggestions later.

Step 7. Rotate roles.   Everyone should have a chance to serve as interviewer, client, and observer. Divide your time equally!

Some general reminders.   It is not necessary to compress a complete interview into 3 minutes. Behave as if you expected the session to last a longer time, and the timer can break in after 3 minutes. The purpose of the role-play sessions is to observe skills in action. Thus, you should attempt to practice skills, not solve problems. Clients have often taken years to develop their interests and concerns, so do not expect to solve their problem in a 3-minute role-play session. Written feedback, if carefully done, is an invaluable part of a program of interview skill development.

Attending Behavior Feedback Sheet

_____ (Date)

_____   _____

(Name of Interviewer)   (Name of Person Completing Form)

Instructions: Provide written feedback that is specific and observable, nonjudgmental and supportive.

1. _Eye contact._ Facilitative? Staring? Avoiding? At what points, if any, did the interviewer break contact? Facilitatively? Disruptively?

2. _Body language._ Leaning? Gestures? Facial expression? At what points, if any, did the interviewer shift position or show a marked change in body language? Number of facilitative body language movements?

3. _Vocal qualities._ Vocal tone? Speech rate? Volume? Accent? Points at which these changed in response to client actions? Number of major changes or speech hesitations?

4. _Verbal tracking and selective attention._ Staying on topic? Number of major topic jumps? Did shifts seem to indicate interviewer interest patterns? Did interviewer demonstrate selective attention in pursuing one issue rather than another?

5. _Specific positive aspects of the interview._

Self-Assessment and Follow-Up

The purpose of this section is to examine your own patterns of attending. Special attention will be given to your level of mastery of attending. The mastery levels may prompt additional suggestions for practice in this basic skill.

1. What single idea stood out for you from among all those presented in this chapter?

_____

_____

_____

2. What is your natural style of attending?

Are you able to understand a problem or concern from the other person's point of view, or do you typically try very early to provide an answer or solve a problem? What are your natural nonverbal habits of attending?

_____

_____

_____

_____

_____

_____

3. To what topics are you most likely to attend easily?

What topics do you find more difficult? What topics might you overemphasize?

_____

_____

_____

_____

4. Mastery of attending skills

Attending behavior may be considered to have four basic levels of mastery: identification, basic mastery, active mastery, and teaching mastery. Indicate the competencies you have mastered below. You may wish to practice those you find more difficult for further mastery. In each case, on the lines provided give brief and specific evidence that you have mastered the competency.

Identification. You will be able to identify and count eye contact breaks, major shifts in body posture, patterns of vocal qualities, and major topic jumps on the part of the counselor and client during the interview. You will be able to demonstrate a beginning awareness of cultural differences in these dimensions.

_____ Ability to write attending and nonattending statements.

_____ Ability to identify, through observation, specific individual and cultural differences in the attending styles of clients and other people.

Basic mastery. You will be able to demonstrate basic attending skills in the interview. You will be able to maintain culturally appropriate eye contact, body language, and vocal tone. In particular, you will be able to stay on the client's topic rather than introducing a new topic of your own. Your talk-time will be reduced while the client's increases.

_____ Ability to demonstrate culturally appropriate eye contact, body language, vocal qualities, and verbal tracking.

_____ Ability to increase client talk-time while reducing your own.

_____ Ability to stay on a client's topic without introducing any new topics of your own.

Active mastery. You will be able to use attending skills intentionally to facilitate client talk or to discourage it. You will be able to encourage clients to talk about specific topics and issues through selective attention. The effectiveness of your skill usage is measured by what your client does, not by your behavior.

_____ Ability through inattention, topic changes, and nonverbal behavior to assist clients to talk about topics that are more productive and growth producing.

_____

_____

_____ Ability to show an increased awareness of the client's pattern of attending. What topics does the client attend to or ignore?

_____

_____

_____ Ability to modify your own patterns of attending to establish rapport with an individual of a different style, background, or culture. Eye contact is not always appropriate!

_____

_____

_____ Ability to formulate your own definition of the mastery of attending skills.

_____

_____

Teaching mastery.   The ability to teach attending to others may be defined as the highest level of mastery. The effectiveness of your teaching can be measured by your students' ability to achieve identification, basic mastery, and active mastery levels of competence. Ideas for teaching attending behavior are outlined in the Appendix of this book. You will find that some clients benefit directly from your teaching them attending and listening skills. This is particularly true of those who lack social skills or who may be depressed.

For a first exercise in teaching microskills, you obviously don't want to do a workshop. However, you will find that some clients can benefit immensely by learning the four ideas of attending behavior as part of your counseling with them. This can be done effectively in a variety of ways:

1. You may simply tell a client during the interview about one or more of the four dimensions of attending behavior. Such direct instruction has helped mothers in talking with their children, managers with their employees, and many others.
2. With disturbed clients, it may be wise to mention or teach only *one* aspect of attending. More may confuse them or be forgotten.
3. Some counselors and therapists have their clients practice role-plays in the interview. As part of your treatment, role-play ineffective and effective listening in the session. Then, talk with your client about how he or she can practice listening skills with friends and with those at work.
4. You will find that some clients find reading about the ideas helpful.

Try one or more of the above suggestions for teaching and indicate your results below.

_____

_____

_____

_____

_____

_____

_____

_____

5. Read the discussion titled "Becoming a Samurai Swordsman" that follows

How do its concepts relate to your own experience of learning the single skills of the interview?

_____

_____

_____

6. Given your experience with attending behavior, what single personal attending goal might you set for yourself in the future?

_____

_____

_____

_____

▲ Becoming a Samurai Swordsman[3]

Japanese master swordsmen learn their skills through a complex set of highly detailed training exercises. The process of masterful swordsmanship is broken down into specific components that are studied carefully, one at a time. In this process of mastery, the naturally skilled person often suffers and finds handling the sword awkward. The skilled individual may even find his performance worsening during the practice of single skills. *Being aware of what one is doing can interfere with coordination and smoothness.*

---

[3]I am indebted to Lanette Shizuru, University of Hawaii, for the example of the samurai swordsman.

Once the individual skills are practiced and learned to perfection, the samurai retire to a mountaintop to meditate. They deliberately forget what they have learned. When they return they find the distinct skills have been naturally integrated into their style or way of being. The samurai then seldom have to think about skills at all: they have become samurai swordsmen.

The same holds true for ballet, tennis, golf, cooking, and many other activities of life. The rehearsal and practice of basic skills builds mastery, which later becomes integrated into our own natural style. The new, unique whole is often larger than the sum of the distinct parts.

You may likely have found discomfort in practicing the single skill of attending. Later you'll find the same problem with other skills. This happens to both the beginner and the advanced counselor. Improving and studying our natural skills often results in a temporary and sometimes frustrating decrease in competence, just as it does for the samurai.

Consider driving. When you first sat at the wheel, you had to coordinate many tasks, particularly if you drove a car with a shift lever. The clutch, the gas pedal, the steering wheel, and the gear ratios had to be coordinated smoothly with what you saw through the windshield. When you gave primary attention to the process of shifting, you might have lost sight of where you were going. But practice and experience soon led you to forget the specific skills, and you were able to coordinate them automatically and give full attention to the world beyond the windshield. The mastery of single skills led you to achieve your objectives.

II Listening to and Observing the Client: How to Organize an Interview

Attending behavior forms the base of the microskills hierarchy. Without individually and culturally appropriate attending behavior, there can be no interviewing, counseling, or psychotherapy.

This section adds to the foundation skill of attending by presenting the *basic listening sequence* that will enable you to elicit the major facts and feelings pertinent to a client's concern. Through the skills of questioning, encouraging, paraphrasing, reflecting feelings, and summarization, you will learn how to draw out your clients and understand the way they think about their problems.

Questioning skills open this section, but in addition to obtaining data you also need to observe what happens to the client as a result of your interventions. Thus an entire chapter on observation skills is included so that you may practice noting your impact on clients' verbal and nonverbal behavior. The remainder of the basic listening sequence is then presented.

Once you have mastered the basic listening sequence and observation skills, you are prepared to conduct a full well-formed interview, consisting of five stages. You will be able to conduct this interview using only listening and observation skills. Furthermore, it is important that you be able to evaluate your interviews and those of others for their level of empathic understanding. It is not only important to listen; it is also important to listen empathically.

This section, then, has ambitious goals. By the time you have completed Chapter 7, you'll have attained several major objectives, enabling you to move on to the more advanced skills of interpersonal change, growth, and development. At a mastery level of competence, you may aim to accomplish the following:

1. Master the basic listening sequence and be able to draw out the facts and feelings relevant to clients' concerns.
2. Observe clients' reactions to your skill usage and modify your skills and attending behaviors to complement their uniqueness.
3. Conduct an interview using only listening and observing skills.
4. Evaluate that interview for its level of empathy; in effect, examine yourself and your ability to communicate warmth, positive regard, and other, more subjective, dimensions of interviewing and counseling.

When you've mastered these tasks, you may find that your client has a surprising ability to solve his or her own problems. Furthermore, you may also gain a sense of confidence in your own ability as an interviewer or counselor. The motto of this book's first seven chapters, then, is "When in doubt, listen!"

CHAPTER

3 Questions: Opening Communication

How can questions help you and your clients?

Major function

If you use open questions effectively, you can expect the client to talk more freely and openly. Closed questions will elicit shorter responses and may provide you with information and specifics.

Like attending behavior, questions can encourage or discourage client talk. With questions, however, the stimulus comes mainly from the interviewer. The client is often talking within your frame of reference.

Secondary functions

Knowledge and skill in questioning result in the following:

▲ Bringing out additional specifics of the client's world.
▲ Making an effective diagnosis of a client's concern or issue.
▲ Guiding the manner in which a client talks about an issue. For example, *what* questions often lead to talk about facts, *how* questions to feelings or process, and *why* questions to reasons.
▲ The ability to open or close client talk according to the individual needs of the interview.

▲ Introduction

While attending behavior forms the foundation of the microskills hierarchy, it is questioning skills that provide a systematic framework for directing the interview. Questions help an interview begin and move along smoothly. They open new areas for discussion, assist in pinpointing and clarifying issues, and aid in clients' self-exploration. However, some theorists do not like questions and suggest that the interviewer never ask them. Your central task in this chapter is to examine this skill and to determine where you stand on the issue of questions in the interview.

Why do some people object to questions? Take a minute to recall and explore some of your own experiences with questions in the past. Perhaps you had a teacher or a parent who used questions in a certain manner that resulted in your feeling a particular way. Write below one of your negative experiences with questions and the feelings and thoughts the questioning process produced in you.

My experience with questions was as follows:

_____

_____

_____

_____

The thoughts and feelings this experience produced in me were as follows:

_____

_____

_____

_____

Many people respond to this exercise by describing situations in which they were "put on the spot" and "grilled" by someone else. They may associate questions with anger and guilt. Many of us have had negative experiences with questions. Furthermore, questions may be used to direct and control client talk. If your objective is to enable clients to truly find their own way, questions may inhibit your reaching that goal, particularly if they are used ineffectively. It is for these reasons that some helping authorities, particularly those humanistically oriented, object to questions in the interview. In addition, in many non-Western cultures questions are inappropriate and may be considered offensive.

Nevertheless, questions remain a fact of life in our culture. We encounter them everywhere. The physician or nurse, the salesperson, the government official, and many others find questioning clients basic to their profession. Most counseling theories use questions extensively. The issue, then, is how to question wisely and intentionally. The goal of this section is to explore some aspects of questions and, eventually, to determine their place in your communication skills repertoire. The basic focus of this chapter on questioning skills is on open and closed questions.

Open questions are those that can't be answered in a few words. They encourage others to talk and provide you with maximum information. Typically, open questions begin with *what, how, why,* or *could:* for example, "Could you tell me what brings you here today?"

Closed questions can be answered in a few words or sentences. They have the advantage of focusing the interview and obtaining information, but the burden of guiding the talk remains on the interviewer. Closed questions often begin with *is, are,* or *do:* for example, "Are you living with your family?"

▲ Example Interviews

In the following examples we see how counseling skills can be used in business management. In the first example, the manager uses closed questions almost exclusively to achieve his objective; in a contrasting example, he uses open questions to achieve a different objective. The open questions are used to clarify the situation and assist the other person to resolve her own problems.

Closed-Question Example

Don: Hi, Suzie. What's up?

Suzie: Well, I'm having a problem with Jo again.

Don: Is she arguing with people again?

Suzie: Yes, she's having a difficult time getting along with the other people.

Don: Does she get to work on time?

Suzie: She gets to work on time. That's not the problem. (Suzie appears somewhat frustrated and confused. Don is leaning forward, taking some of her space. Suzie, having experienced this type of behavior before, holds her own ground.)

Don: Does she try hard?

Suzie: She tries hard. That's not the problem.

Don: So, it's a personality problem?

Suzie: Yeah. (This is said with some relief, as Don has finally heard what she wanted him to hear. Don, however, is working much harder to get that information than is really necessary.)

Don: Does she get along with Jane?

Suzie: Well, some of the time. I mean, not really . . . ah . . . I mean, everybody has a hard time with Jane.

Don: Do you get along . . . how about Sam?

Suzie: Not really anybody. Any time she has to do something for somebody else she, you know, she can't follow through, she has a hard time.

Don: Does she follow your orders?

Suzie: (surprised) Not as much as I'd like . . .

Don: Are you being clear when you give her orders, Suzie?

Suzie: . . . I try to be . . . I . . .

Don: Sometimes you're pretty vague.

Suzie: Probably that's right. I expect her to . . . you're right . . . I probably expect her to do things on her own a little bit more than she's able. She needs more direction . . . (Don is playing the game of "Who's got the monkey?" Rather than take time to determine what is really happening via open questions, he uses closed questions to validate his own prior assumptions and is placing the blame, or "monkey," with Suzie. While this may often be effective, it doesn't allow Suzie much room.)

Don: Do you think you maybe need to be a little bit more clear?

Suzie: Probably, but I wonder if she has a hard time hearing people. I often wonder if she misses things.

Don: Sounds like you need to give her clearer orders. Do you think you can do that?

Suzie: I think so . . .

> *Comment:* Closed questions are helpful in obtaining specifics. This example should not deter you from their use. The overuse of closed questions, however, is a distinct problem in many supervisory and counseling interviews.

Open-Question Example

Don: Hi, Suzie, what's up?

Suzie: Hi, Don. I'm having a problem with Jo—you know, the woman I hired this fall to work for me. (Attending behavior serves as a solid foundation for this interview. Suzie is more relaxed and attentive herself. Throughout the session there is an atmosphere of respect and ease between the interviewer and the interviewee.)

Don: Oh, yeah. Could you tell me generally what's been going on? (an open question beginning with the maximally open *could*)

Suzie: Well, Jo's just been having a hard time working with everybody, everybody on our staff. You know. . . she'll often interrupt them. Jo talks incessantly and, you know, takes a lot of time. People are very busy and have to stop and listen to her. And, to give her instructions, I have to do it over and over again. Then *I* have to listen to what she has to say about something. It's taking a great deal of time, and people find it offensive.

Don: How do you feel about her, Suzie? (open question dealing with feelings, beginning with *how*)

Suzie: Well, she's a nice woman and she means well, but I have a hard time listening to her. She's just . . . she seems to talk so much about everything, and it's difficult. I don't have all that much time, either, you know, and I have to keep moving. I have lots to do and don't have time to sit and listen to her all the time.

Don: Repeating the question, Suzie, how do you feel about her? I do hear you think *she* is nice. (Don has a solid prior relationship with Suzie and so can force the issue a bit more. Suzie and he both know she often avoids talking about her feelings. Feelings can be important in determining action. Without a solid relationship this string of questions would be too aggressive.)

Suzie: She's just hard to work with. She makes me feel a bit sad and even angry. She means well, but I have a hard time relating to her. I have a hard time liking her, too, because she's so intrusive.

Don: Uh-huh.

Suzie: Also, her voice is very difficult to listen to.

Don: Why do you think she does this? (*Why* questions tend to bring out reasons and interpretations of the situation. However, *why* often puts people on the defensive, and many authorities argue against *why* questions. How often did your parents ask you the same question?)

Suzie: I think she probably wants to do a good job, but she has a need to control. She wants to be in charge and therefore seems to want to direct and talk to people all the time. I think she's going to go about getting her way no matter what, even if it means talking to everybody until they are absolutely sick of her . . . and then, finally, she gets her way.

Don: So far, Suzie, I've heard you say that you're having trouble with Jo and that it's kind of an ongoing problem.

Suzie: Uh-huh.

Don: Ah . . . it seems that one of the important things is that she isn't getting along too well with others. She talks a lot and is intrusive. You, too, feel angry with her, particularly at her intrusiveness. You have a hard time liking her. I gather that you feel she needs to control. Am I hearing you accurately so far? (This is a *summarization,* a skill that is discussed in more detail in Chapter 5. Questions bring out considerable data, and you will find it helpful if you summarize what you are hearing from time to time. The closed question at the end is a *perception check* or *check-out.* This is an important aspect of the interview. In the microskills system, this provides room for the client or other person to react to what you have said. It is a way of sharing ownership of the interview.)

Suzie: Yes, that's exactly accurate. (She smiles.)

Don: Now, maybe it would help if you could give a very specific example. Could you give me a specific example of one situation where she caused this type of reaction? (Up to this point Suzie has talked in generalities about Jo. Asking the client for a specific example is an important interviewer skill. It brings concreteness to the interview. The phrase *hard time,* for example, means different things to different people. But when we get a concrete description of observable behavior, we have something both interviewer and counselee can agree to. In fact, "Could you give me a specific example of . . . ?" may be the most useful question in your repertoire.)

Suzie: Okay, she was assigned work with the R-and-D department, in which she had to do some purchase plans with the supervisor. She had her own ideas for the project. She wanted to change the design of the form, while the R-and-D super wanted quicker feedback from us. I suppose Jo had a good idea, but she ended up arguing with the super and caused a lot of dissension between the two groups. Sure, we need the new form, but we also need to get along with R and D. And . . . she didn't schedule the appointment, either. You know Bill, the R-and-D super, wants the status treatment. Jo thinks that's foolish, and she insists on doing it her way.

Comment: This interview illustrates the use of just a few open questions. If you have a verbal client, extensive data emerges in a relatively short time. Note that the responsibility rests with the client in this session and with the supervisor in the closed-question session. Client talk-time is increased with open questions.

▲ Instructional Reading

Clients come to the interview seeking to say something about their interests and concerns. If it is an employment interview, they want to talk about their positive assets and make a good impression. In many sales, management, or medical situations, the client wants to express ideas clearly and concisely so that help may be obtained for some problem or need. Clients in counseling and therapy want to express themselves also, but they sometimes find it difficult.

In all these diverse situations, skill with open and closed questions can facilitate client self-disclosure and enable interviews to achieve their objectives more completely. At the same time, a barrage of probing, insensitive questions may put the client on guard and impede open communication. Several basic points about open and closed questions are noted below.

1. Questions help begin the interview

With verbal clients the open question facilitates free discussion and leaves plenty of room to talk. Here are some examples:

"What would you like to talk about today?"
"Could you tell me what you'd like to see me about?"
"How have things been since we last talked together?"
"The last time we met we talked about your tension while watching the baseball game. How did it go this week?"

The first three open questions provide considerable room, in that the client can talk about virtually anything. The last question is open but provides some focus for the session, building on material from the preceding week.

Such open questions may be more than a nontalkative client can handle, however. In such cases, a gentle series of closed questions—"Did you go to the baseball game last week?" "Who won?" "Were you tense once again?" and the like—may provide structure for the interview. These can be followed by more open questions as the client begins to talk more freely.

2. Open questions help elaborate and enrich the interview

A beginning interviewer often asks one or two questions and then wonders what to do next. Even more experienced interviewers at times find themselves hard put to know what to do. An open question on some topic the client presented earlier in the interview helps the session start again and keep moving:

"Could you tell me more about that?"

"How did you feel when that happened?"

"Given what you've said, what would be your ideal solution to the problem?"

3. Questions help bring out concrete specifics of the client's world

If there is one single open question that appears to be useful in most theoretical persuasions or in most practice situations, it is that which aims for concreteness and specifics in the client's situation. Again, the model question "Could you give me a specific example?" is the most useful open question available to any interviewer. Many clients tend to talk in vague generalities, and specific, concrete examples enrich the interview and provide data for action. Some additional open questions that aim for concreteness and specifics are illustrated below:

Client: George makes me so mad!

Counselor: Could you give me a specific example of what George does? *or*
What does George do specifically that brings out your anger? *or*
What do you mean by "makes me mad?" *or*
Could you specify what you do before and after George makes you mad?

Closed questions, of course, can bring out specifics as well, but they place more responsibility on the interviewer. However, if the interviewer knows specifically the desired direction of the interview, closed questions such as "Did George show his anger by striking you?" "Does George tease you often?" "Is George on drugs?" and so on may prove invaluable. Yet even well-directed closed questions may take the initiative away from the client.

4. Questions are critical in the diagnosis and assessment of a problem

Physicians must diagnose their clients' physical symptoms. Managers may have to diagnose a problem on the production line. Vocational counselors need to diagnose a client's vocational history. Questions are the meat of effective diagnosis. George Kelly, the personality theorist, has suggested for general client problem diagnosis the following set of questions, which roughly follow the *who, what, when, where, how, why* of newspaper reporters:

Who is the client? What is the client's personal background? Who else may be involved?

What is the client's problem? What is happening? What are the specific details of the situation?

When does the problem occur? When did it begin? What immediately preceded the occurrence of the problem?

Where does the problem occur? In what environments and situations?

How does the client react to the problem? How does the client feel about it?

Why does the problem occur?

Needless to say, the *who, what, when, where, how, why* series of questions also provides the interviewer with a ready system for helping the client elaborate or be more specific on an issue at any time during a session.

5. The first word of certain open questions partially determines client verbalizations

Often, but not always, key question stems result in predictable outcomes.

What questions most often lead to facts. "What happened?" "What are you going to do?"

How questions often lead to a discussion about processes or sequences or to feelings. "How could that be explained?" "How do you feel about that?"

Why questions most often lead to a discussion of reasons. "Why did you allow that to happen?" "Why do you think that is so?"

Could questions are considered maximally open and contain some of the advantages of closed questions in that the client is free to say "No, I don't want to talk about that." *Could* questions reflect less control and command than others. "Could you tell me more about your situation?" "Could you give me a specific example?" "Could you tell me what you'd like to talk about today?"

6. Questions have certain potential problems

While questions can have immense value in the interview, we must not forget their potential problems. Among these are the following:

Bombardment/grilling.   Too many questions will tend to put many clients on the defensive. They may also give too much control to the interviewer.

Multiple questions.   Interviewers may confuse their clients by throwing out several questions at once. This is another form of bombardment, although at times it may be helpful to some clients.

Questions as statements.   Some interviewers may use questions as a way to sell their own points of view. "Don't you think it would be helpful if you studied more?" "What do you think of trying relaxation exercises instead of what you are doing now?" This form of question, just like multiple questions, can be helpful at times. Awareness of the nature of the question, however, may suggest alternative and more direct routes to reach the client. A useful rule of thumb is that if you are going to make a statement, it is best not to frame it as a question.

Questions and cultural differences.   The rapid-fire questioning style of our culture is often received less favorably in non-Western groups. If you are working with a member of a cultural group different from your own, be aware that excessive use of questions sometimes results in distrust of the counselor.

Why questions.   Most of us experienced some form of the "Why did you do that?" question as children. *Why* questions often put interviewees on the defensive and cause discomfort. This same discomfort can be produced by any question that evokes a sense of being grilled.

Questions and control.   The person who asks the questions is usually in control of the interview. He or she is determining who talks about what, when the talk will occur, and under what conditions it will occur. At times, questions can be helpful in bringing out-of-control interviews under control and direction. At the same time, questions can be used unfairly and intrusively for the interviewer's gain rather than the client's.

7. Questions can be used to monitor the comfort and pace of the interview

Questions, used effectively, can help the counselor or interviewer pace the session. If a client finds himself or herself revealing too much and the counselor senses this discomfort, a series of closed questions can help the client slow down and regain composure. Similarly, open questions can provide room for the client to open up and explore things in greater depth. The skilled, intentional use of questioning can help produce an interview that meets the client's needs and wishes.

Box 3-1. Key Points

Why?	Questions help begin the interview, open new areas for discussion, assist in pin-pointing and clarifying issues, and assist the client in self-exploration.
What?	Questions can be described as open or closed: *Open questions* are those that can't be answered in a few short words. They encourage others to talk and provide you with maximum information. Typically, open questions begin with *how, why,* or *could.* One of the most helpful of all open questions is "Could you give a specific example of . . . ?"
	Closed questions are those that can be answered in a few words or sentences. They have the advantage of focusing the interview and bringing out specifics, but they place the prime responsibility for talk on the interviewer. Closed questions often begin with *is, are,* or *do.* An example is "Where do you live?"
	It is important to note that a question, open or closed, on a topic of deep interest to the client will often result in extensive talk-time *if* it is interesting enough and important enough. If an interview is flowing well, the distinction between open and closed questions is less important.
How?	A general framework for diagnosis and question asking is provided by the newspaper reporter framework of *who, what, when, where, how, why?*
	Who is the client? What are key personal background factors? Who else is involved? *What* is the problem? What are the specific details of the situation? *When* does the problem occur? What immediately preceded and followed the situation? *Where* does the problem occur? In what environments and situations? *How* does the client react? How does he or she feel about it? *Why* does the problem occur?
	Interviewing is about more than problems. The same set of questions could be asked to discover what events and issues surround a positive situation or accomplishment. Too much interview training emphasizes problems and difficulties. A positive approach is needed for balance.

(continued)

Box 3-1 (continued)

| *With whom?* | Questions may turn off some clients. Some cultural groups find North American rapid-fire questions rude and intrusive. Yet questions are very much a part of our culture and provide a way to obtain information that most clients find helpful. |
| *And?* | The first word of open questions often leads to a variety of results. For example, *what* questions lead to facts, *how* to feelings and process, *why* to reasons. *Could* is often the most open: "Could you tell me more?" "Could you give me an example?" |

▲ Practice Exercises and Self-Assessment

How are you going to use questions in your own interviewing practice? The following exercises are designed to increase your mastery of questioning skills and to encourage you to decide if and how you want to use questions.

Individual Practice

Exercise 1. Which of the following questions are open (O) and which closed (C)?

_____ Do you come here often?
_____ Where does your daughter live?
_____ Do you get along with Joe?
_____ What important things have happened during the week?
_____ Could you tell me about your family?
_____ How do you imagine she feels about that?
_____ Why do you think Harry quit his job?

Exercise 2. Writing questions that may be expected to affect client talk

A client tells you the following:

My check is lost. I think I left it on the bureau, but I looked there, and it is gone. I worry that my son might have taken it and used it for drugs.

Write below open questions that will tend to bring out general information, specific facts, feelings, and reasons.

Could _____ ?

What _____ ?

How _____ ?

Why _____ ?

Now, generate three closed questions that might bring out some specifics of the situation.

Do _____ ?

Are _____ ?

Where _____ ?

Finally, what questions might be used to get specific examples and details that might enlarge and make the problem more concrete?

_____

_____

Exercise 3. Observation of questions in your daily interactions

This chapter has talked about the basic question stems *what, how, why,* and *could,* and how clients respond differently to each. During a conversation with a friend or acquaintance, try sequentially these four basic question stems:

Could you tell me generally what happened?
What are the critical facts?
How do you feel about the situation?
Why do you think it happened?

Record your observations below. Were the predictions of the book fulfilled? Did the person provide you in order with (1) a general picture of the situation, (2) the relevant facts, (3) personal feelings about the situation, and (4) background reasons that might be causing the situation?

_____

_____

_____

_____

_____

_____

_____

_____

Systematic Group Practice

Two systematic exercises are suggested for practice with questions. The first focuses on the use of open and closed questions, the second on the diagnosis of a client's concern or problem. The instructional steps for practice are abbreviated from those described in Chapter 2, on attending behavior. As necessary, refer back to those instructions for more detail on the steps for systematic practice.

Exercise 1. Systematic group practice on open and closed questions

Step 1. Divide into practice groups.

Step 2. Select a group leader.

Step 3. Assign roles for the first practice session.

▲ Role-played client
▲ Interviewer
▲ Observer 1
▲ Observer 2, who runs equipment and keeps time

Step 4. Planning.   The interviewer should plan to use both open and closed questions. It is important in the practice session that the key *what, how, why,* and *could* questions be used.

For active mastery, planning should include efforts to produce specific client results as indicated in the active-mastery list of competencies in the Self-Assessment and Follow-Up section. Specifically, the interviewer should be able to elicit the overall situation, the key facts, the feelings related to those facts, and the reasons underlying the situation.

The suggested topic for this role-play is a real situation in which the client did something he or she felt good about. To repeat an important point, counseling and interviewing too often focus on negative behaviors and problems. Some time given to assets in the interview will provide an opportunity to balance negative thinking.

Suggested alternative topics might include the following:

A friend or family member who does something well
A problem I find interesting and stimulating
A positive addiction I have (such as jogging, health food, biking, team sports)

Observers should take this time to examine feedback forms and to plan their own sessions.

Step 5. Conduct a 3-minute practice session using only questions.   The interviewer should practice open and closed questions and may wish to have handy a list of suggested question stems (*could, what, how, why*). The client should be relatively cooperative and talkative, but not respond at such length that the interviewer has a limited opportunity to ask questions.

Step 6. Review the practice session and provide feedback to the interviewer for 12 minutes.   Be sure to use the feedback form that follows these group exercises to ensure that the interviewer's questions have been recorded accurately. Feedback based on impressions is not nearly as valuable as feedback citing specific, observable data. The interviewer, too, should examine his or her performance—were the planned objectives achieved?

Remember to stop the audio- or videotape periodically and listen to or view key happenings several times for increased clarity. Generally speaking, it is wise to provide some feedback before reviewing the tape, but this sometimes results in a failure to view or listen to the tape at all.

Step 7. Rotate roles.

A reminder.   The question "Could you give me a specific example?" tends to be one of the most helpful of all questions as it helps the client or other person become much more specific and concrete. Too much interviewing takes place in broad generalities rather than behavioral specifics understandable to all. You will often find that this question changes and clarifies your impression of the client and the client's problems.

Exercise 2. Systematic practice in elementary assessment

This exercise focuses on the use of the newspaper formula (*who, what, when where, how,* and *why*) to obtain a basic summary of a client's problem or issue. The steps of the exercise are identical to the preceding series of seven steps. The same feedback form may be used.

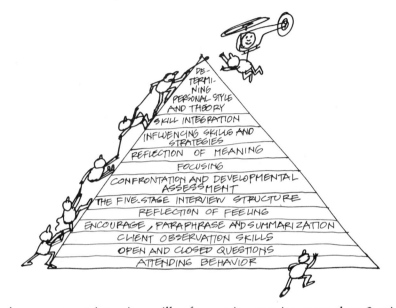

An assessment interview will, of necessity, require more than 3 minutes. The broad questions of the newspaper formula will need amplification by further open and closed questions. The key question "Could you give me a specific example?" will often prove useful. The assessment interview may run 15 minutes or more in a practice session.

Here are some suggested topics for the practice assessment interview:

Difficulty with a present or past academic course
Work problems, past or present
A past illness or experience with a family member who was ill
Views on alcohol, drugs, sexuality

Questions Feedback Sheet

_____ (Date)

_____   _____
(Name of Interviewer)   (Name of Person Completing Form)

Instructions: List below the questions asked by the interviewer as completely as possible. At a minimum, indicate the first key words of the question (_what, why, how, do, are_, and so on). Indicate whether each question was open (O) or closed (C).

_____   1. _____

_____   2. _____

_____   3. _____

_____   4. _____

_____   5. _____

_____   6. _____

_____   7. _____

_____   8. _____

_____   9. _____

_____   10. _____

1. Which questions seemed to provide the most useful client information?

2. Provide specific feedback on the attending skills of the interviewer.

3. Give your general impressions of the interview.

Self Assessment and Follow-Up

How do you feel and think about questions? The purpose of this section is to help you think through your position on questions and examine your level of mastery of questioning skills.

1. Questions are a controversial skill in the helping professions. Do you want to use them at all? If so, how?

_____

_____

_____

_____

_____

_____

_____

_____

_____

2. What is your position on the use of _why_ questions in the interview?

_____

_____

_____

_____

3. What specific questioning competencies have you mastered? Give evidence for each level of mastery in the space provided.

**Identification.**   You will be able to identify and classify open and closed questions and to note their specific impact in the interview.

_____ Ability to classify questions as open or closed.

_____

_____

_____ Ability to note the impact of open and closed questions and specific question stems on clients and other persons.

_____

_____

**Basic mastery.**   You will be able to demonstrate the use of open and closed questions in a role-played interview and will be able to use those questions deliberately in daily life.

_____   Ability to use questions in a role-played interview.

_____

_____

_____   Ability to use questions in daily life situations.

_____

_____

Active mastery.   You will be able to use questioning skills to achieve a specific, demonstrable impact on client talk in the interview. At issue is what the client does in response to your questioning skills. At this point, aim to produce a specific result from your verbal intervention. Evidence of your ability can be provided by audiotapes and/or written journal examples.

_____   Use of open questions to enable clients to bring out more data.
_____   Use of closed questions to close off and/or direct client talk to specifics.
_____   Use of *could* questions to elicit the general picture or a summary of a situation.
_____   Use of *what* questions to elicit facts and information.
_____   Use of *how* questions to enable clients to talk about feelings and/or process.
_____   Use of *why* questions to bring out reasons.
_____   Ability to assist clients to produce specifics via the "Could you give me a specific example?" type of question.
_____   Use of the newspaper formula to bring out the basic facts of a client's problem for an elementary assessment.
_____   Use of questions to enable a client to talk about facts, then feelings, then facts again, thus providing a change of pace and demonstrating your ability to facilitate client talk in different directions.
_____   Ability to start a client talking about a subject, then to stop and move to another subject via questioning.

Teaching mastery.   You will demonstrate the ability to teach questions to clients and other persons. The impact of your teaching will be measured by your students' achievements based on the above criteria. This skill may be particularly helpful to clients who lack skills in speaking to others or who feel shy. Foreign students coming to the United States and Canada have benefited by learning how to ask questions; it appears to be a most useful skill in social situations to help others start talking. You may want to take a friend or client through the systematic Group Practice in this chapter. First, have your client read the Key Points box, then work through the exercises. Additional suggestions will be found in the Appendix.

_____

_____

4. Given your experience with questioning skills, what one single goal for increasing your mastery might you set for yourself at this point?

_____

_____

_____

_____

_____

_____

4 Client Observation Skills

How can client observation skills help you and your clients?

Major function   Client observation skills enable you to note and understand clients' behavior in the interview and their patterns of description of key situations. This understanding will help you choose useful interviewing skills and counseling interventions to facilitate client growth and development.

Secondary functions   Knowledge and skill in client observation result in an increased ability to note the following:

▲ Client nonverbal behavior
▲ Client verbal behavior
▲ Client discrepancies, conflicts, and incongruities

▲ Introduction

The skilled interviewer is concerned with facilitating human development, but understanding your clients, their behavior, and thoughts will be central to those efforts. It is therefore important that you become skilled in observing client behaviors in your interviewing sessions. This chapter is concerned with sharpening those powers of observation. You will find that the basic skills of attending and questioning continue to be useful in this process.

What should you observe about client behavior in the interview? From your own life experience you are already aware of many things that are important for a counselor or interviewer to notice about other people and clients. Brainstorm from what you already know and make a list below:

_____

_____

_____

_____

_____

_____

_____

There is an almost infinite array of things you can observe about clients. How can you organize all these data in a meaningful way? Some unifying principles are necessary if we are to make sense of our clients' often confusing worlds. Psychological theories help us make sense of and organize our own understanding of client behavior; however, this chapter does not deal with theory. Rather, it presents three key dimensions that will help you to understand your client's world *before* you start applying a formal theory of your own viewpoint to the client's situation.

1. *Client nonverbal behavior.* Some authorities have claimed that 85% or more of client communication of meaning is nonverbal. Client eye contact patterns, body language, and vocal qualities should be observed. Supplementary information on body language will be presented in this chapter that can be added to that of Chapter 2 on attending behavior.

2. *Client verbal behavior.* Words form the basis of most interviewing and counseling sessions. Clients tend to focus on certain key words and constructs. Through selective attention and verbal tracking, you can better enter clients' worlds and understand their patterns of thinking.

3. *Client discrepancies.* Incongruities, mixed messages, contradictions, and conflict are often the reasons clients come to the interview; in other words, because of some discrepancy within themselves or in relation to someone or something else. Careful observation of client verbal and nonverbal behavior will provide the counselor or interviewer with extensive data on conflict and discrepancies in the client's world. It is often these data that provide the framework for attacking client problems.

More information will be presented in this chapter than most readers will be able to use immediately, but the concepts will be repeated and used throughout the remainder of this book to provide further practice.

You will now have an opportunity to read a transcript of the early stages of an interview, in which the counselor uses attending and questioning skills exclusively to reveal a basic discrepancy in a client. The task at this point is not to problem-solve, but rather to understand "where the client is coming from," or how she or he views the world. Important here is observing key aspects of verbal and nonverbal communication.

▲ Example Interview

Our task in examining the following interview is different from that in the preceding two chapters. There we examined interviewer behavior with minimal attention to the client. This interview has been edited extensively and condensed to provide as many examples as possible to illustrate issues critical to include in your observation.

Jane: You were saying that you are troubled by your relationship with your parents, that they aren't satisfied with your job or your relationship with Carol. I sense anger, frustration, and hurt. Could you tell me a little more about it?

Ralph: Yeah . . . It seems that they are always on me. Dad is a driver . . . uh . . . he's made a mint in sales. He thinks I should do as well as he did at the same age. (As Ralph talks, he looks at the floor; he sits in a slumped, dejected fashion; his speech is slow and deliberate. There is one speech hesitation. There are no gestures.)

Jane: Could you give me a specific example of when you and your father disagreed?

Ralph: Well, last night I was going out with Carol. We were going to go to the movies. He saw me backing the car out of the driveway and came running up. I can see the fire in his eyes. He started shouting, saying that I hadn't asked permission. And it just looked impossible, and I couldn't say anything. (Ralph looks up and talks more animatedly while discussing this concrete example. At the end, when he talks about his inability to say anything, his eyes drop, his face flushes, and his right hand clenches in a fist. Note that Ralph is using visual imagery in his statements "*saw* me backing . . . ," "*see* the fire . . . ," "*looked* impossible . . . ")

Jane: So things *looked* impossible to you. How did you feel when that happened? What do you *visualize* was happening inside you? (Note that Jane has matched Ralph's visual imagery. She is now searching for feelings.)

Ralph: I *see* myself as *focusing* on tension, my *image* is of tight muscles, moving away. (Ralph closes his eyes, and his hands move to cover his stomach.)

Jane: You felt tense. What *perspective* or meaning does this have for you? What sense do you make out of it? (Jane is searching here for the meaning of the situation for Ralph.)

Ralph: I do want to please my father, but he makes it impossible for me to meet the *picture* he demands of me. I've got my own *image* of myself. (As Ralph talks, his right hand is tense and closed, his left hand open.)

Jane: So what I *see* is that you have been saying that the *pictures* you have of yourself and those of your father conflict. There seem to be different *perspectives* on what you are and want to be. (Jane points out the incongruity or discrepancy between the son's and the father's pictures of the situation. It is these discrepancies that provide data for the bulk of the interview.)

Ralph: Yeah . . . that *looks* right, the *picture* is fuzzy, but we sure do have different ideas of what I seem to *look like* and need. It gets to me. (At this point, Ralph seems a bit more relaxed, his eyes are more frequently on the interviewer. His body is somewhat more congruent with his speech, although he is sitting toward the edge of the chair with his shoulders slightly hunched.)

Comment: So far in the interview you should be able to see, hear, and feel that a considerable amount of client data have been produced. Making sense of all those data is one skill of the successful interviewer or counselor. The conflict with the father is the major discrepancy that has been identified. While it may need further honing (for example, "Tell me more about your father" or "Describe some other interactions with him") and exploration of feelings and meanings, a basic problem definition has been established. Ralph's key words (verbal descriptors) should also be noted. The father is described as a driver who made a mint in sales. Ralph's brief description of himself includes some important key words including *impossible, couldn't say anything,* and *moving away.* Key descriptive words used by clients usually indicate their understanding of a person or situation and may indicate the meaning the situation has to them. A task of the interviewer is to note the meaning behind the descriptors and help the client develop alternative meanings and actions.

Jane: It would help if you could describe a situation where you and your father were able to *see* each other *clearly* and perhaps had more feelings in tune with each other. (The interviewer is still within Ralph's visual imagery, but is adding feeling and auditory images or concepts as well. The search for a positive experience may reveal strengths in the client.)

Ralph: One thing Dad and I have been able to work together on is when we do something around the house, like paint or build a new closet. (Ralph talks with a little more animation, his body is more relaxed. No nonverbal discrepancies may be observed.)

Jane: *Looks* and *sounds* like you were *able* to do something. Tell me more about it. (Jane has matched Ralph's visual system and adds a secondary system of auditory listening to strengthen the impression. She has also picked up on the word *able.* Note that *able* is a contrast to the words *impossible* and *moving away* mentioned earlier as key descriptors.)

Ralph: For example, when we built the closet, I was able to meet my father's demands. In fact, it was fun . . . we both enjoyed the *appearance* of the end product. We were able to work together. (Ralph continues to appear more relaxed and evidences a slight smile.)

Jane: So, when you were working together with mutual goals, things went differently . . . it *looked* and *felt* good, it *sounds* to me. Remember that positive *feeling* and *image.* Now put it together with the feelings of inadequacy and impossibility you were talking about as you gave me the picture of the two of you driving out of the driveway. What sense do you make of the two images?

Ralph: Hummmm . . . I *see* myself in one situation doing what Dad and I wanted to do together. It really *felt good.* But now it seems that he wants me to do everything he says. Yet he always stressed the importance of me "being my own man." It seems confusing and impossible. (Ralph starts slowly with a major speech hesitation. His shoulders hunch again, and his eyes squint. When he says *felt good,* he relaxes for a moment and smiles slightly. A tone of bitterness and frustration enters when he talks about being his own man and his feelings of confusion.)

Jane: What do those words *confusing* and *impossible* mean to you? (At this point, Jane is searching for the underlying, deeper meanings of two key words.)

Comment: There are extensive data in this condensed interview, even though it is very brief. The task of the beginning interviewer and counselor at the first stage is simply to note the data and organize it into verbal and nonverbal dimensions. Later, concepts of discrepancy, incongruity, and conflict can be added. There is always room for increased sophistication and awareness of the behavior of the client. Those verbal and nonverbal data give us specific suggestions for when to open the interview further, to narrow or focus it, or even to change the topic completely.

▲ Instructional Reading

Three organizing principles for understanding client behavior are stressed in this chapter: nonverbal behavior, verbal behavior, and discrepancies or incongruities. Over time, you will gain considerable skill in drawing out and working with the client's view of the world.

Nonverbal Behavior

Attending behavior patterns are important to observe in clients. Clients may be expected to break eye contact, exhibit bodily movement, and change vocal qualities when they are talking about topics of varying levels of comfort to them. You may observe clients crossing their arms or legs when they want to close off a topic, rapid alternations of eye contact during periods of confusion, or increased stammering or speech hesitations while pursuing difficult topics. This chapter includes a nonverbal behavior observation form that you may use to increase your awareness of these and other behaviors.

Facial expressions are particularly important to observe. The brow may furrow, lips may tighten or loosen, flushing may occur, a client may smile at an inappropriate time. Even more careful observation will reveal subtle color changes in the face as blood flow changes with emotional reactions. Breathing may change or stop temporarily. The lips may swell, and pupils may dilate or contract. These seemingly small responses are important clues to what a client is experiencing; to notice them takes work and practice. You may want to select one or two aspects and study them for a few days in your regular daily interactions and then move on to others as part of a systematic program to heighten your powers of observation.

Particularly important are discrepancies in nonverbal behavior. When a client is talking casually about a friend, for example, one hand may be tightly clenched in a fist and the other relaxed and open, possibly indicating mixed feelings toward the friend or something related to the friend.

Dramatic and interesting patterns of movement exist between people. It is useful to observe their degree of harmony of movement with others. Often people who are communicating well will "mirror" each other's body language. They may unconsciously sit in identical positions and even make complex hand movements together as if in a ballet. This is termed *movement synchrony*. Other paired movements may not be identical, but still harmonious, as in *movement complementarity*. For instance, one person talks and the other nods in agreement. You may observe a hand movement at the end of one person's statement that is answered by a related hand movement as the other takes the conversational "ball" and starts talking.

Needless to say, patterns of *movement dissynchrony* should also be observed. Lack of harmony in movement is common between people who disagree markedly or even between those who have subtle conflicts that they may not be aware of.

You as interviewer will want to observe your degree of body harmony with your clients. How do your movements relate to theirs? Discreetly but deliberately assuming their posture and some of their movements may help you to get in touch with their experience. Many expert counselors and therapists practice "mirroring" their clients. Experience has shown them that matching body language, breathing rates, and key words of the client can heighten their understanding of how the other perceives and experiences the world.

Verbal Behavior

Many clients will demonstrate problems of verbal tracking and selective attention. They may either stay on a single topic to the exclusion of other important issues or change the topic, either subtly or abruptly, when they want to avoid talking about a difficult issue. Perhaps the most difficult task of the beginning counselor or interviewer is to help the client stay on the topic without being overcontrolling. Observing client topic changes is particularly important. At times it may be helpful to comment, for instance, "A few minutes ago we were talking about X." Another possibility is to follow up that observation by asking how the client might explain the shift in topic.

"I statements"

Clients often give you clues by repeating statements that are particularly important to them. These sentences may be stated rather clearly and take the form of "I statements" (for example, "I am depressed" or "I am thinking of having an abortion" or "I can't get along with Bob"). "I statements" may be implicit and/or confused ("I don't know what's wrong with me" or "I feel lost; I don't know what to say"). The task of the interviewer in both cases is to note these key sentences and to help clients explore the facts and concrete specifics of the situation, the way they feel about them, and what they mean to them. For example:

Client: I'm having a terrible time getting along on the production line. I can't make my quota, and the foreman is pushing me. I'm afraid I'll be fired.

Counselor: (searching for more facts underlying the key sentence) Could you tell me *specifically* what the foreman said to you?

Counselor: (listening for feelings about the situation) How do you feel toward the foreman?

Counselor: (determining meaning to the client) And what does this all mean to you personally?

Key words

If you listen carefully to clients, you will find that certain words appear again and again in their descriptions of situations. Noting their key words and helping them explore the facts, feelings, and meanings underlying those words may be useful. Key descriptive words are often the constructs by which a client organizes the world; they may reveal underlying meanings. *Verbal underlining* through vocal emphasis is another helpful clue to determining what is most important to a client. Through intonation and volume, clients tend to stress the single words or phrases that are most important to them.

You will find that joining clients by using their key words facilitates your understanding and communication with them. If their words are negative and self-demeaning, reflect those perceptions early in the interview, but later help them use more positive descriptions of the same situations or events. Often you will aim to help the client change from "I can't" to "I can."

Individual verbal styles of perceiving the world

Finally, clients have individual ways of receiving information from the world, which is reflected in their choice of language. Some of us obtain our data primarily through visual means: we need to "see the situation." Others may be auditorily oriented and "hear what is happening." Still others are kinesthetically inclined and need physical representations before full understanding is gained: they may need to "feel out the situation." You will find it helpful to note the words used by your clients and to match your language to facilitate their expression. Some example words follow:

Visual	*Auditory*	*Kinesthetic*
see	hear	feel
perceive	sounds	touch
view	in tune	wrap around
visualize	harmony	let's dance
imagine	that rings a bell	swinging
draw a picture	dissonant	blow away
flat	sharp	sharp
dull	flat	that grabs me
flaming	noisy	cool
sunny	quiet	warm

In addition, some people may use taste words ("a sweet person") or olfactory words ("that stinks").

The concept of individual verbal style is rooted in a long-held theory of education that holds that children have different learning styles. Some learn best by looking at words, others by sounding them out, and still others by touching cloth cutouts of words and letters. Apparently these learning styles continue through adult life and are illustrated by individual language usage. Many people have mixed styles, however, and such concepts cannot be relied upon entirely. With some experimentation you will find that matching language systems with the client truly helps in the development of rapport and understanding. However, to make your counseling interventions successful, you will find it more helpful to use all modalities rather than just the client's primary language system. For example, "Can you *picture* an ideal outcome to your problem? How would it *feel*? What would it *sound* like?"

Overlapping (Lankton, 1980) is a term that emphasizes this usefulness of multiple perceptual systems in helping a client describe an event. You may find a client talking about a problem with a spouse, for example, in rather abstract terms. Ask that client for a concrete example of the problem; then follow up with questions about how the spouse and situation are visualized, what sounds may be heard, and, finally, what feelings well up in the client. If you are empathic and use the concept of overlapping sensitively, you may obtain a much deeper understanding of what the client is saying. You will find that you have *recreated* much of the problem and anchored the client's reaction to that problem to the "here and now" in the counseling interview.

Thus, through effective observation and listening skills, you can help your clients recreate problems or situations that they have experienced. Many, perhaps most, clients would rather talk about (or around) their problems than re-experience them directly. Using the following technique can help such clients bring the problem alive. First, ask them to relax, perhaps to close their eyes. Then ask them to see the person in their mind's eye. Follow that by asking them to hear the person talking to them and remember what they were saying. Your observation skills will tell you when your client is "into" the experience. Finally, ask the client what he or she is feeling. Through this use of overlapping, you will have recreated the sights, sounds, and feelings of a past situation. This may be used for deeper understanding on your part and on the client's part as well.

Discrepancies

The variety of discrepancies clients may manifest is perhaps best illustrated by the following statements:

"My son is perfect, but he just doesn't respect me."

"I really love my brother." (said in a quiet tone with averted eyes)

"I can't get along with Charlie." (discrepancy between the client and another person)

"I deserve to pass the course." (from a student who has done no homework and just failed the final examination)

"That question doesn't bother me." (said with a flushed face and a closed fist)

Once the client is relatively comfortable and some beginning steps have been taken toward rapport and understanding, a major task of the counselor or interviewer is to identify basic discrepancies, mixed messages, conflicts, or incongruities in the client's behavior and life. A common goal in most interviews, counseling, and therapy is to assist clients in working through discrepancies and conflict, but first these have to be identified clearly.

Discrepancies can be of several types:

Between nonverbal behaviors.   A client may be talking smoothly on a topic, but careful observation may reveal that her smile is coupled with a tightly closed fist. Mixed messages are often conveyed when parts of the body lack congruence.

Between two statements.   In a single sentence a client may express two completely contradictory ideas ("My son is perfect, but he just doesn't respect me" or "This is a lovely office you have; it's too bad that it's in this neighborhood"). Over a longer time, a positive statement about one's job may be qualified by an extensive discussion of problems. Most of us have mixed feelings toward our loved ones, our work, and other situations—it is helpful to aid others in understanding their ambivalences.

Between what one says and one does.   A parent may talk of love for a child but be guilty of child abuse. A student may say that he or she deserved a higher grade than examination scores suggest.

Between statements and nonverbal behavior.   "That question doesn't bother me." (said with a flushed face and a closed first)

Between people.   Conflict can be described as a discrepancy between people. Noting interpersonal conflict is a key task of the interviewer, counselor, or therapist.

Between a client and a situation.   "I want to be admitted to medical school, but I didn't make it." "I just found out I have early symptoms of arthritis." "I can't find a job." In such situations the client's ideal world is often incongruent with what really *is*. The counselor's task is to work through these issues in terms of behaviors or attitudes.

Most clients are aware, at some level, of the conflicts and discrepancies in their life; however, they are usually not fully attuned to the full dimensions of those discrepancies. When observing the conflicts cited above, it is particularly important to notice mixed and ambivalent feelings and emotions. The skilled counselor does not necessarily attack client cognitive or emotional discrepancies immediately but may hold back and observe verbal and nonverbal behavior carefully so that other discrepancies—perhaps even more important ones—may be noted. However, in certain forms of time-limited interviewing and in certain counseling theories (such as Gestalt), immediate, direct confrontation of such discrepancies may be essential.

Chapter 8 builds on this discussion of the observation of discrepancies and suggests that in these dimensions and their resolution lies much of what we term counseling and therapy.

▲ Summary

The interviewer seeks to observe client verbal and nonverbal behavior with an eye to identifying discrepancies, mixed messages, incongruity, and conflict. Counseling and therapy in particular but also interviewing frequently focus on problems and their resolution. A discrepancy is often a problem. At the same time, discrepancies in many forms are part of life and may even be enjoyed. Humor, for example, is based on conflict and discrepancies. It is necessary for counselors and interviewers to work on client problems, but that emphasis often results in a tendency to view life as a problem to be solved rather than as an opportunity to be enjoyed. Even while working with the most complex case, it is wise to focus on client strengths and assets from time to time. The exercise used in the preceding chapter on questions ("Talk about something you feel good about") is ideally part of every interview. The focus on positive assets is necessary to combat the tendency to search constantly for problems and difficulties. People solve problems with their strengths, not with their weaknesses!

Box 4-1. Key Points

Why?	The most effective interviewer is constantly aware of the client. Clients tell us about their world by nonverbal and verbal means. Client observation skills are a critical tool in determining how the client interprets the world.
What?	Client observation skills focus on three areas:

1. *Client nonverbal behavior.* Client eye contact patterns, body language, and vocal qualities are, of course, important. Shifts and changes in these may be indicative of client interest or discomfort. A client may lean forward, indicating excitement about an idea, or cross his arms to close it off. Facial clues (brow furrowing, lip tightening or loosening, flushing, pulse rate visible at temples) are especially important. Larger-scale body movements may indicate shifts in clients' reactions, thoughts, or the topic.

2. *Client verbal behavior.* Noting patterns of verbal tracking is particularly important. At what point do clients change topic, and to what topics do they shift? Clients tend to use certain key words to describe their behavior and situations; noting these descriptive words and repetitive themes is helpful. Some clients use primarily auditory ("hear," "sounds like"), visual ("see," "looks like"), or kinesthetic ("feel," "touch") words to describe their way of interacting with the world; it is helpful to match these words. Using all three sensory modalities through *overlapping* will strengthen the impact of many interviews.

3. *Client discrepancies.* Incongruities, mixed messages, contradiction, and conflict are manifest in many and perhaps all interviews. The effective interviewer is able to identify these discrepancies, to name them appropriately, and, sometimes, to feed them back to the client. These discrepancies may be between nonverbal behaviors, between two statements, between what clients say and what they do, or between statements and nonverbal behavior. They may also represent a conflict between people or between a client and a situation.

How?	Simple, careful observation of your client is basic. What can you see, hear, and feel from the client's world? Note your impact on the client: how does what you say change or relate to the client's behavior? Use those data to adjust your microskill or interviewing technique.
With whom?	Observation skills are essential with all clients. Note individual and cultural differences in verbal and nonverbal behavior. Always remember that some individuals and some cultures may have a different meaning for a movement, use of language, or a discrepancy from your own personal meaning. Use caution!

(continued)

Box 4-1 (continued)

And?	Movement harmonics are particularly interesting and provide a basic concept that explains much verbal and nonverbal communication. When two people are talking together and communicating well, they often exhibit *movement synchrony* or *movement complementarity* in that their bodies move in harmonious fashion. When people are not communicating clearly, *movement dissynchrony* will appear: body shifts, jerks, and pulling away are readily apparent.

▲ Practice Exercises and Self-Assessment

Many concepts have been presented in this chapter; it will take time to master them and make them a useful part of your interviewing. Therefore, the exercises here should be considered introductory. Further, it is suggested that you continue to work on these concepts throughout the time that you read this book. For example, in the next chapter on paraphrasing you will want to continue to practice observing clients' key words and their visual, auditory, and kinesthetic descriptors. In practicing the skill of reflection of feeling (see Chapter 6) you will want to observe nonverbal expressions of emotion. In Chapter 7 you will have the opportunity to note "I statements" and whether the nature of the statements changes in a positive direction later in the interview. If you keep practicing the concepts in this chapter throughout the book, material that might now seem confusing will gradually be clarified.

Individual Practice

Exercise 1. Observation of client nonverbal patterns

Observe a counseling interview, a television interview, or any two people talking. Give special attention to the person being interviewed or who seems to be talking less. Note the following:

Eye contact patterns.   Do people maintain eye contact more while talking or while listening? Does the "client" break eye contact more often while discussing certain subjects than others? Can you observe changes in pupil dilation as an expression of interest?

Body language.   Note gestures, shifts of posture, leaning, patterns of breathing, and use of space. Give special attention to facial expressions such as changes in skin color, flushing, and lip movements. Note appropriate and inappropriate smiling, furrowing of the brow, and so on.

Vocal qualities.   Note speech rate and changes in intonation or volume. Give special attention to speech "hitches" or hesitations.

For each of the variables listed above, use the Client Observation Form that follows to record your observations under the following three categories:

1. *Context.* Describe the situation in which the observations occur: for example, "Interview in which a client is talking about vocational history."
2. *Observation.* Describe in clear behavioral terms what you see or hear during the observation: for example, "Eye contact break accompanied by sitting back in chair, shortness of breath coupled with a rise in vocal volume in response to counselor question 'Are you married?'"
3. *Impression.* Speculate on what you observe: for example, "Client feels anxious in some way about issue of marriage."

Exercise 2. Observation of movement harmonics

Observe an interview or conversation, but this time note the behavior of both people. Give primary attention to examples of movement harmonics. Note points at which the bodies of the two communicators mirror one another. You may find complex movement patterns being mirrored; at the same time, you will most likely note examples of dissynchrony. Record your observations using the Client Observation Form or the space provided below. For example, consider the following context, observation, and impression:

1. *Context.* Counselor and client were talking about sexual difficulties experienced during the last week.
2. *Observation.* Counselor and client were sitting in mirror positions until this topic came up. Counselor sat back, put hand to chin, and lowered voice. Client in turn hesitated, moved back, and raised voice, speaking more quickly.
3. *Impression.* Counselor and client appeared to be in harmony until this topic came up. Counselor may be uncomfortable in this area. Clearly they are not communicating as well as they were earlier in the session.

_____

_____

_____

_____

_____

_____

_____

_____

_____

Exercise 3. Observation of nonverbal communication discrepancies

After a variety of observation situations in which you demonstrate your ability to note nonverbal communication and movement harmonics, give special attention to discrepant nonverbal behavior. You may note the picking of lint off clothes

Client observation form

Context	Observation	Impression

as if to brush off the other person's comments, inappropriate smiling, sitting back in a chair as if to gain distance from the other, and the like. The nonverbal discrepancies may be within one person (for example, a closed fist in one hand and an open palm in the other) or between two people. Again it is important to separate context, observation, and impression. Record your remarks below or on the Client Observation Form.

Exercise 4. Observation of client verbal tracking and selective attention

Listen carefully to clients (or other people in your daily interactions) and note when they change topics. Do those to whom you listen have varying abilities and interests in staying on certain topics? Are some topic changes abrupt and others more subtle?

It is particularly important to note selective attention patterns. Some clients, for example, will selectively attend only to negative elements in their life situation, while others attend only to positive strengths. Some people attend only to discussions in which sexuality is an issue, whereas others will avoid the topic. In the same format of context, observation, and impression, summarize your observations of others either in an interview or in conversations, using the space below or the Client Observation Form.

Exercise 5. Noting "I statements" descriptive of the self

Clients tell you a lot about themselves if you listen carefully. Much of counseling and interviewing involves understanding client self-statements, or "I statements." Clients will often present clear statements about their condition: "I am depressed," "I am lonely," "I feel sad," "I am pregnant." Note that these key sentences are often the issue around which the interview or counseling session will turn. Further, the sentences often (though not always) follow a form in which the subject is the self (*I*), followed by a verb of being (*am*), and ending with an adjective descriptor referring to the self (*depressed*).

One task of the interviewer or counselor is to change, through the process of counseling, the "I statements" from negative to positive self-descriptors—for example, to change "I am lonely" to "I have friends and I am a happy person."

Once an "I statement" has been identified, the task of the interviewer is to clarify its meaning and obtain more specifics. Note in the following examples how a sequence of questions can discover more data underlying the original "I statement."

Client:	Joan really bugs me. I don't know what to do. ("I statement" = "I don't know what to do.")
Counselor:	Could you tell me generally what is going on between you? (search for general summary via the *could* question)
Counselor:	Could you give me a specific example of when the conflict occurred? What did she do? What did you do? (search for concrete facts)
Counselor:	How do you feel when this happens? (search for feelings)
Counselor:	What does all this mean to you? (search for meaning)

The data generated by this series of questions clarify for the interviewer the total situation in which the client is living. Armed with more concrete specifics and facts derived from the original "I statement," the counselor may aid the client in a search for solutions. The effectiveness of the interview may be determined by the "I statement" of the client as he or she leaves the session actually determined on a new action—for instance, "I am going to do X," said in an affirmative tone.

For this exercise, you will note a negative "I statement" of a client or another person and use the questioning sequence suggested above to clarify the situation that brought about the negative "I statement." Summarize your experience below:

Negative "I statement":

_____

Result of systematic questioning:

_____

_____

_____

_____

Positive "I statement" that might be generated by the client after successful interviewing or counseling:

_____

Exercise 6. Noting client modes of receiving information

Refer back to the lists of sensory descriptors under "Individual Verbal Styles of Perceiving Reality." Spend 15 minutes a day for at least 4 days noting other people's modes of receiving information. Deliberately match their reception mode through your use of vocabulary. Alternatively, deliberately mismatch your modes and note any difficulties that arise in communication. Summarize your discoveries below:

_____

_____

_____

_____

_____

Exercise 7. Overlapping and recreation of experience

To experience overlapping, take a moment to think of a place where you were particularly comfortable and happy. Then try to see the place; once you do, look around it. Then hear the sounds of the place; perhaps you can conjure up the scent, as well. Finally, notice any bodily sensations that arise during this exercise.

To follow up, ask a friend to work with you and talk him or her through the same experience. Move slowly and use client observation skills so that you are in tune with your friend and not moving too rapidly. You will find that your "client" can recreate past positive experiences. Summarize your observations here:

_____

_____

_____

_____

When you work with clients who have difficulty expressing themselves regarding a past relationship or problem, you will find that this same exercise will help them bring the old experience to life. However, use this exercise carefully and ethically, and only with clients with whom you have solid rapport and trust.

Exercise 8. Observation of discrepancies in your daily life

The skilled counselor and interviewer will be able to note discrepancies, mixed messages, incongruity, and conflicts during any interview. The six types of discrepancies discussed are (1) between nonverbal behaviors (see Exercise 3), (2) between two statements, (3) between what clients say and what they do, (4) between statements and nonverbal behavior, (5) between people, and (6) between people and situations. For 3 days give special attention to the observation of discrepancies among those you meet. Search especially for mixed feelings; for example, toward one's parents, toward a job, and so on. Summarize your observations below:

_____

_____

_____

_____

_____

Systematic Group Practice

Several client observation skills have been discussed in this chapter:

Observation of client nonverbal patterns
Observation of movement harmonics
Observation of discrepancies in nonverbal communication
Observation of client verbal tracking and selective attention
Noting "I statements"
Noting client modes of receiving information
Observation of other discrepancies

It is obviously not possible to master all these skills in one single role-played interview. However, practice can serve as a foundation for elaboration at a later time. This exercise has been selected to summarize the central ideas of the chapter.

Step 1. Divide into practice groups.

Step 2. Select a group leader.

Step 3. Assign roles for the first practice session.

▲ Role-played client, who responds naturally and is talkative. The client may give the interviewer a hard time.
▲ Interviewer, who follows a set list of questions.
▲ Observer 1, who observes nonverbal communication.
▲ Observer 2, who observes verbal communication.

Step 4. Planning. State the goals of the session. As the central task is observation, the interviewer should give primary attention to asking the stock questions listed in Step 5. After the role-play is over, the interviewer should report personal observation of the client made during that time and demonstrate basic or active mastery skills.

The suggested topic for the practice role-play is "Something or someone with whom I have a present conflict or have had a past conflict." Alternative topics include the following:

My positive and negative feelings toward my parents or other significant persons
The mixed blessings of my work, home community, or present living situation

The two interviewers may use this session as an opportunity both for providing feedback to the interviewer and for sharpening their own observation skills.

Step 5. *Conduct a 6-minute practice session.* The interviewer should follow the suggested set of open questions below, using each one in order. It will be useful to have the questions available in one's lap and to use language relatively close to theirs. The feedback emphasis in this chapter will be on client verbal and nonverbal behavior, not on the interviewer. The suggested questions are as follows:

▲ "Could you give me a general summary of your conflict situation?" (Or positive and negative feelings about parents, work, home community, or area of the country.)
▲ *Search for facts.* "Could you give me a specific example of when the conflict occurred? What did they say? What did you do?" (Or an example of a positive and negative thing one's parents did or similar specific examples for work, home community, or living situation.)
▲ *Search for feelings.* "How did you feel when that happened?" "What feelings or emotions did the positive event elicit in you?"
▲ *Search for meaning.* "What does all this mean to you?" "What kind of sense does this make to you?" "What do your thoughts and feelings about this situation say about you as a person?"

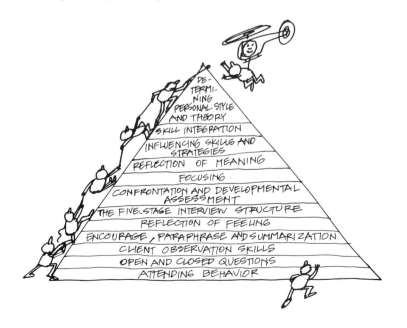

Step 6.   Review the practice session and provide feedback for 14 minutes.
Remember to stop the audiotape or videotape periodically and listen to or view key items several times for increased clarity. Observers should give special attention to careful completion of the feedback sheet throughout the session.

Step 7. Rotate roles.

Some general reminders.   Again, it is important that the interviewer feel free to have notes on his or her lap and refer to them when desired. This session focuses on bringing out client facts, feelings, and meanings and then examining client behavior—not on counselor behavior.

Client Observation Feedback Sheet

_____ (Date)

_____   _____
(Name of Interviewer)   (Name of Person Completing Form)

Instructions: Observe the client carefully during the role-played session and immediately afterward complete the nonverbal feedback portion of the form. As you view the videotape or listen to the audiotape, give special attention to verbal behavior and note discrepancies. If no recording equipment is available, one observer should note nonverbal behavior and the other verbal behavior during the interview itself.

Nonverbal behavior checklist

1. *Eyes.* At what points did eye contact breaks occur? Staring? Did the client maintain eye contact more when talking or when listening? Changes in pupil dilation?

2. *Face.* At what points did changes in expression occur? Changes in skin color, flushing, swelling or contracting of lips? Appropriate or inappropriate smiling? Head nods? Brow furrowing?

3. *Body language.* General style and changes in hands and arms, trunk, legs? Open or closed gestures? Tight fist? Playing with hands or objects? Physical tension: relaxed or tight? Body oriented toward or away from interviewer? Sudden body shifts? Twitching? Distance? Breathing changes?

4. *Vocal qualities.* When did speech hesitations occur? Changes in tone and volume? What single words or short phrases were emphasized?

(continued)

Client Observation Feedback Sheet (continued)

5. *Movement harmonics.* Examples of movement complementarity, synchrony, or dissynchrony? At what times did these occur?

6. *Nonverbal discrepancies.* Did one part of the body say something different from another? With what topics did this occur?

Verbal behavior checklist

1. *Verbal tracking and selective attention.* At what points did the client fail to stay on the topic? To what topics did the client give most attention?

2. *Client "I statements."* While discussing the conflict or confusing situation, what self-statements did the client make? Which might be desirable to change, given a longer interview?

3. *Client mode of receiving information.* Is this client visually, auditorily, or kinesthetically oriented? How well did the interviewer track the language system of the client?

4. *Key words.* List here the most important key words used by the client; these are important for deeper analysis.

(continued)

Client Observation Feedback Sheet (continued)

Other client discrepancies

Write here observations of verbal discrepancies between two statements, between what was said and what the client did, between statements and nonverbal behavior, between people, and between the client and situations.

_____

_____

_____

_____

_____

_____

_____

_____

_____

Self-Assessment and Follow-Up

Observation of clients' verbal and nonverbal behavior is a central skill of effective interviewers and counselors. As you progress, you will improve your skills. Do not expect to be fully conversant with the concepts in this chapter after only one reading and a few practice exercises. Even the most skilled individual, after years of experience, is constantly learning new ways to understand and interpret client behavior.

Use the self-assessment and follow-up ideas here as beginning steps toward eventual mastery of the complex art of observing others.

1. What single dimension stood out for you in this chapter as either a significant learning or an interesting and helpful concept?

Use this knowledge and interest as your base for further study of client verbal and nonverbal behavior.

_____

_____

_____

_____

2. Which concept stood out for you as least relevant and least helpful?

Could you summarize your reasons here? It is important that you develop your own position on these issues.

_____

_____

_____

_____

_____

3. Mastery of client observation skills

What specific competencies have you mastered? Provide specific evidence of your mastery of each level below. Additional evidence may be provided by tapes, transcripts, and case studies.

Identification.   You will be able to note a wide variety of nonverbal behavior and verbal behavior in clients and others and be able to identify discrepancies among those behaviors.

_____ Ability to note eye contact patterns, particularly changes in patterns.

_____

_____

_____ Ability to note facial expression and body language, particularly shifts or changes in relation to certain topics.

_____

_____

_____ Ability to note vocal qualities, particularly changes and hesitations.

_____

_____

_____ Ability to note movement harmonics.

_____

_____

_____ Ability to note client verbal tracking and selective attention.

_____

_____

_____ Ability to note explicit and implicit client "I statements."

_____

_____

_____ Ability to note client mode of receiving information (auditory, visual, or kinesthetic).

_____

_____

Ability to note discrepancies in verbal and nonverbal behavior:

_____ Between nonverbal behaviors.

_____

_____

_____ Between two statements.

_____

_____

_____ Between statements and nonverbal behavior.

_____

_____

_____ Between people.

_____

_____

_____ Between people and situations.

_____

_____

_____ Between what one says and what one does.

_____

_____

Basic mastery. You will be able to demonstrate the same observation skills in your own interviewing practice. For example, you will note body shifts, changes in eye contact or skin coloration, and repetitive verbal patterns. Provide one specific example of your own observations in an interview of nonverbal, verbal, and discrepant behavior.

_____ Ability to note nonverbal behavior.

_____
_____
_____

_____ Ability to note verbal behavior patterns.

_____
_____
_____

_____ Ability to note client discrepancies.

_____
_____
_____

Active mastery. You will be able to note client verbal and nonverbal behaviors in the interview and be able to match your behavior to the client's. When necessary, you will be able to mismatch behaviors to promote client movement. For example, if you first join the negative body language of a depressed client and then take a more positive position, the client may follow and adopt a more assertive posture. You will be able to note your own verbal and nonverbal responses to the client. You will be able to note discrepancies between yourself and the client and work to resolve those discrepancies.

One route toward demonstrating this level of mastery is to take each of the specific observation areas in "Identification" and provide evidence that you are able to use these concepts effectively in the interview. For the first stages of active mastery, the following competencies are suggested as most important:

_____ Ability to mirror nonverbal patterns of the client. The interviewer mirrors body position, eye contact patterns, facial expression, and vocal qualities.

_____
_____
_____

_____ Ability to identify client patterns of selective attention and use those patterns either to bring talk back to the original topic *or* to move knowingly to the new topic provided by the client.

_____
_____
_____

_____ Ability to identify key client "I statements" and feed them back to the client accurately, thus enabling the client to describe and define what they mean more fully. (Helpful for this exercise is the series of questions listed in Exercise 5.)

_____

_____

_____

_____ Ability to match your language system with the client's mode of processing the experience (auditory, visual, or kinesthetic) and to enable clients to recreate their past experiences vividly.

_____

_____

_____

_____ Ability to note client discrepancies and feed them back to the client accurately. (Note that this is the important skill of *confrontation*; it is discussed in detail in Chapter 8.) The client in turn will be able to accept the confrontation and use the feedback for further effective self-exploration.

_____

_____

_____

Teaching mastery.   You will demonstrate your ability to teach others client observation skills. Your achievement of this level can be determined by how well your students can be rated on the basic competencies of this self-assessment form. Certain of your clients in counseling may be quite insensitive to obvious patterns of nonverbal and verbal communication. Teaching them beginning methods of observing others can be most helpful to them. Do not introduce more than one or two concepts to a client per interview, however!

_____

_____

_____

4. Given your experience with client observation skills, what single goal might you set for yourself at this point?

_____

_____

_____

_____

▲ **Reference**   Lankton, S. (1980). *Practical magic*. Cupertino, Calif.: Meta Publications.

5 Encouraging, Paraphrasing, and Summarizing: Hearing the Client Accurately

---

How can these three skills help you and your clients?

Major function	Clients need to know that the interviewer has *heard* what they have been saying, *seen* their point of view, and *felt* their world as they experience it. Encouragers and restatements, paraphrases, and summarizations are basic to helping a client feel understood. Once clients' positions have been truly heard, it becomes possible to free them for further development.
Secondary function	Knowledge and skill in these dimensions result in the following:

▲ Clarifying for the client what he or she has said.
▲ Clarifying for the interviewer what the client has said. By feeding back what you have heard, you can check on the accuracy of your listening.
▲ Helping clients to talk in more detail about issues of concern to them.
▲ Helping an overly talkative client stop repeating the same facts or story, thus speeding up and clarifying the interview process.

▲ Introduction

Attending, questioning, and client observation skills form the basis of culturally intentional helping. They all facilitate client talk, allowing the sharing of concerns and issues. Yet simply helping the client talk is not enough; clients need to know they have been *heard* by another human being. And the more accurate the listening process, the more likely the client is to continue exploring issues in greater depth.

Encouraging, paraphrasing, and summarizing all communicate to clients that they have indeed been heard. In these accurate-listening skills you do not mix your own ideas with what the client has been saying. You may feed back the client's ideas in your own words that distill, perhaps shorten, and clarify what the client has said. Even then, however, it is wise to use the client's key words and ideas for particularly delicate topics.

Hearing another person accurately is not easy, nor necessarily common. A simple exercise will illustrate this fact. Ask a friend to tell you about a recent life event. Ask a series of open questions so that considerable information is generated. Then feed back what the friend told you and ask how accurate your summary was. Note, too, how your friend felt about your feedback. Use this space for your observations about your friend's reactions:

_____

_____

_____

_____

_____

_____

Paraphrasing and summarizing communicate to clients that they have been listened to. Encouraging helps clients explore their feelings and thoughts more completely. A brief definition of these skills follows:

Encouragers are a variety of verbal and nonverbal means the counselor or interviewer can use to prompt clients to continue talking. They include head nods, openhanded gestures, phrases such as "Uh-hum," and the simple repetition of key words the client has uttered.

Paraphrases feed back to the client the essence of what has just been said by shortening and clarifying client comments. Paraphrasing is not parroting; it is using some of your own words plus the important main words of the client.

Summarizations are similar to paraphrases but cover a longer time span and more information. Summarizations may be used to begin or end an interview, as a transition to a new topic, or to clarify lengthy and complex client issues.

▲ Example Interview[1]

With this example, we again turn our attention to the options open to the counselor. In the following excerpt, note how the counselor uses the three skills of this chapter while at the same time remaining aware of needed client observation skills. The counselor begins with a summary of the last interview. Note that the three skills are often helpful in clarifying issues more precisely for both the client and the counselor.

Marsha: The last time we talked, Jesse, you were saying you weren't sure what you wanted to do. You had this interesting job possibility way across the country, but there were some things holding you here, too. We were discussing some details of the job, and I noted how pleased and excited you were about it. Could you go on and tell me what's been happening this week? (This is a summary of the main points discussed earlier, followed by an open question to keep the dialogue going and to open the discussion more fully.)

Jesse: Well, what's been happening since we last talked, Marsha, is that I did get the job offer . . . and it's exciting. The salary is higher, and it's in Florida, and I've

---

[1]Several of the paraphrases and summaries in this transcript contain reflections of feeling, a skill closely related to paraphrasing that is discussed in the next chapter.

always wanted to be in a place with more sun, and it really sounds great. On the other hand, the family isn't too enthusiastic about it. Ah . . . May likes the idea of being here in the Rockies. It's the type of life she likes. She likes horses and all that. The kids didn't seem too thrilled either . . . they are kind of down in the dumps. I came home with big news, and no one responded. It's kind of a downer.

Marsha: So, you're pretty excited about making this move, but there are some other issues that need to be addressed. (This brief paraphrase catches the essence of the conflict, at least as discussed thus far. It also contains elements of a basic confrontation, in that incongruity between Jesse and his family is identified.)

Jesse: Yes, there seem to be two things happening. The job looks good, but the family is really down. I've been thinking about it, too. I've enjoyed being on the bowling team here . . . ah, I have a lot of friends. I understand housing is going to be more expensive down there. And . . . there are a lot of things to decide . . . and then the family comes in and complicates it.

Marsha: Complicates it? (This single-word encourager may be expected to produce more talk from Jesse about his meaning and understanding of his words. Single-word encouragers stated in a questioning tone facilitate client talk in more depth.)

Jesse: Yeah . . . complicates it, in that I thought the decision was made last week. If I got the offer, we'd go. Now it seems more complex.

Marsha: So it's really hard to go ahead and make this move. (This paraphrase catches the essence of what Jesse has been saying so far in the interview. There are some dimensions of reflection of feeling—"it's really hard"—in the paraphrase.)

Jesse: Yeah, I think you've got it right on target. I've thought a lot about it, but . . . I really want to go . . . I don't really feel comfortable about the move. I did before. (Jesse talks in a less certain tone of voice. He is seeing the decision as more complex than he originally thought. Note that almost every counselor statement has resulted in a "Yeah," indicating that the counselor is accurate in her paraphrases. You will note clients using affirmatives frequently when your paraphrasing is effective.)

Marsha: Could you tell me more of these thoughts?

Jesse: I'm getting older, and the kids are almost through high school. I like the house here, and it's expensive down in Florida. I'm not sure we'd be happy down there.

Marsha: You're not sure you'd be happy down there. (an encourager in the form of a restatement)

Jesse: Yes, it'd be very disruptive. Yet on the other hand, I'm awfully bored with this job. I feel I could do it blindfolded.

Marsha: Blindfolded? (encourager)

Jesse: Yeah, it's a snap. I feel like I'm going to seed and am stuck. There just isn't a lot of opportunity here. The salary is okay, but there isn't much of a challenge anymore.

Marsha: So, you've got to weigh the potential disruption of your life with some of the boredom and repetitiveness you feel right now on the job. (This paraphrase again catches a basic dilemma and involves elements of a confrontation, in that the conflict is distilled and clarified.)

Jesse: Exactly! That's exactly how I feel. And the decision is really tough. I almost feel like it comes down to a chance to do something new. The more bored I get, the harder I get to live with around the house. That isn't so good; that might get us into trouble. (Note that, as the paraphrasing continues, Jesse continues to expand on the complexity of the decision.)

Marsha: So, while you're worried about your life being disrupted, sounds like you're very worried about being bored where you are now. (This paraphrase is a little less effective than the previous one, as it misses the possible dimension of conflict between husband and wife. However, this omission may be deliberate, and even wise, as the conflict may be discussed later.)

Jesse: Yeah . . . (hesitant), I think so. (Jesse indicates the paraphrase wasn't fully on target through vocal tone and speech hesitation.)

Marsha: Could you give me an idea of what might be needed to make the job here more interesting to you? (This open question follows up on Jesse's need to stay in the Rockies and opens the discussion for new options.)

Jesse: Well, I don't get along too well with the guy across the hall. He's always disagreeable. He's in good with the boss. I get along okay, but not as well as I would like.

Marsha: What you're saying now is that difficulties on the job may be as much a moti-vator to leave as the attractions of Florida. At the same time, you find your family wants to stay here. Perhaps it might be worthwhile to explore for a while some of these new dimensions you're talking about. But before I go on, let me check out if I have been hearing you accurately so far.

Last week, you said quite definitely that if the job came you'd take it. Now it seems that you have the job offer you wanted, but a set of new issues has come up. Important among them are your family's reactions and your own reactions to leaving a place and people you like. Issues of boredom on the job and the guy across the hall seem to be strong motivators to leave. Now we've started talking a bit about what might be done to make the job here more comfortable. Have I heard you correctly? Shall we take a look at the setting here?

Comment: This summary brings together two interviews to this point and focuses potential discussion for the next stage of the interview. As often happens, a "simple" choice has become increasingly complex as the deeper issues under-lying the move are explored. Still to be considered are the possible family conflict, ways in which the current setting could be made more satisfactory, and further exploration of the positive and negative aspects of the potential move.

This particular excerpt may strike some as unrealistic, as it uses so many of the reflective listening skills. In fact, it is a portion of an actual interview. It is possible to engage a client fully using only encouraging, paraphrasing, and summarizing. The questions used help to open up new areas where, again, the three skills can be helpful in clarifying. In your own practice sessions you may at first find it difficult to paraphrase even once in a brief interview. Work to build up your skill, and you will be surprised at the power you have to facilitate others' making their own decisions—and with relatively little input from you. The counselor or interviewer who paraphrases seeks to tread as lightly as possible on the client's world.

▲ Instructional Reading

Encouraging, paraphrasing, and summarizing help the client clarify issues and move into deeper exploration of issues and concerns. The three skills are related, but each has special advantages and purposes, which are discussed below.

Encouraging

Encouragers have been defined as head nods, open gestures, and positive facial expressions that encourage the client to keep talking. Minimal verbal utterances such as "Ummm" and "Uh-huh" have the same effect. Silence, accompanied by appropriate nonverbal communication, can be another type of encourager. All these encouragers affect the direction of client talk only minimally; clients are simply encouraged to keep talking.

Restatement and repetition of key words, on the other hand, have more influence on the direction of client progress. Consider the following client statement:

"And then it happened again. The grocery store clerk gave me a dirty look and I got angry. It reminded me of my last job, where I had so much trouble getting along. Why are they always after me?"

There are several key words in the above statement; repetition of any one of them would tend to lead the interview in a very different direction. The counselor could use a variety of short encouragers in a questioning tone of voice ("Angry?" "Last job?" "Trouble getting along?" "After you?"), and in each case the client would move in a different direction and talk about different topics. These short encouragers are a form of selective attention on the part of the interviewer and direct the interview much more than casual observation would suggest. It is important that you note your patterning of single-word encouraging responses in interviews; you may be directing clients more than you think.

A restatement is another type of encourager in which the counselor or interviewer repeats back short phrases ("The clerk gave you a dirty look" "You got angry" "You had trouble getting along in your last job" "You wonder why they are always after you"). Like short encouragers, different types of restatements lead the client in different directions. Restatements can be used with a questioning tone of voice; they then function much like the single-word encourager. When they simply parrot a client's words, they function more as brief paraphrases. In that case they highlight points noted by the counselor or interviewer but tend to close off discussion: vocal tone may determine the difference.

It may be helpful if you reread the paragraphs above, saying aloud the suggested encouragers and restatements. Use different vocal tones and note how your verbal style can facilitate others' talking—or can stop them cold.

All types of encouragers facilitate client talk unless they are overused or used badly. Excessive head nodding or gestures and excessive parroting can be annoying and frustrating to the client. Observation of many interviewers suggests that too many encouragers are wooden and unexpressive. Well-placed encouragers help to maintain flow and continually communicate that the client is being listened to. Single word encouragers often facilitate client talk toward deeper meanings.

Paraphrasing

At first glance, paraphrasing appears to be a simple skill, only slightly more complex than encouraging. In restatement and encouraging, exact words and phrases are fed back to the client, but in a shortened and clarified form. If you are able to give an accurate paraphrase to a client, you are likely to be rewarded with a "That's right" or "Yes . . . ," and the client will go on to explore the issue in more depth. Further, accurate paraphrasing will help the client stop repeating a story. Some clients have complex problems that no one has ever bothered to hear accurately, and they literally need to tell their story over and over until someone indicates they have been heard clearly. Once clients know they have been heard, they are often able to move on to new topics. The goal of paraphrasing is the facilitation of client exploration and the clarification of issues. The tone of your voice and your body language accompanying the paraphrasing also indicate to the client whether you are interested in listening in more depth or wish the client to move on.

How do you paraphrase? Client observation skills are important in accurate paraphrasing. You need to hear the client's important words and use them in your paraphrase much as the client does. Other aspects of the paraphrase may be in your own words, but the main ideas and concepts should reflect the client's view of the world, not yours!

An accurate paraphrase, then, usually consists of four dimensions:

1. A *sentence stem* using, insofar as possible, some aspect of the client's mode of receiving information. Visual clients tend to respond best to visual words ("*Looks* like you're saying you *see* the situation from this *point of view* . . . "); auditory clients respond best to tonal words ("As I *hear* you, *sounds* like . . . does that *ring a bell*?"); and kinesthetic clients respond to feeling words ("So the situation *touches* you like . . . and how does that *grab* you?"). With many clients a mixture of visual, auditory, and kinesthetic words will be even more powerful. A stem, of course, is not always necessary.

2. The *key words and construct systems* used by the client to describe the situation or person. Again, drawing on client observation skills, the effort is to include main ideas that come from the client and some of his or her exact words. This aspect of the paraphrase is sometimes confused with the encouraging restatement. A restatement, however, is almost entirely in the client's own words and covers only limited amounts of material.

3. The *essence of what the client has said* in summarized form. It is here that the interviewer's skill in transforming the client's sometimes confused statements into succinct, meaningful, and clarifying statements is most manifest. The counselor has the difficult task of keeping true to the client's ideas, but not repeating them exactly.

4. A *check-out* for accuracy. The check-out is a brief question at the end of the paraphrase, asking the client for feedback on whether or not the paraphrase (or summary or other microskill) was relatively correct and useful. Some example check-outs include "Am I hearing you correctly?" "Is that close?" "Does that ring a bell?" and "Does that touch the situation?" It is also possible to paraphrase with an implied check-out by raising your voice at the end of the sentence as if the paraphrase were a question.

Here is a client statement followed by its sample key-word encouragers, restatements, and a paraphrase:

"I'm terribly concerned about my wife. She has this feeling that she has to get out of the house, see the world, and get a job. I'm the breadwinner and I imagine that I have a good income. The children view Sally as a picture-perfect mother, and I do too. But last night, we really saw the problem differently and had a terrible argument."

▲ Key-word encouragers: "Argument?" "Terribly concerned?"
▲ Restatement encouragers: "You're terribly concerned over your wife." "She's a picture-perfect mother." "You had a terrible argument."
▲ Paraphrase: "Let me see if I can visualize the situation. You're concerned over your picture-perfect wife who wants to work even though you have a good income, which has resulted in a terrible argument. Is that how you see it?"

The above example shows that the key-word encourager, the restatement, and the paraphrase are all different points on a continuum. In each case the emphasis is on hearing the client and feeding back what has been said. Both short paraphrases and longer key-word encouragers will resemble restatements. A long paraphrase is close to a summary. All can be helpful in an interview—or they can be overdone.

Summarizing

Summarizations fall along the same continuum as do the key-word encourager, restatement, and paraphrase. Summarizations, however, encompass a longer period of conversation—at times they may cover an entire interview or even issues discussed by the client over several interviews.

In a summarization the interviewer attends to verbal and nonverbal comments from the client over a period of time and then selectively attends to key concepts and dimensions, restating them for the client as accurately as possible. A check-out at the end for accuracy is an important part of the summarization. The following are examples of summarizations.

To begin a session:

"Let's see, last time we talked about your feelings toward your mother-in-law and we discussed the argument you had with her around the time the new baby arrived. You saw yourself as guilty and anxious. Since then you haven't gotten along too well. We also discussed a plan of action for today. How did that go?"

Midway in the interview: "So far, I've seen that the plan didn't work too well. You felt guilty again when you saw the idea as manipulative. Yet one idea did work. You were able to talk with her about her garden, and it was the first time you had been able to talk about anything without an argument. You visualize the possibility of following up on the plan next week. Is that about it?"

At the end of the session: "In this interview we've reviewed your feelings toward your mother-in-law in more detail. Some of the following things seem to stand out: First, our plan didn't work completely, but you were able to talk about one thing without yelling. As we talked, we identified some behaviors on your part that could be changed. They include better eye contact, relaxing more, and changing the topic when you start to see yourself getting angry. I liked your idea at the end of talking with your father-in-law. Does that sum it up?"

▲ Summary

The skills of encouraging are particularly important in helping a client to keep moving, open up, and talk more freely. Paraphrasing and summarization will communicate that the client has been heard, allowing explanation in further depth. Using a delicate balance of the client's words and your own is essential. If you are too close to what the client is saying, you may be guilty of parroting, and very little is gained. If you are too far from what the client has said, you may be guilty of imposing your own ideas on the client's world. An accurate style of paraphrasing is critical for the counselor or interviewer who seeks to develop empathy with clients.

Box 5-1.   Key Points

Why?	Clients need to know they have been *heard*. Attending, questioning, and other skills help the client open up, but accurate listening through the skills of encouraging, paraphrasing, and summarizing is needed to communicate that you have indeed heard the other person fully.
What?	Three skills of accurate listening help communicate your ability to attend:

1. *Encouragers* are a variety of verbal and nonverbal means the counselor or interviewer can use to encourage others to continue talking. They include head nods, an open palm, "Uh-huh," and the simple repetition of key words the client has uttered.
2. *Paraphrases* feed back to the client the essence of what has just been said by shortening and clarifying client comments. Paraphrasing is not parroting; it is using some of your own words plus the important main words of the client.
3. *Summarizations* are similar to paraphrases except that a longer time and more information are involved. Summarizations may be used to begin or end an interview, for transition to a new topic, or to provide clarity in lengthy and complex client issues or statements.

(continued)

Box 5-1 (continued)

How?	Encouragers are described above. It is important to add that the so-called "simple" repetition of key words is more important than appears at first glance. Key words repeated back to the client usually lead to the client elaborating in greater detail on the meaning of that word to him or her. Interviewers and counselors find it interesting and sometimes challenging to note their own selective attention patterns as they use this first "simple" skill.

Paraphrasing involves four dimensions:

1. *A sentence stem* using, insofar as possible, some of the client's mode of receiving information: auditory, visual, or kinesthetic ("You *appear* to be saying . . . ").
2. The *key descriptors* and concepts the client used to describe the situation or person. Use the client's own words for the most important things.
3. The *essence of what the client has said* in summarized form. The interviewer transforms a confusing longer statement or series of statements into relatively brief form.
4. A *check-out* for accuracy. Implicitly or explicitly, the interviewer checks to see if hearing has been accurate ("Am I hearing you correctly?").

With whom? These skills are useful with virtually any client. However, some find repetition tiresome and may ask "Didn't I just say that?" Consequently, when you use the skill you should employ your client-observation skills.

And? All of these skills involve active listening, encouraging others to talk freely. They communicate your interest and help clarify the world of the client for both you and the client. This skill is one of the most difficult in the microtraining framework for many people.

▲ Practice Exercises and Self-Assessment

The three skills of encouraging, paraphrasing, and summarizing are much less controversial than questions. Virtually all interviewing theories recommend and endorse these key skills of active listening.

Individual Practice

Exercise 1. Identification of skills

Which of the following would you identify as encouragers (E), restatements (R), paraphrases (P), or summarizations (S)? Keep in mind that restatements are considered a variation on the encourager.

_____ "Uh-huh . . . "
_____ Silence, with facilitative body language.
_____ "Fearful?"
_____ "Change your mind?"
_____ "You'd like to return to college."
_____ "I hear you saying that you've changed your mind, that you are considering returning to college, but that finances may be a real problem. Is that right?"
_____ "In the last interview, we talked about your returning to college and some of your mixed feelings about it, and we agreed that you'd try a visit to your sister's campus to look at it again."

Exercise 2. Generating written encouragers, restatements, paraphrases, and summarizations

"I've just broken up with Dan. I couldn't take his drinking any longer. It was great when he was sober, but it wasn't that often he was. Yet that leaves me alone. I don't know what I'm going to do about money, the kids, or even where to start looking for work."

Write three different types of minimal encouragers for the client statement above.

_____

_____

_____

Write a restatement:

_____

Write a paraphrase (include a check-out):

_____

_____

Write a summarization (generate data by imagining previous interviews):

_____

_____

_____

_____

_____

Exercise 3: Observation

Use the Feedback Sheet for this chapter to observe an "interview": during the coming week, observe conversations for the use of encouragers, paraphrases, restatements, and summarizations. One thing you may expect to find is that these skills are not used very frequently in conversations, though TV talk shows make use of them at times. Note below your observations and the impact of the skills on the "client."

_____

_____

_____

_____

_____

Exercise 4. Practice of skills in other settings

Encouraging.   During conversations with friends or in your own interviews, deliberately use single-word encouragers and brief restatements. Note their impact on your friends' participation and interest. You may find that the flow of conversation changes in response to your brief encouragers. Summarize some of your observations below.

_____

_____

_____

_____

_____

_____

_____

_____

Paraphrasing and summarizing.   Continue practicing the client-observation skills of Chapter 4. Note the key words that other people use and their primary modes of processing information (visual, auditory, or kinesthetic) and then paraphrase to them what they have been saying. Sometimes the paraphrase will produce further talk and elaboration; at other times it may close off a topic and lead to a change in the discussion. The tone of the paraphrase may be crucial. A questioning inflection at the end of a paraphrase tends to bring out further talk, while in contrast, a diving inflection (particularly if coupled with a check-out) tends to close off discussion, leaving the other person feeling accurately heard. The check-out may provide you with useful data on the accuracy of your paraphrases and summarizations. Summarize your own important observations below.

_____

_____

_____

_____

_____

_____

_____

_____

Systematic Group Practice

Experience has shown that the skills of this chapter are often difficult to master. It is easy to try to feed back what another person has said, but to do it *accurately*, so that the client feels truly heard, is another matter.

Step 1. Divide into practice groups.

Step 2. Select a group leader.

Step 3. Assign roles for the first practice session.

▲ Role-played client
▲ Interviewer
▲ Observer 1
▲ Observer 2

Step 4. Planning.   Establish and state clear goals for the practice session. The interviewer should plan a role-play in which open questions are used to elicit the client's problem. Once this is done, use encouragers to help bring out more details and deeper meanings. Use more open and closed questions as appropriate, but give primary attention to the paraphrase and the encourager. End the interview with a summary (this is often forgotten). Check the accuracy of your summary with a check-out ("Am I hearing you correctly?").

For real mastery, seek to use only the three skills of this chapter and use questions only as a last resort.

Ideally, the topic for this practice session should be continued in the next chapter's practice on reflection of feeling. Thus, you will have the opportunity to work through the same problem or concern emphasizing two different skill areas. Select the topic for practice with particular care, therefore; consider the following, as each involves the observation of interpersonal or intrapersonal discrepancies:

Something toward which or someone toward whom I have conflicted feelings
Positive and negative feelings toward my parents or other significant persons
Mixed blessings of my work setting, home community, or area of the country
A conflict about a decision regarding work, school, or a major purchase

Observers may use planning time to examine feedback forms and to plan their own interviews.

Step 5. Conduct a 3-minute practice session.

Step 6. Review the practice session and provide feedback to the interviewer for 12 minutes.   Be sure to use the Feedback Sheet to ensure that the interviewer's statements are available for discussion. This sheet provides a helpful log of the session, which greatly facilitates discussion. If you have an audio- or videotape, start and stop the tape periodically and rewind it to hear and observe important points in the interview. Did the interviewer achieve his or her goals? What mastery level was demonstrated?

Step 7. Rotate roles.

Some general reminders. It is important that clients talk freely in the role-plays. As you become more confident in the practice session, you may want your clients to become more "difficult" so you can test your skills in more stressful situations. You'll find that difficult clients are often easier to work with after they feel they have been heard.

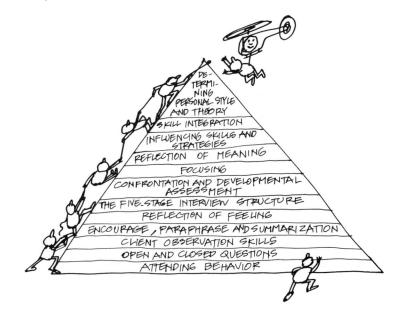

Encouraging, Paraphrasing, and Summarizing Feedback Sheet

_____ (Date)

_____   _____
(Name of Interviewer)   (Name of Person Completing Form)

Instructions: Write below as much as you can of each counselor statement. Then classify the statement as a question, an encourager, a paraphrase, a summarization, or other. Rate each of the last three skills on a scale of 1 (low) to 5 (high) for its accuracy.

Counselor statement	Open question	Closed question	Encourager	Paraphrase	Summarization	Other	Accuracy rating
1.							
2.							
3.							
4.							
5.							
6.							
7.							
8.							
9.							
10.							

1. What were the key discrepancies demonstrated by the client?

2. General interview observations.

Self-Assessment and Follow-Up

1. Is paraphrasing a skill you had from the past?

Were you aware of its impact? Encouraging? Summarizing? Comment below.

_____

_____

_____

_____

_____

2. Mastery of encouraging, paraphrasing, and summarizing

What specific competencies have you mastered? Provide evidence for each level of mastery in the space provided or via audio- or videotapes, case studies, or related demonstrations.

Identification.   You will be able to identify and differentiate between encouragers, restatements, paraphrases, and summarizations in the interview. You will note their impact on the client.

_____   Ability to classify and differentiate the skills.

_____

_____

_____   Ability to note the impact of the skills on the client.

_____

_____

Basic mastery.   You will be able to demonstrate the use of encouragers, paraphrases, and summarization in the interview.

_____   Ability to use the skills in a role-played interview.

_____

_____

_____   Ability to use these skills in daily life situations.

_____

Active mastery.   You will be able to use these skills in the interview and (1) through the use of encouragers and restatements facilitate further client talk on a topic; (2) paraphrase accurately what the client has said and, through your use of the skill, encourage either further talk or introduction of a new topic; (3) summarize what the client has been saying accurately and, through the summarization, begin the interview, provide structure at key points in the session, and wrap up the interview at the end.

Provide evidence of your mastery of each of the following via supplementary written or taped materials.

_____ Are you able to use a variety of nonverbal encouragers (head nods, gestures, and the like) in such a way that they encourage client talk?

_____ Can you, through the single-word encourager or brief restatement, assist clients in talking in more depth and detail about specific topic areas?

_____ By changing the single-word encourager or brief restatement can you change the content of client talk?

_____ Through accurate paraphrasing can you encourage a client to talk further about a topic?

_____ Through accurate paraphrasing can you assist a client to stop unnecessary repetition and move on to new topics of discussion?

_____ Are you able to distinguish between an accurate and an inaccurate paraphrase and change your paraphrase when you discover inaccuracies?

_____ Are you able to summarize the main strands of a client's conversation over time accurately and use these data to provide the following?

    _____ A summary at the beginning of the interview when necessary

    _____ A periodic summary to clarify and organize what the client has said

    _____ Summaries to close off sections of the interview or organize the entire interview

Teaching mastery.   Are you able to teach these skills to others, with demonstrable competence on their part? In teaching these skills to clients, you are sharing an important life competence. Husbands need to know that they have been heard by their wives and vice versa. Employees need to know that their ideas have been heard by others. A natural skill of the effective elementary teacher is constant paraphrasing and encouraging of the children. Many of your clients will benefit from learning this skill, which results in better family, job, and interpersonal communication.

_____

_____

3. Do you agree with this chapter's strong emphasis on the importance of hearing other people accurately and encouraging them to talk in greater depth on the topic?

In review, how do you feel this skill fits with your natural style?

_____

_____

_____

_____

_____

6 Noting and Reflecting Feelings: A Foundation of Client Experience

How can reflection of feeling help you and your clients?

Major function	Underlying clients' words and behaviors are feelings and emotions. The purpose of reflection of feeling is to make these implicit, sometimes hidden, emotions explicit and clear to the client.
Secondary functions	Knowledge and skill in reflection of feeling result in the following:

▲ Bringing out additional specifics of the client's emotional world.
▲ Noting that most clients have mixed or ambivalent feelings toward significant events and others. You can use the skill to help clients sort out these complex feelings and thoughts.
▲ Grounding the counselor and client from time to time in basic experience. There is a tendency in much interviewing to intellectualize and move away from deeper goals and feelings.

▲ Introduction

"I'm feeling down right now. I just got word that I got turned down by graduate school. Now I *really* don't know what to do. It just seems that I've tried everything. If only Professor Jones hadn't treated me so unfairly, I might have made it. He really ticks me off! But maybe I should have worked harder. I just feel so confused about what to do next."

Paraphrasing is concerned with feeding back to the client the essence of what has been said. Reflection of feeling, in contrast, involves observing client emotions and feeding key feelings back to the client. To clarify the distinction, take a moment right now to write a paraphrase of the client statement above:

_____

_____

When you reflect feelings, you add to the paraphrase those affective, or feeling, words that are in tune with the client's emotional experience. Before reading further, write down the above client's feeling words and your impression of what some of the unspoken feeling words might have been if they were expressed:

Client-expressed feelings (explicit feelings):

_____

_____

_____

Unexpressed feelings the client may have (implicit feelings):

_____

_____

_____

Feeling words explicit in the client's statement are *feeling down, ticked off,* and *confusion.* The unexpressed, implicit feelings could be sadness, depression, worry, anxiety, anger, guilt, fear, and many others.

In a reflection of feeling the counselor focuses on the client's emotions. In this case the counselor could say, "You feel down and confused, and I sense some anger there as well." As emotions form the base of much of life experience, noting key feelings and helping the client clarify them can be one of the most facilitative things an interviewer can do. This is particularly true in situations where emotions are confused or mixed: it often helps if we know *how* we feel before we act.

Before continuing it would be helpful if you generated your own personal list of feeling words. If you are to reflect feelings, you need a vocabulary of emotional labels. Words such as *happy, glad, sad,* and *confused* may give you a start. Also think of different intensities of the same emotion—for example, *annoyed, angry, furious.*

_____	_____	_____
_____	_____	_____
_____	_____	_____
_____	_____	_____
_____	_____	_____
_____	_____	_____

▲ Example Interview

The following transcript illustrates reflection of feeling in action.

Sylvia: So, Beth, how are things with your mother? (open question)

Beth: Well, the tests that she had taken recently came back looking pretty good. But with cancer you never can tell. I'm just really worried. It's hard to feel relaxed about her illness.

Sylvia: You sound like you feel tight and worried. (Reflection of feeling. Note kinesthetic mode used by Beth.)

Beth: Well, since she had her first bout with cancer . . . ah . . . I've just felt real concerned. She just doesn't look as well as she used to, and she seems to need a lot more rest. I guess I keep worrying that it's all going to, you know, turn out badly for her.

Sylvia: I can sense you felt upset and concerned. At the same time, are there any positives in the situation? Anything at all encouraging? (The reflection of feeling was followed by an open question oriented toward the search for something positive in the situation. Some counselors and interviewers focus solely on the negative and can literally cause depression and immobility. Some attention to positive dimensions is essential.)

Beth: Well . . . the doctors seem to feel that she's doing real well. She's basically made a good recovery. Most of my worry about her, Sylvia, is that I never know when it's going to hit again. You know . . .

Sylvia: Um-hum . . .

Beth: It's the unknown that's really leaving me up in the air.

Sylvia: So you do feel a little bit optimistic about the fact that she has recovered so quickly, is that right? (The reflection of feeling focuses on positive feelings. This seems important so that the counselor and client can attack problem areas from a base of strength rather than pessimism.)

Beth: Yeah, I feel good about that.

Sylvia: At the same time, you feel concerned about the fact that you don't know just what's going to happen. (This reflection is a return to Beth's real concerns of the moment.)

Beth: You know, ah . . . I've always seen her as a healthy person and now this thing has come up, I just worry about her all over the place. You know, little things that I never used to think about get me pretty jumpy.

Sylvia: You've got real deep feelings of caring about her. (This reflection of feeling differs from earlier reflections in that the words *deep feelings of caring* come more from the counselor than from the client. This reflection potentially "adds" to Beth's understanding and again emphasizes positive assets on her part.)

Beth: Yes, that's really correct. It made me realize that . . . how much I love her and how much she means to me. And . . . it's all real crazy 'cause that makes me worry about her even more.

Sylvia: It's almost as if the more you care, the more you worry. This feeling becomes very powerful. (In this reflection the positive feelings are pointed out to be part of the problem. Specifically, positive feelings toward a person can lead to even more anxiety than if you didn't care a lot. This, of course, is a basic human issue. The price of the joy of caring for another is possible loss, a real issue underlying the difficulty many people find in being committed to each other.)

Beth: That's right; it's like a vicious circle. I just . . . you know . . . realize how much she means to me and then I worry more . . . and I think you're right—there isn't that much to worry about. (Note that Beth continually begins her statements with affirmations of the counselor's reflections, such as "Yes" and "That's right." Beth's last sentence comes from Beth, not from the counselor. Through the process of working through feelings, she is beginning to resolve issues: "But . . . ah . . . it's just real hard right now.")

Sylvia: So in one sense you feel there's really not that much to worry about. But there is . . . and there's not much you can do about it. Is that correct? (This reflection of feeling is particularly important as Sylvia has reflected in summary form the main feelings that Beth has talked about so far. The feelings are mixed— that is, a desire to do something and anxiety and worry about not being able to, feelings of deep caring and love, and Beth's beginning awareness that she will have to *accept* things as they are. That acceptance is the beginning of some emotional relief in the situation.)

Beth: Yeah, it's the helplessness I feel. It's that, if she is really sick, it's out of my hands . . .

Sylvia: Ummmm . . .

Beth: Maybe that's what's really bothering me . . . that I used to think I had a lot of control over my life and her life, and now I realize that . . . ah . . . there's nothing I really can do anything about.

Sylvia: Sounds like it's a deeply troubling thing, but it's something that you're beginning to accept. Am I hearing you correctly there? (The reflection of feeling focuses on the mixed feelings of being bothered or troubled and the beginning of acceptance. As the counselor is now in more murky or difficult areas, the check-outs or perception checks at the end of her last two reflections of feeling are important to ensure accuracy and more open communication. The perception checks were not consciously planned in this interview, but at times they should be deliberately planned.)

Beth: That's right. I guess I'm having to learn how to do that right now.

Comment: The counselor in this case did not plan to use almost exclusively reflections of feeling. Yet this particular topic segment was such that the client seemed to want and need deeper exploration of feelings. Out of that exploration the client developed a new awareness. Now that this phase is completed, it would be appropriate to bring in other skills and work more concretely toward thinking through content issues or deciding on specific actions.

In your own practice with reflection of feeling, attempt to use the skill as frequently as possible. In the early stages of mastery it is wise to combine the skill with questioning, encouraging, and paraphrasing—most people find it awkward to use a single skill at a time. Full mastery of a skill will appear when a person can conduct a long segment of an interview effectively using a single skill almost constantly. Over the years the most effective interviewer, counselor, or therapist often develops—consciously or unconsciously—a level of skill such that the specific skill being used makes relatively little difference. Each is used so well that positive client benefits can be produced. Effectiveness and competence, then, do not necessarily depend on the particular skill, but upon the art of using it effectively. Nonetheless, being aware of and competent in each skill facilitates general personal and professional development as an interviewer.

▲ Instructional Reading

Many authorities argue that our thoughts and actions are only extensions of our basic feelings and emotional experience. The skill of reflection of feeling is aimed at assisting others to sense and experience the most basic part of themselves—how they really feel about another person or life event.

A basic feeling we have toward our parents, family, and best friends is love and caring. This is a deep-seated emotion in most individuals. At the same time, over years of intimate contact, negative feelings about the same people may also appear, possibly overwhelming and hiding positive feelings—or negative feelings may be buried. A common task of many counselors is to help clients sort out mixed feelings toward significant people in their lives. Many people want a simple resolution and want to run away from complex mixed emotions. However, ideally the counselor should help the client discover and sort out both positive and negative feelings.

At another level our work and social relationships and the decisions we make are often based on emotional experience. In an interviewing situation it is often helpful to assist the client to identify feelings clearly. For example, an employee making a move to a new location may have positive feelings of satisfaction, joy, and accomplishment about the opportunity, but simultaneously feel worried, anxious, and hesitant about new possibilities. The effective interviewer notes both dimensions and recognizes them as a valid part of life experience.

At the most elementary level, the brief encounters we have with people throughout the day involve our emotions. Some are pleasant; others can be fraught with tension and conflict even though the interaction may be only with a telephone operator about a bad connection, with a hurried clerk in a store, or with the police as they stop you for speeding. Feelings undergird these situations just as the more complex feelings we have toward significant others underpin more intimate relationships. Becoming aware of others' feelings can help you move through the tensions of the day more gracefully and can be helpful to other individuals in many small ways. Rather than reflecting clients' feelings about these situations, you may find a brief, simple acknowledgment of feeling is helpful. The same structure is used in an acknowledgment as in a full reflection, but much less emphasis is given to feeling, and interaction moves on more quickly.

If you address client feelings and emotions in an interview, the following specifics are important to keep in mind.

Noting Client Verbal and Nonverbal Feelings

When a client says "I feel sad"—or "glad" or "gloomy"—and supports this statement with appropriate nonverbal behavior, identifying emotions is easy. However, many clients present subtle or discrepant messages, for often they are not sure how they feel about a person or situation. In such cases the counselor will have to identify and label the implicit feelings.

The most obvious technique for identifying client feelings is simply to ask the client an open question ("How do you feel about that?" "Could you explore any emotions that come to mind about your parents?" "What feelings come to mind when you talk about the loss?"). With some quieter clients, a closed question in which the counselor supplies the missing feeling word may be helpful ("Does that feel hurtful to you?" "Could it be that you feel angry at them?" "Are you glad?").

At other times the counselor will want to infer, or even guess, the client's feelings through observation of verbal and nonverbal cues such as discrepancies between what the client says about a person and his or her actions, or a slight body movement contradicting the client's words. As many clients have mixed feelings about the most significant events and people in their lives, inference of unstated feelings becomes one of the important observational skills of the counselor. A client may be talking about caring for and loving parents while holding his or her fist closed. The mixed emotions may be obvious to the observer though not to the client.

It is important to realize that different clients have different patterns of feeling-word constructs, which provide you with important information about how they think about the world. For example, Beth, the client in this chapter's example interview, used the following feeling words: *worried, relaxed, real concerned, good, jumpy, love, helplessness, out of my hands,* and *control. Worry* was used in many of her statements, and, although it has some negative evaluative connotations, it is best considered a mixed feeling representing a synthesis of all the other more specific words. The other words may be categorized into feelings of activity–passivity (*real concerned, relaxed, jumpy*), potency–impotency (*helplessness, out of my hands, control*), and positive or negative evaluation (*good, love*). Some possible goals for Beth would be to acknowledge and validate the general worry; to become more relaxed; to accept the fact that in some ways she cannot control her mother's illness, though she can control other aspects of the situation; and to give more weight to her positive feelings.

The intentional counselor does not necessarily respond to every emotion, congruent or discrepant, that has been noted; reflections of feeling must be timed to meet the needs of the individual client. Sometimes it is best simply to note the emotion and keep it in mind for possible comment later.

The Techniques of Reflecting Feeling

Somewhat like the paraphrase, reflection of feeling involves a typical set of verbal responses that can be used in a variety of ways. The classic reflection of feeling consists of the following dimensions:

1. A *sentence stem* using, insofar as possible, the client's mode of receiving information (auditory, visual, or kinesthetic) often begins the reflection of feeling ("I hear you say you feel . . . " "Feels like . . . "). Unfortunately, these sentence stems have been used so often that they can almost sound like comical stereo-

types. As you practice, you will want to vary sentence stems and sometimes omit them completely. Using the client's name and the pronoun *you* helps soften and personalize the sentence stem.

2. A *feeling label* or emotional word is added to the stem ("John, you seem to feel badly about . . . " "Looks like you're happy" "Sounds like you're discouraged today; you look like you feel really down"). For mixed feelings more than one emotional word may be used ("Sally, you appear both glad and sad . . . ").

3. A *context or brief paraphrase* may be added to broaden the reflection of feeling. (To use the examples above, "John, you seem to feel badly about *all the things that have happened in the past two weeks*" "Sally, you appear both glad and sad *about leaving home*.") The words *about, when,* and *because* are only three of many that add context to a reflection of feeling.

4. The *tense* of the reflection may be important. Reflections in the present tense (Right now, you *are* angry") tend to be more useful than those in the past ("You felt angry then"). Some clients will have difficulty with the present tense, whereas others may need more of it.

5. A *check-out* may be used to see if the reflection is accurate. This is especially helpful if the feeling is implicit ("You feel angry today—am I hearing you correctly?").

▲ Summary

Reflection has been described as basic to the counseling process, yet it can be overdone. Many times a short and accurate reflection may be the most helpful. With friends, family, and fellow employees, a quick acknowledgment of feeling ("If I were you, I'd feel angry about that . . . " or "You must be tired today") followed by continued normal conversational flow may be most helpful in developing better relationships. In an interaction with a harried waiter or salesperson, an acknowledgment of feeling may change the whole tone of a meal or business interchange. Similarly, with many clients a brief reflection of feeling may be more useful than the more detailed emphasis outlined here. Identifying implicit feelings can be helpful, and as clients move toward complex issues, the sorting out of mixed feelings may be the central ingredient of successful counseling, be it vocational interviewing, personal decision making, or in-depth individual counseling and therapy.

Nevertheless, it is important to remember that not all people will appreciate or welcome your noting their feelings. Clients will prefer to disclose feelings after rapport and trust have been developed. Less verbal clients may find reflection puzzling at times, or may say, for instance, "Of course I'm angry; why did you say that?" With some cultural groups, reflection of feeling may be inappropriate and represent cultural insensitivity. Male blue-collar workers, for example, may believe that expression of feelings is "unmanly," yet a brief reflection may be helpful to them. Be aware that an empathic reflection can sometimes have a confrontational quality that causes clients to look at themselves from a different perspective; it may therefore seem intrusive to some clients. Though noting feelings in the interview is essential, acting on your observations may not always be in the best interests of the client. Timing is particularly important with this skill.

Box 6-1.   Key Points

Why?	Emotions undergird our life experience. Out of emotions spring many of our thoughts and actions. If we can identify and sort out clients' feelings, we have a foundation for further action.
What?	Emotions and feelings may be identified through labeling client behavior with affective words such as *angry, happy, sad, scared,* or *confused.* The counselor will want to develop an array of ways to note and label client emotions. Important in labeling client feelings are noting the following: 1. Emotional words used by the client 2. Implicit emotional words not actually spoken 3. Nonverbally expressed emotions seen through the observation of body movement 4. Mixed verbal and nonverbal emotional cues, which may represent a variety of discrepancies
How?	Emotions may be observed directly, drawn out through questions ("How do you feel about that?" "Do you feel angry?"), and then reflected through the following steps: 1. Begin with a sentence stem such as "You feel" or "Sounds like you feel" or "Could it be you feel." Use the client's name. 2. Feeling word(s) may be added (*sad, happy, glad*). 3. The context may be added through a paraphrase or a repetition of key content ("Looks like you feel happy *about the excellent rating*"). 4. In many cases a present-tense reflection is more powerful than one in the past or future tense. "You feel happy right now" rather than "You felt" or "You will feel." 5. Following an implicit identification of feeling, the check-out may be most useful. "Am I hearing you correctly?" "Is that close?" This lets the client correct you if you are either incorrect or uncomfortably close to a truth that he or she is not yet ready to admit.
With whom?	Brief reflections of feeling may be particularly helpful with friends, family, and people met during the day. Deeper reflections and a stronger emphasis on this skill may be appropriate in many counseling situations, but they require a relatively verbal client. The skill may be inappropriate with clients of certain cultural backgrounds.
And?	The client observation skills of Chapter 4 will prove especially helpful in improving your skill in reflecting feeling. The concept of concreteness (see Chapter 7) may be useful to add to reflection of feeling. For example, "You seem to be angry with your spouse. Could you give me a specific example of a situation in which you feel this anger?" Following this, other feelings and thoughts may be identified, and the question "What does this mean to you?" may be helpful. Just because you observe a feeling does not mean it should be reflected. Too much reflection may overintensify the feeling; also, some counselors focus too much attention on negative feelings. Accentuate the positive too! Where you discover a strong negative feeling, there is frequently an unseen positive contrasting feeling as well.

▲ Practice Exercises and Self-Assessment

Feelings are basic to human experience. Although we may observe them in daily interaction, we usually ignore them. In counseling and helping situations, however, they can be central to the process of understanding another person. Further, you will find that increased attention to feelings and emotions may enrich your daily life and bring you to a closer understanding of those with whom you live and work.

Individual Practice

Exercise 1. Increasing your feeling vocabulary by categorizing feelings

Return to the list of affective words you generated at the beginning of this chapter. Take some more time to add to that list. One way to lengthen that list is to consider five categories of feeling words that would give you some idea of how the client thinks about the world.

The first category is words that represent mixed or ambivalent feelings. In such cases the feelings are often very unclear, and your task is to help the client sort out the deeper emotions underlying the surface, expressed word. List below words that represent confused or vague feelings (for instance, *confused, anxious, ambivalent, torn, ripped, mixed*).

Mixed, vague feeling words:

_____   _____   _____

_____   _____   _____

_____   _____   _____

_____   _____   _____

_____   _____   _____

A common mistake is to assume that these words represent the root feelings. Most often they cover deeper feelings. The word *anxiety* is especially important to consider in this context: it is sometimes a vague indicator of mixed feelings. If you accept client anxiety as a basic feeling, counseling may proceed slowly. An important task of the interviewer when noting mixed feeling words is to use questions and reflection of feeling to help the client discover the deeper feelings underlying the surface ambivalence. Underlying anxiety or confusion, for example, you may find anger, hurt, love, and concern over financial need.

The next three categories of emotional words were suggested by Osgood, Suci, and Tannenbaum (1957), who categorize adjectives into bipolar opposites (good–bad, wise–foolish, strong–weak, and such). Emotional words can likewise be categorized. You will find that more words can be generated to increase your feeling vocabulary via the process described below. *Also, you will find that identifying client words that fit into the pattern of opposites provides you with a map of the client's feelings.*

Take your list of words from earlier in the chapter and categorize them below according to which seem to represent activity, potency, or evaluation. In some cases, you will list words in more than one category. Space has also been provided for you to list opposite feeling words.

Feelings of activity (active–passive, fast–slow, depressed–hyperactive)

Active Word   Passive Opposite

_____   _____

_____   _____

_____   _____

_____   _____

_____   _____

_____   _____

Feelings of potency (potent–impotent, strong–weak, skillful–clumsy)

Potency Word   Impotency Opposite

_____   _____

_____   _____

_____   _____

_____   _____

_____   _____

_____   _____

Feelings of evaluation (good–bad, bored–interested, nice–awful)

Positive Word   Negative Opposite

_____   _____

_____   _____

_____   _____

_____   _____

_____   _____

_____   _____

Fifth, feelings are often presented through metaphors, concrete examples, and similes. It is often more descriptive of your emotions to say that you feel like a limp dishrag than to say you are tired and exhausted. Other examples might include "dry as a desert," "empty as a dish," "wheeling along," "proud as a lion," "birdlike." Metaphors can also represent confused, active, evaluative, or potency emotions. Because metaphors are often masks for more complex feelings, at times it is inappropriate to accept such descriptions as presented—you may want to search for the underlying feelings. After you have developed a list of at least ten metaphors below, you may wish to generate a list of opposite metaphors and examples.

Metaphors, similes, and concrete examples of feelings

Metaphor   Opposite Metaphor

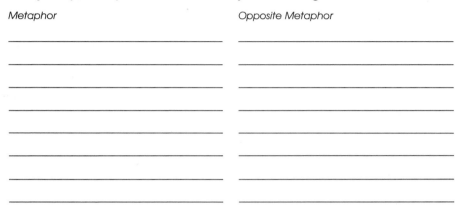

Exercise 2. Observation of feelings

The patterns of feeling-word constructs that clients use can provide you with information on how they think about the world. Some words may represent mixed feelings; other words may be grouped into pairs of more general polar opposites such as feelings of activity–passivity, potency–impotency, and positive or negative evaluation. Some goals you might help clients work toward are to acknowledge and validate their mixed feelings, to recognize what aspects of a situation they can and cannot control, and to accentuate their positive feelings.

Observe an interview or listen to a discussion and note below the feeling words used by the client. Develop polar opposites that may give you some idea of how the client constructs the world. Keep in mind that the polar opposites are your words, not those of the other person.

Feeling Words   Polar Opposite

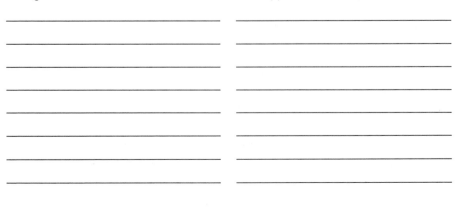

Given the concepts of activity, potency, and evaluation, what concepts or ideas can you generate to describe the client and possible goals to help the client develop?

_____

_____

_____

_____

_____

_____

_____

_____

_____

_____

_____

_____

_____

Exercise 3. Distinguishing a reflection of feeling from a paraphrase

The key feature that distinguishes a reflection of feeling from a paraphrase is the affective word. Many paraphrases contain reflections of feeling—such counselor statements are classified as both. Consider the two examples below. In the first example, you are to indicate which of the leads is a paraphrase (P), which a reflection of feeling (RF), and which an encourager (E).

"I am really discouraged. I can't find anywhere to live. I've looked at so many apartments, but they are all so expensive. I'm tired and I don't know where to turn."

Mark the following counselor responses with an E, P, RF, or combination if more than one skill is used.

_____ "Where to turn?"
_____ "Tired . . . "
_____ "You feel very tired and discouraged."
_____ "Searching for an apartment simply hasn't been successful; they're all so expensive."
_____ "You look tired and discouraged; you've looked hard but haven't been able to find an apartment you can afford."

For the example below, write an encourager, paraphrase, reflection of feeling, and a combination paraphrase/reflection of feeling in response to the client.

"Right, I do feel tired and frustrated. In fact, I'm really angry. At one place they treated me like dirt!"

Encourager: _____

Paraphrase: _____

_____

Reflection of feeling: _____

_____

Combination paraphrase and reflection of feeling: _____

_____

_____

Exercise 4. Acknowledgment of feeling

We have seen that the brief reflection of feeling (or acknowledgment of feeling) may be useful in your interactions with busy and harried people during the day. At least once a day, deliberately tune in to a waitress, teacher, service station attendant, telephone operator, or friend, and give a brief acknowledgment of feeling ("You seem terribly busy and pushed"). Follow this with a brief self-statement ("Can I help?" "Should I come back?" "I've been pushed today myself, as well") and note below what happens:

_____

_____

_____

_____

_____

Exercise 5. Examining your own feeling vocabulary

Write a 200-word essay on any topic of interest to you. Alternatively, examine a letter you have written to a friend or family member. In either case, list below your feeling words and metaphors:

_____ _____ _____

_____ _____ _____

_____ _____ _____

_____ _____ _____

_____ _____ _____

_____ _____ _____

_____ _____ _____

Now classify your feeling words in terms of activity, potency, and evaluation. What do you discover?

_____

_____

_____

_____

_____

Systematic Group Practice

One of the most difficult skills for people in our culture to learn is the reflection of feeling. Mastering this skill is critical to effective counseling and interviewing.

Step 1. Divide into practice groups.

Step 2. Select a group leader.

Step 3. Assign roles for the first practice session.

▲ Role-played client
▲ Interviewer
▲ Observer 1, who gives special attention to noting client feelings
▲ Observer 2, who gives special attention to interviewer behavior

Step 4. Planning.   Establish clear goals for the session. A useful way for the interviewer to begin, if the topic is the same as in Chapter 5's practice session, is with a summary of the previous interview. This can be followed by questioning, paraphrasing, and encouraging to bring out data. Periodically, the interviewer should reflect feelings. This may be facilitated by one-word encouragers that focus on feeling words and by open questions ("How did you feel when that happened?"). The practice session should end with a summarization of both the feelings and the facts of the situation. Examine the basic and active mastery goals in the "Self-Assessment and Follow-Up" section to determine your personal objectives for the interview.

It is critical that the client talk about feelings if the interviewer is going to reflect them. The same topics are suggested as those that were recommended for paraphrasing:

Something with which or someone with whom I have a present or past conflict
Positive and negative feelings toward my parents or other significant persons
Mixed blessings of my work setting, home community, or area of the country
A conflict revolving around a decision regarding work, school, or a major
    purchase

The observers should use this time to examine the feedback forms and to plan their own sessions.

Step 5. Conduct a 5-minute practice session using this skill.

Step 6. Review the practice session and provide feedback to the interviewer for 10 minutes.   How well did the interviewer achieve goals and mastery objectives? As skills and client role-plays become more complex, you'll find that this time is not sufficient for in-depth practice sessions, and you'll want to contract for practice time outside the session with your group. Again, it is particularly important that the observers and the interviewer note the level of mastery achieved by the interviewer. Was the interviewer able to achieve specific objectives with a specific impact on the client?

Step 7. Rotate roles.

A reminder.   The role-played client may be "difficult" if he or she wishes, but must be talkative—this can help generalize learning to real situations. Remember that this is a practice session, and unless affective issues are discussed, the interviewer will have no opportunity to practice the skill.

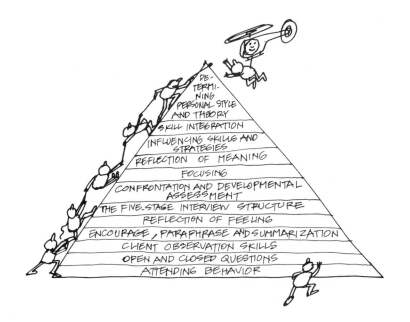

Noting and Reflecting Feelings Feedback Sheet

_____ (Date)

_____   _____
(Name of Interviewer)   (Name of Person Completing Form)

Instructions: Observer 1 will give special attention to client feelings via notations of verbal and nonverbal behavior. Observer 2 will write down the wording of interviewer reflections of feeling as closely as possible and comment on their accuracy and value.

1. *Verbal feelings expressed by the client.* List here all words that relate to emotions.

2. *Nonverbal indications of feeling states in the client.* Facial flush? Body movements? Others?

3. *Implicit feelings not actually stated by the client* Check these out with the client later for validity.

4. *Reflections of feelings used by the interviewer.* As closely as possible, use the exact words of the interviewer and record them on a separate sheet of paper.
5. *Comments on the reflections of feeling.* What sentence stems were typically used? Were the feeling words reflected by the interviewer implicitly, or explicitly expressed by the client? Was the interviewer's use of the skill accurate and valid? Was the check-out used?

Self-Assessment and Follow-Up

The questions and self-assessment topics presented below are designed to help you determine your present mastery level for the reflection of feeling skill and to determine possible directions for the future.

1. Reflection of feeling is seen by many interviewers and counselors as the central interviewing skill, enabling the interviewer to reach and understand client emotional experience

Without understanding of emotional experience and feelings, many say, no real counseling or effective interviewing can exist. Do you agree or disagree with this statement? Explain your position below.

_____

_____

_____

_____

_____

_____

2. Mastery of reflection of feeling

What specific competencies have you mastered with this skill? Give evidence of each level of mastery in the space provided and/or information from tapes, transcripts, or case studies.

Identification.   You will be able to classify the skill of reflection of feeling as it is shown in the interview. You will be able to develop an extensive list of affective words to assist you in reflecting feelings.

_____   Ability to generate an extensive list of affective words.

_____

_____

_____   Ability to categorize these affective words as mixed or metaphorical feelings or as activity, potency, or evaluative words.

_____

_____

_____   Ability to identify reflection of feeling as it is demonstrated in an interview.

_____

_____

_____   Ability to acknowledge feelings briefly in daily interactions with people outside of counseling situations (in restaurants, grocery stores, and the like).

_____

_____

Basic mastery.   You will be able to demonstrate the skill of reflection of feeling in a role-played interview.

_____   Ability to use the skill in a role-played interview.

_____

_____

_____   Ability to use the skill in real interviews.

_____

_____

Active mastery.   You will be able to use this skill in the interview and to identify client feelings accurately. A client may be expected to say "That's right . . . " at times in response to your reflection. Through the careful use of this skill, you may open up a client to further expressions of personal feeling and emotion. You may combine reflection of feeling with paraphrasing and summarization. You will enable a client to talk about emotions and to sort through mixed emotions.

Provide evidence of your mastery of each of the following from tapes, transcripts, or case studies.

_____   In response to your reflections of feeling, do clients often say "That's right . . . " and continue their talk?

_____   Through reflection of feeling (often coupled with questioning) can you facilitate exploration of feelings?

_____   Can you match the client's auditory, visual, or kinesthetic system?

_____   Through this skill (often coupled with closed questions) can you close off a discussion of feelings?

_____   Can you use activity, potency, and evaluative dimensions to classify feelings more accurately in the session?

_____   Can you sort out and discover the feelings underlying words such as *confused* and *ambivalent*?

_____   In a problem-solving interview or a session in which a client talks about an important relationship, can you bring out the positive and negative feelings about each alternative or about the relationship?

_____   Either in a role-played practice or in a real interview or personal interaction, can you help the other person sort out confused feelings about significant relationships or issues through questions, paraphrasing, encouragers, and reflection of feeling?

Teaching mastery.   Are you able to teach the skill of reflection of feeling to clients and other persons? This skill is particularly important to teach those who have interpersonal difficulties with families and friends or on the job. Learning to recognize feelings in other people is central to interpersonal empathy and success in relationships.

_____

_____

3. What one single goal would you set for yourself with regard to the skill of reflection of feeling?

_____

_____

_____

_____

▲ **Reference**

Osgood, C., Suci, G., and Tannenbaum, P. (1957) *The measurement of meaning*. Urbana, Ill.: University of Illinois Press.

Selecting and Structuring Skills to Meet Client Needs: How to Conduct a Complete Interview Using Only Listening Skills

7

How can the concepts of this chapter be used to help you and your clients?

Being heard by another person is a true gift. One of the best tests of your ability to hear and to listen is to complete a full, well-formed interview using listening skills alone. With a solid mastery of attending, observation, and the basic listening sequence, you will be prepared to study more advanced skills and to consider alternative theoretical approaches to counseling.

This chapter covers four basic concepts. Brief definitions and the function of each follow:

Concept and Definition

Basic listening sequence (BLS). The skills of questioning, encouraging, paraphrasing, reflection of feeling, and summarizing make up the BLS. The BLS appears in a similar form in such varied fields as counseling, management, medicine, and social work.

Positive asset search. The positive asset search uses the BLS to draw out specific positive assets of the client that may be brought to bear on a problem.

Empathy. Viewing the world from the client's frame of reference requires the skilled use of attending. Empathy can be divided into specific dimensions, such as concreteness, immediacy, and a nonjudgmental attitude. You will find concepts of empathic understanding helpful in evaluating the quality of your responses to a client.

Structuring the interview. An interview has five stages: (1) establishing rapport and structuring, (2) gathering information, (3) defining outcomes, (4) confronting client incongruity and generating alternatives, and (5) generalizing and transferring learning.

Function

To assist in defining a client's problem and/or the desired outcome of the interview. Emphasis is on the client's frame of reference. The BLS helps ensure that the interviewer understands the problem as the client experiences it.

To identify and emphasize client strengths. Too often counseling and interviewing focus on weakness and difficulty. The positive asset search provides the client with a solid base for personal growth.

To improve the quality of the interview and the helpfulness of the attending and influencing skills used. Furthermore, it provides you with a scale by which you can evaluate the quality of your listening skills (and, later, your influencing skills as well).

To ensure purpose and direction in the interview, and to help define and achieve specific outcomes. Different theories of interviewing give varying attention to each stage. The ability to conduct a well-formed interview using only listening skills may be considered a prime competency of the culturally intentional interviewer or counselor.

▲ Introduction

To recapitulate the definition of Chapter 1, *intentionality* means determining your goals and aims and then choosing from a range of alternative actions. The intentional interviewer has more than one action, thought, or behavior available

for use in the continually changing atmosphere of the intel ___ ... ____intional interviewer generates alternative possibilities in a given interview situation and selects from many different theories using a variety of skills and techniques. The intentional interviewer can act decisively, note feedback in response to that action, and then act in accordance with the new data, adapting the style to suit different cultural groups.

Remember, if something doesn't work, don't try more of the same . . . try something different! Each client you face in the interview is unique and will respond individually to the skills you present. What works with one person at one time may not work 5 minutes later. Yet it is possible to have skills, skill sequences and structures, and techniques with which to achieve specific objectives in your sessions.

Once you have mastered the several skills of attending, observation, and listening, it is important to put them together in a smoothly flowing, integrated interview. This chapter provides a framework for integrating the skills into the interview and presents additional integrative formulations that are important to becoming a skilled interviewer. The practice exercises at the conclusion of the chapter will assist in the process of skill integration.

▲ Instructional Reading

The Basic Listening Sequence

Observations of interviews in counseling and therapy as well as in management, medicine, and other settings have revealed a common thread of skill usage. As we saw in Chapter 1, many successful interviewers begin their sessions with an open question followed by closed questions for diagnosis and clarification. The paraphrase checks out the content of what the client is saying, and the reflection of feeling (usually brief in the early stages) examines key emotions. These skills are followed by a summary of the concern expressed by the client. Encouragers may be used throughout the interview to enrich it and help evoke details.

Though the above set of skills appears in many different situations, it is not a rigid sequence. Each counselor or interviewer adapts these skills to meet the needs of the client and the situation. The effective interviewer uses client observation skills to note client reactions and intentionally *flexes* at that moment to provide the support the client needs. As you learn other skills and observe individual and cultural differences, you may find it appropriate to begin some interviews with a self-disclosure or even a directive instead of the usual open question.

Your goal in using the basic listening sequence is threefold. Whenever you are working with a client on any topic, you will want to elicit the following:

1. *An overall summary of the issue.* This is done initially through the open question "Could you tell me about that?" or through simple attending. At the close of a section of the interview, you may want to summarize the client's main facts and feelings.
2. *The key facts of a situation.* These are obtained through *what* questions, encouragers, and paraphrases.

3. *The central emotions and feelings.* You reach these through questions, such as "Could you share your feelings about that issue?" reflection of feeling, and encouragers that focus on emotional words.

The basic listening sequence provides you with an array of skills to ensure that you understand the basic structure of the client's thinking. Later, depending on your theoretical orientation and natural style, you may want to add other thoughts, behaviors, and meanings to the basic listening sequence.

For the beginning counselor or interviewer, mastery of the basic listening sequence can be most beneficial. Table 7-1 gives examples of the basic listening sequence in counseling, management, and medical interviewing. A special advantage of mastering this sequence is that once a basic set of skills is defined it can be used in many different situations. It is not unusual for a person skilled in the concepts of intentional interviewing to be conducting vocational counseling at a college in the morning, training parents in communication skills in the afternoon, and working as a management consultant on group meeting skills in the evening. The microskills approach can be applied in many settings. In each case the BLS has the objective of bringing out client data—facts and feelings—for later interviewer and client action.

Table 7-1. Three examples of the Basic Listening Sequence

Skill	Counseling	Management	Medicine
Open question	"Could you tell me what you'd like to talk to me about . . . "		
Closed question	"Did you graduate from high school?" "What specific careers have you looked at?"	"Who was involved with the production line problem?" "Did you check the main belt?"	"Is the headache on the left side or on the right? How long have you had it?"
Encouragers	Repetition of key words and restatement of longer phrases.		
Paraphrases	"So you're considering returning to college."	"Sounds like you've consulted with almost everyone."	"It looks like you feel it's on the left side and may be a result of the car accident."
Reflection of feeling	"You feel confident of your ability but worry about getting in."	"I sense you're upset and troubled by Hank's reaction."	"It appears you've been feeling very anxious and tense lately."
Summarization	In each case the effective counselor, manager, or physician summarizes the problem from the client's point of view *before* diagnosing from the interviewer's point of view.		

The Positive Asset Search

Counseling, interviewing, and psychotherapy can be difficult experiences for some clients. They have come to discuss their problems and resolve conflicts, so the session can rapidly become a depressing litany of failures and fears.

People grow from their strengths, not from their weaknesses. The positive asset search is a useful method to ensure a more optimistic and directed interview. Rather than just ask about problems, the effective interviewer seeks constantly to find positive assets upon which the client can focus. Even in very complex issues, it is possible to find good things about the client and things that he or she does right. Emphasizing positive assets also gives the client a sense of personal power in the interview.

To conduct a positive asset search the interviewer simply uses the BLS to draw out the client's positive aspects and then reflects them back. This may be done systematically, as a separate part of the interview, or used constantly throughout the session. Specifically, the positive asset search appears in the interview in the following ways:

1. The interviewer may begin a session by asking what has happened recently that the client feels good about. Or the interviewer may comment on some positive strength in the client.

2. In the problem-definition phase of the interview, the interviewer may use the BLS to bring out positive client assets in detail. For example, a response to a client who has just lost a job and feels depressed and worried might be "You say you're worried and feel lost. At the same time, I know you held that job for four years. Could you tell me one thing you liked about the job or felt you did well?"

3. If a client constantly repeats negative self-statements, these may be paraphrased and then followed by feedback from a more positive viewpoint. For example, "Yes, losing a job is traumatic and really hurts. At the same time, I see that you have several strengths—a good sense of humor, some valuable skills, and a history of perseverance in the face of difficulty. All of these will help you work through this."

Highlighting specific concrete assets of the client in the context of real problems is a very helpful way of promoting positive change, and is central to any intelligent approach to human problems.

The positive asset search is a new concept in the helping field. Theoretically, it may be described as a psychoeducational intervention that emphasizes human development rather than the "medical model" that emphasizes remediation of problems. The positive asset search will reappear in later portions of this book, and other ways to help clients positively reframe life experiences will be presented. The concept appears under many different guises in the varying forms of interviewing, counseling, and therapy. At times, the positive asset search can obviate the need for traditional problem solving in the session, as client strengths naturally overcome their weaknesses.

Empathy: Qualitative Aspects of Skill Usage

The skills of attending and influencing are not always sufficient in themselves to provide quality relationships with clients. Most basic is the quality of empathy—experiencing the client's world as if *you* were the client. This means moving into the client's frame of reference. The attending skills—particularly paraphrasing, reflection of feeling, and reflection of meaning—are deeply involved in developing basic empathy. Empathy manifests itself in the interview behaviorally when the interviewer or counselor truly understands the client and is able to paraphrase the client's main ideas accurately. In such cases the counselor will often be found using the important words of the client, but distilling and shortening the main ideas.

In *basic empathy,* described above, counselor responses are roughly interchangeable with those of the client. In *additive empathy* the counselor or interviewer uses influencing skills and *adds* congruent ideas and feelings from another frame of reference to facilitate client exploration. Attending skills, used well, can themselves be additive. Reflection of meaning, especially, operates from the client's frame of reference and adds depth beyond the mere reflection of feeling and paraphrasing.

Empathy, then, is a major goal of both attending and influencing skills. If the skills are used ineffectively, however, they may subtract from the client's experience. Lack of empathy *subtracts* from the helping process: subtractive responses take something away from the client and usually indicate poor listening skills, although inappropriate influencing skills are often subtractive as well.

It is possible to rate empathy on a rough 5-point scale, and you may wish to examine each of your responses for the degree to which it manifests empathy. (See also Carkhuff, 1969, for further discussion of these concepts.) Here are examples of five levels of empathy in response to a client:

Client: I don't know what to do. I've gone over this problem again and again. My husband just doesn't seem to understand that I don't really care anymore. He just keeps trying, but it doesn't seem worth bothering with him anymore.

Level-1 Counselor: (subtractive) That's not a very good way to talk. I think you ought to consider his feelings, too.

Level-2 Counselor: (slightly subtractive) Seems like you've just about given up on him. You don't want to try anymore.

Level-3 Counselor: (basic empathy or interchangeable response) You're discouraged and confused. You've worked over the issues with your husband, but he just doesn't seem to understand. At the moment, you feel he's not worth bothering with. You don't really *care.*

Level-4 Counselor: (slightly additive) You've gone over the problem with him again and again to the point that you don't really *care* right now. You've tried hard. What does this mean to you?

Level-5 Counselor: (additive) I sense your hurt and confusion and that right now you really don't care anymore. Given what you've told me, your thoughts and feelings make a lot of sense to me. At the same time, you've had a reason for trying so hard. You've talked about some deep feelings of caring for him in the past. How do you put that together right now with what you are feeling?

To be empathic means to take risks, and higher-level responses are not always well received by clients. As the counselor attempts to move toward additive responses, the risk goes up. Risk, in this case, means "risk of error." You may have excellent listening skills, but when you seek to add your own perceptions you may be out of synchrony with client needs.

A Level-3 interchangeable response is fairly safe and direct. When the counselor strives for higher-level, additive responses, they may sometimes be completely off the mark, and the client will respond negatively. This does not mean the counselor response was necessarily that bad; it may be simply that the client wasn't ready at that moment, or the client's developmental level on that topic was too low. (Chapter 8 will provide a scale of rating developmental change in the client.)

In any case, how the client responds to your interviewing lead is more important than any external rating of the response. No interviewer can always predict client responses to leads. It is here that client observation skills and the ability of the interviewer to flex and change the next lead to fit the needs of the client are most important. Flexing requires the interviewer to note the client's response to interventions and intentionally provide another intervention more in synchrony with the client's needs at that moment. The following 1–2–3 pattern illustrates the flow necessary for flexing and true empathic responding.

1. The interviewer observes the client's verbal and nonverbal behavior and consciously or unconsciously selects a verbal lead (skill) with the potential for facilitating client development. (The counselor in the example above might select the Level-5 response as likely to facilitate talk and deeper exploration.)

2. The client reacts to the counselor's statement with verbal and nonverbal behavior. (In this case, the client might say angrily, "I don't put that together. What I want at the moment is to get away. Are you pushing me back toward him?")

3. The interviewer again observes the client's verbal and nonverbal behavior and selects another verbal lead (skill) with the possibility of facilitating client development. (After the client's angry response the counselor might try a Level-3 response: "What I just said made you feel angry. You want very much to get away from him right now.")

Number 1 in the pattern is the behavior of the counselor, number 2 the reaction of the client, and number 3 the consequent behavior of the counselor. True empathy requires the interviewer constantly to flex and be ready to change and adapt to each unique client. While many counselors are anxious to move to the deeper Level-4 and 5 responses, if they are used out of context and without regard to client readiness, failure of even the "best" responses is inevitable. True empathy requires you to be where the client is able to hear you.

A number of authorities have given extensive attention to empathy (Carkhuff, 1969; Egan, 1986; Ivey & Authier, 1978; Rogers, 1961); Carkhuff and Rogers are considered the basic authorities. As they point out, to produce quality helping relationships, it is often useful to consider positive regard, respect and warmth, concreteness, immediacy, nonjudgmental attitudes, and authenticity or congruence as the foundations of empathy. These dimensions have arisen explicitly and implicitly throughout this book and can now be briefly summarized with suggestions for noting them in the interview.

Positive regard

Positive regard may be defined as selecting positive aspects of clients' experience and selectively attending to positive aspects of client statements. A 5-point scale may be developed to measure positive regard (as well as other qualities discussed in this section), with the same points of reference as for empathy.

Level	1	2	3	4	5
	Subtractive		Interchangeable		Additive

In a subtractive response, the counselor finds something wrong with the client. In an interchangeable response, the counselor notes or reflects accurately what the client has talked about. In an additive response the counselor points out how, even in the most difficult situation, the client is doing something positive. For example, the counselor may say the following to a client suffering from depression and talking about many problems: "John, I respect your ability to describe your problems so clearly. You've got your reasons for feeling so depressed. Tell me a bit more about your ability to define problems in the present and past." Carl Rogers was particularly good at delving into the most complex problems or person and finding positive qualities. Positive regard is perhaps the most basic aspect of true empathy.

Respect and warmth

Respect and warmth may be most easily rated from a kinesthetic and nonverbal point of view. You show respect and warmth by your posture, your smile, and your vocal qualities. Your ability to keep your comments congruent with your body language and your willingness to touch (in appropriate situations) are indicators of respect and warmth.

Concreteness

Concreteness has been stressed throughout this book and a concrete counselor promptly seeks specifics rather than vague generalities. As interviewers, we are most often interested in specific feelings, specific thoughts, and specific examples of actions. As has been stressed many times, one of the most useful of all open questions is "Could you give me a specific example of . . . ?" Concreteness makes the interview live and real. Likewise, communication *from* the interviewer—the directive, the feedback skill, and interpretation—needs to be highly specific or it may become lost in the busy world of the client.

There are times, nevertheless, when concreteness is not the most appropriate response. Some problems are best discussed in more general terms, and some cultural groups tend to be less specific. Cultural differences of expression in empathy, respect and warmth, and concreteness must always be kept in mind.

Immediacy

Immediacy is a useful concept to give the interview timeliness. It is most easily described in terms of language. You may respond to a client who is angry in three tenses: "You *were* angry... you *are* angry... you *will be* angry." We tend to respond to others in the same tense in which they are speaking. You will find that some clients always talk in the past tense; they may profit from present-tense discussion. Other clients are always thinking of the future; still others are constantly in the present. The most useful response is generally made in the present tense. A change of tense may be used to speed up or slow down the interview. It seems, however, that for counseling styles of many types, responses that include all three tenses tend to be the most powerful of all.

Another way to view immediacy is in terms of the relationship between the counselor and the client. The more personal the relationship is, the more immediate it is. As issues of closeness between interviewer and client arise, this type of immediacy may become very powerful. A relationship is made immediate in this sense by a focus on the counselor and client ("I – you" talk) and by staying in the present tense.

You will find that as interviews move more to present tense immediacy your presence in the interview will become more powerful and important. You may even find that clients start responding to you in the here and now similarly to ways they responded to significant people from their past. It is in such instances that the immediacy of "I – you" talk between counselor and client becomes especially important. The skill of artful self-disclosure (see Chapter 11) will be useful here.

Nonjudgmental attitude

A nonjudgmental attitude is difficult to describe. Closely related to positive regard and respect, a nonjudgmental attitude requires that you suspend your own opinions and attitudes and assume a value neutrality in relation to your client. Many clients have attitudes toward their issues and concerns that may be counter to your own beliefs and values. If you listen to your clients carefully, you will come to an understanding of why they might have taken that position or action. People who are working through difficulties and issues do not need to be judged or evaluated; they need acceptance for themselves and their actions as they are.

A nonjudgmental attitude is expressed through vocal qualities and body language and by statements that indicate neither approval nor disapproval. However, as with all qualities and skills, there are times when your judgment may facilitate client exploration. There are no absolutes in counseling and interviewing.

Authenticity and congruence

Authenticity and congruence are the reverse of discrepancies and mixed messages, which were discussed in Chapter 6. The hope is that the counselor or interviewer can be congruent and genuine and not display many discrepancies. Needless to say, however, life is full of discrepancies and paradoxes, and your ability to flex in response to the client may be the most basic demonstration of your authenticity.

A Basic Structure for the Well-Formed Interview

Not only do basic listening skills cut across different areas of interpersonal relationships and professions, but they also may be used to organize an effective, well-formed interview. This section summarizes one basic structure for the interview and illustrates how the listening skills can be used effectively in each of its different segments. This interviewing structure can be used in many different settings with appropriate adaptations for the person and situation.

The structure is based on a decisional or problem-solving model that focuses on defining the problem, defining the goals, and resolving the discrepancies between problem and goals. Much of interviewing, counseling, and therapy are about problem solving and decision making. Alternative theories, of course, approach decisions very differently. Thus this is not the only interviewing structure, but you will find it provides an organization that can produce results. Later in this book, you will discover that this structure can be used in many approaches to counseling and therapy, even though the theories appear to be very different from one another. The interview can be organized into five basic stages (see Table 7-2).

Table 7-2.   A simple five-stage structure for the interview

Definition of Stage	Function and Purpose of Stage	Commonly Used Skills
1. *Rapport and structuring.* "Hello _____."	To build a working alliance with the client and to enable the client to feel comfortable with the interviewer. Structuring may be needed to explain the purpose of the interview. Structuring helps keep the session on task and to inform the client of what the counselor can and cannot do.	Attending behavior to establish contact with the client and client-observation skills to determine appropriate method to build rapport. Structuring most often involves the influencing skill of information giving and instructions.

(continued)

Table 7-2 (continued)

Definition of Stage	Function and Purpose of Stage	Commonly Used Skills
2. *Gathering information, defining the problem, and identifying assets.* "What's the problem?"	To find out why the client has come to the interview and how he or she views the problem. Skillful problem definition will help avoid aimless topic jumping and give the interview purpose and direction. Also to identify clearly positive strengths of the client.	Most common are the attending skills, especially the basic listening sequence. Other skills may be used as necessary. If problems aren't clear, you may need more influencing skills. The positive asset search often reveals capabilities in the client that are useful in problem resolution.
3. *Determining outcomes. Where does the client want to go?* "What do you want to have happen?"	To find out the ideal world of the client. How would the client like to be? How would things be if the problem were solved? This stage is important in that it enables the interviewer to know what the client wants. The desired direction of the client and counselor should be reasonably harmonious. With some clients, skip Stage 2 and define goals first.	Most common are the attending skills, especially the basic listening sequence. Other skills used as necessary. If outcome is still unclear, more influencing skills may be helpful. With clients from other cultures and those who are less verbal, this phase should often precede Stage 2.
4. *Exploring alternatives and confronting client incongruities.* "What are we going to do about it?"	To work toward resolution of the client's issue. This may involve the creative problem-solving model of generating alternatives and deciding among those alternatives. It also may involve lengthy exploration of personal dynamics. This stage of the interview may be the longest.	May begin with a summary of the major discrepancies. Depending on the issue and theory of the interviewer, a heavy use of influencing skills may be expected. Attending skills still used for balance.
5. *Generalization and transfer of learning.* "Will you do it?"	To facilitate changes in thoughts, feelings, and behaviors in the client's daily life. Many clients go through an interview and then do nothing to change their behavior, remaining in the same world they came from.	Influencing skills, such as directives and information/explanation, are particularly important. Attending skills used to check out client understanding of importance of the stage.

Stage 1. Rapport and structuring

"Hello ____ ." As a prime rule for establishing rapport, use the client's name. Some interviewers give extensive attention to the rapport stage, whereas others simply assume rapport and start immediately. Introducing the interview and building rapport obviously are most important in the first interview with a client. In some cases rapport building may be quite lengthy and blend into treatment—for example, in reality therapy with a delinquent youth, where playing Ping-Pong and getting to know the client on a personal basis may be part of the treatment. In most counseling and interviewing, however, this stage is quite short. After a brief "Hello" the interviewer immediately moves to a discussion of what the client wants.

The most important microskills for building rapport are basic attending behavior and client observation skills. Basic attending is used to demonstrate that you understand the client and are interested. Client observation is critical at this stage of the interview. Is the client comfortable and relaxed? Is this client oriented in a primarily auditory, visual, or kinesthetic manner? All observations are helpful in the process of rapport development. Self-disclosure on your part may be helpful with some clients, as well. In a continuing series of sessions, summarization may be used so that past interviews are integrated with the current session to maintain rapport.

The positive asset search may be an important part of rapport building. With a nervous or insecure client, taking time to outline specific and concrete client assets provides the client with a secure base from which to confront difficult problems. What is most important is that the interviewer be open, authentic, and congruent with the client, and flexibly meet the needs expressed by that client.

Nevertheless, you should remember that many—perhaps most—interviews begin with some variation on "Could you tell me how I might be of help?" In much of interviewing rapport can be assumed, but when it is necessary, it is the most important issue in the entire interview. Unless the client has some liking for and trust in you, you won't get far. Again, your ability to observe clients will tell you when it is appropriate to move to Stage 2. One of the best clues as to when to start is the point at which the client starts talking spontaneously about concerns and/or you note that body language is mirrored between you and the client. Movement symmetry or movement complementarity are excellent ways to judge the level of empathy between you and the client.

Structuring is the second part of this first stage. Ordinarily it involves some form of telling the client what to expect from the interview. When you conduct an interview using only attending and listening skills, it may be helpful to inform your client that you are going to listen to him or her carefully. Later, as you make a more detailed theoretical commitment, you will want to inform your client of the purposes of your interview, your general methods, and other structural issues important to the relationship.

Some clients need to have the interview explained for them. This may be their first interview and they may not know how to behave. Setting the stage for this type of client can be extremely important. In such cases the interviewer explains the purpose of the interview and what he or she can or cannot do. Welfare interviewers, for example, find that they can better assist clients if they indicate very early in the session what their powers are. If the client has a different need, immediate referral is possible, with minimal frustration for both client and interviewer.

Stage 2. Gathering information, defining the problem, and identifying assets

"What's the problem?" The first task of the interviewer is to find out why the client is there and what the problem is. Coupled with that is gathering necessary information about the client and the problem. Clients often confuse interviewers with a long list of issues and concerns. One simple rule is that the *last* item a client presents in a "laundry list" of problems is often the one of central concern—watch for it, but be prepared to redefine the problem as you listen further.

The basic listening sequence is crucial to defining problems and gathering information. Open and closed questions will help define the issue as the client views it. Encouragers and paraphrases will provide additional clarity and an opportunity for you to check out that you have heard correctly. Acknowledgment of emotions through reflection of feeling will provide an important beginning understanding of the emotional underpinnings. And finally, summarization provides a good way to put the several ideas the client has presented into an orderly format.

The central task at this point is defining the problem as the client feels it. This can be supplemented by gathering information and data about the client and his perceptions. The basic *who, what, where, when, how,* and *why* series of questions provides one short and often useful framework to make sure you have covered the most important aspects of information gathering and problem definition.

In your attempts to define the central client concerns, always ask yourself, what is the real world of the client? What problem seeks resolution, or what opportunity needs to be actualized? Failure to clearly answer these questions often results in an interview that wanders and lacks purpose.

At the same time, it is important to give attention to client strengths. The positive asset search should be part of this stage of the interview or systematically included later in the session. Always remember a very central point of this text: *clients grow from strength.*

Stage 3. Determining outcomes

The third stage focuses on client goals: where does the client want to go? Many counselors and interviewers will summarize the problem of the client and then ask a question such as "What would you imagine the ideal solution to be?" "Where do you want to go with this?" "Could you take a moment to draw back and develop a fantasy of what you would like to have happen?" or some variation on this theme. After the client proposes some solutions, you may use

the basic listening sequence, and more details of the client's thoughts and feelings about ideal situations will be generated. Often clients can solve their own problems in this stage of the interview.

Some clients prefer to have this stage of the interview early in the session, even before problem definition. For example, with high school discipline problems, less verbal clients, and those of some cultural groups, moving quickly to defining a clear outcome may help rapport development. Some clients dislike lengthy analysis of the problem and want action *now.* If you adapt your interviewing style to meet this simple but obvious need, you will be able to achieve counseling success with many clients that more traditional problem-focused methods cannot reach.

Another type of client who may profit from exploring this phase of the interview is one experiencing vocational indecision. The problem is often vague, confused, and ambiguous. Sorting out a clear goal first may later result in better problem definition and asset identification.

A maxim for the confused interview—be it discipline, vocational, or even marital counseling—is "Define a goal, make the goal explicit, search for assets to help facilitate goal attainment, and only then examine the nature of the problem." At times, clear goal definition and a solid asset search can make problem identification unnecessary.

The phrase *determining outcomes* is useful to focus on as a way to bring specificity to the interview. Whether you are conducting long-term therapy or meeting briefly with a client in an employment agency, asking what the client wants to have come out of the interaction is critical in reaching an outcome. Too often the client and counselor assume they are working toward the same outcome when actually each of them wants to head in a different direction. A client may be satisfied with sleeping better at night, but the counselor wants complete personality reconstruction. The client may want brief advice about how to find a new job, whereas the counselor wants to give extensive vocational testing and suggest a new career. On the other hand, clients often expect and want more than the interviewer can deliver. Clarifying this issue early in the session through questioning can save a great deal of time and effort.

The question of determining outcomes is of interest from a theoretical as well as a practical perspective. Rogers talks about many clients having incongruencies between the real self and the ideal self. Behavioral psychologists often talk about present behavior as compared to desired behavioral goals. Reality therapists talk about fulfilling unmet needs, and trait-and-factor counselors speak of facilitating a client's decision to act. Many theoretical orientations ask "Where is the client, and where does she or he want to go?" "What is the difference between the real world and the desired world?" Blanchard and Johnson (1981), in their primer on effective management, *The One-Minute Manager,* summarize the issue succinctly:

> If you can't tell me what you'd like to be happening . . . you don't have a problem yet. You're just complaining. A problem only exists if there is a difference between what is actually happening and what you desired to be happening (p. 3).

Once the discrepancies—between the real self and the ideal self, between the real situation and the desired situation, between the nature of the relationship now and the desired relationship, and so on—are clear, it is possible to confront issues clearly and precisely. A wide variety of skills, techniques, and theories are available to explore and confront the conflict faced by the client.

For example, consider the following five model sentences:

▲ *Trait and factor decision making:* "On the one hand the problem may be summarized as . . . and on the other hand your desired outcome is . . . and you have the following assets and strengths to help you reach your goals . . . "

▲ *Rogerian:* "Your real self, as you describe yourself, is . . . Yet you see your ideal self as . . . and you have several positive qualities, such as . . . "

▲ *Behavioral:* "Your present behavior is . . . but you would like to behave differently. For example, you would really like to . . . and you note the following positive behaviors and actions from the past . . . "

▲ *Marital counseling:* "Your present relationship is described as . . . but you would like to see it change as follows. . . . As a couple you seem to have several strengths, such as . . . that will be helpful in resolving the conflict."

▲ *Vocational counseling (confused client):* "You are searching for a college major (or life career) and aren't really sure of your possibilities. Yet you've described your short- and long-term goals rather clearly. . . . You've had several positive work experiences in the past. . . . How do you put that together?"

Note that all these model confrontation sentences bring together and point out the discrepancy between the problem definition and the desired outcome. The positive asset summary is used to help the client realize that he or she is personally capable of problem resolution.

Many verbal and high-developmental-level clients can use such a summary as a springboard to action. They will resolve the discrepancy on their own with your support. Clients at lower levels or those extremely emotionally involved with their problems may require more influencing skills and active direction on your part. Observing your client's verbal and nonverbal reaction to this summary will help you determine your style of interview in Stage 4.

Stage 4. Exploring alternatives and confronting client incongruity

"What are we going to do about it?" The purpose of this stage of the interview is problem solving and relief for the client. The problem may lie in deciding between two positive alternatives, making a vocational choice, or in any of the several theoretical orientations described above. The client at this stage is stuck and unable to come up with productive alternatives. The task of the counselor or interviewer is to explore possibilities and to assist the client in finding new ways to act more intentionally in the world.

How does the interviewer confront and explore incongruity? Two major routes appear to be available. First, one could summarize the client conflict and frame of reference and use the basic listening sequence to facilitate the client's problem resolution. Second, one could summarize the client conflict and frame of reference, then *add* one's own frame of reference through influencing skills (feedback, self-disclosure, instruction, directives, interpretation) and/or by applying alternative helping theories (Gestalt, psychodynamic, behavioral). It is preferable for inexperienced interviewers to concentrate on the first alternative, that of facilitating clients through the use of listening skills only.

Let us consider a business manager talking with an employee about a conflict between the purchasing department and the production department. Within the interview structure suggested here, the first task of the manager is to establish rapport with the employee. This is followed by gathering information and defining the problem—here many discrepancies may be identified. Next, the ideal resolution can be determined. Where does the employee (and the manager, in this case) want to go? What outcome is desired? Having defined the real world and the ideal world, the manager can then assist the employee to confront the discrepancies. The manager may self-disclose how he or she solved similar problems in the past. The manager may give the employee some advice or a simple directive to solve the problem. Alternatively, the problem may be solved with the sole use of listening skills.

To bring this employee to Stage 4, the model summarizations described in detail at the end of the description of Stage 3 are especially helpful. "On the one hand, Mr. Employee, the problem you have brought to me is. . . . But you have also defined your goals clearly. They are. . . . Given the problem and your goals, what comes to mind that might serve as a solution to this issue?" Many clients come to counseling with a confusion of issues, problems, and goals. The clear summarization of the present situation together with the ideal situation often clarifies the problem sufficiently so that clients can generate their own ideas.

In addition, you will find that the basic listening sequence and skilled questioning are useful in facilitating client exploration of answers and solutions. Here are some useful questions to assist client problem solving:

"What other alternatives can you think of?"
"Can you brainstorm ideas—just anything that occurs to you?"
"What has worked for you before?"
"What part of the problem is workable if you can't solve it all right now?"
"Which of the ideas that you have generated appeals to you most?"
"What would be the consequence of your taking that alternative?"

In effect, all of the above are oriented toward opening client thought leading to new solutions. You will also find that encouraging skills are useful in helping clients stop and explore possibilities. Repeat key words that might lead the client to new alternatives for action.

Counseling and long-term therapy both try to solve problems in client lives in a similar fashion. The counselor needs to establish rapport, define the problem, and establish certain desired client outcomes. The distinction between the problem and the desired outcome is the major incongruity the therapist seeks to resolve. This incongruity or discrepancy may be resolved in three basic ways. The counselor can use attending skills to clarify the client's frame of reference and then feed back the problem and the goal. Often clients will generate their own synthesis and resolve the problem. If clients do not generate their own answers, then the therapist can add interpretation, self-disclosure, and other influencing skills in an attempt to resolve the discrepancy. In that case, the counselor would be working from a personal frame of reference or theory. Finally, in systematic problem solving the counselor and client might together generate or brainstorm alternatives for action and set priorities for the most effective possibilities.

It is good to keep the basic problem-solving model in mind throughout the interview, particularly in this stage:

1. Define the problem, keeping in mind the goal or desired outcome
2. Generate alternatives
3. Decide on action

During this stage it is particularly important to keep the problem in view while generating alternatives for solution (whether they are practical and commonsensical or theoretical systems of interviewing) and an eventual decision for action. However, decision for action is not enough. You must also plan to make sure that feelings, thoughts, and behaviors generalize beyond the interview itself. Stage 5 of the interview speaks to this task.

Stage 5. Generalization and transfer of learning

"Will you do it?" The information conveyed, the concepts learned in the interview, the new behaviors suggested may all be for naught if systematic thought is not given to the transfer and generalization of the interview to daily life. The complexities of the world are such that taking a new behavior back to the home setting is difficult.

Consider the management and counseling situations again. The manager may give good advice about solving a problem between the production and purchasing departments, but if the employee reverts to the older, more inefficient, "stuck" behavior, the problem will continue. The counselor and client may work through an excellent vocational plan or method of resolving family conflict. But if the client returns to the same work setting or the same family complex, transfer of what has been learned may be extremely difficult or impossible. You and the client may want to work further together to understand and to change larger systems affecting client life.

Many therapies, both traditional and modern, work on the assumption that behavior and attitude change will come out of new unconscious learning; they "trust" that clients will change spontaneously. Change does not come easily, and maintaining any change in thoughts, feelings, or behavior is even more difficult. Behavioral psychology has given considerable thought to the transfer of training and has developed an array of techniques for transfer; even so, clients still revert to earlier, less intentional behaviors. Below are some specific methods different theoretical schools have used to facilitate the transfer of learning from the interview.

Role-playing.   Just as in the practice sessions of this book, the client can practice the new behavior in a role-play with the counselor or interviewer. This emphasizes the specifics of learning and increases the likelihood that the client will recognize the need for the new behavior after the session is over.

Imagery.   Ask the client to imagine the future event and also imagine what he or she will specifically need to do to manage the situation more effectively.

Behavioral charting and progress notes.   The client may keep a record of the number of times certain behaviors occur and report back to the counselor. With other clients an informal diary of personal subjective reactions may be more helpful.

Homework.   The interviewer may suggest specific tasks for the client to try during the week, to follow up on the interview. This is an increasingly common practice in counseling.

Paradoxical instructions.   Through the pioneering work of Viktor Frankl it has been found that directing clients to continue "stuck" behavior or thinking during the next week may be helpful. For example, if a client has difficulty studying, the counselor might suggest that the client *deliberately* procrastinate and avoid work. Out of paradoxical directives such as this, clients often learn to laugh and manage their stuck or out-of-control behavior. *But* paradox is a complex skill and should be used sparingly and with adequate consultation and supervision.

Family or group counseling.   Sometimes individual problems are deeply merged within difficult marriage, family, or work-group arrangements. Therefore, an increasing number of counselors now seek to involve spouses and families in the counseling process. In work settings, too, managers and personnel people increasingly see organizational development and team building as critical to improving individual skills and transfer of behavior.

Follow-up and support.   It may be helpful to ask the client to return periodically to check on the maintenance of behavior. At this time the counselor can also provide social and emotional support through difficult periods.

As you can see, the use of influencing skills is particularly important in the final stages of the interview. When conducting an interview using only listening skills, the last suggestion above is perhaps the most relevant. Here are some questions you can use to facilitate clients planning their own generalization from the interview:

"What one thing from the interview stands out for you right now that you might take home?"

"You've generated several ideas and selected one to try. How are we going to know if you actually do it?"

"What comes to your mind to try as homework next week that we can look at when we get together?"

Each of these can be coupled with the basic listening sequence to draw out the generalization plan in more detail. You may want to ask your client at the close of the interview, "Will you do it?" as a form of contract between the two of you for the future.

These are but a few of the many possibilities to help develop and maintain client change. Each individual will respond differently to these techniques, and client observation skills are called for to determine which technique or set of techniques is most likely to be helpful to a particular person. For maximal impact and behavior transfer, a combination of several techniques is suggested. Evidence makes clear that behavior and attitudes learned in the interview do not necessarily transfer in daily life without careful planning.

Summary

Given the wide variety of models and theories, it is difficult to describe the most effective balance of time and effort to be spent in each stage of the interview. Rather, it seems most effective to use careful client observation to determine the appropriate moment to move from stage to stage. Nevertheless, it is possible to make some generalizations.

For most interviews, a relatively short time is required for rapport building. Problem definition will vary with the complexity of the issue and should not be overlooked. Stage 3, the ideal world of the client, may sometimes be skipped if problem definition is clear, but usually it is helpful to give some time to this stage, for it can open new alternatives you and your client may have overlooked. The work of most interviews takes place in Stage 4. Due to extensive effort here, the fifth stage, generalization, is often forgotten (many times the interviewer is simply tired). The result is that change produced in the interview often doesn't last very long. It is suggested that you not stop your efforts with the fourth stage. Current thinking is that the generalization stage is of importance equal to, if not greater than, the other four stages.

As you work through your first interviews, checking off in your mind whether or not you have used the concepts of each stage will supply a roadmap. Later, as you find your own style and become more comfortable with alternative theories, you will want to develop your own structure for the interview, changing and balancing the stages in your own way to meet the needs of your clients' uniqueness.

Let us now examine how an interview might be conducted using only listening skills.

▲ Example Interview

This interview illustrates how listening skills can be used to help the client understand and cope with interpersonal conflict. The interview has been edited to show portions that demonstrate skill usage and levels of empathy as clearly

as possible. When you conduct your own interview and develop a transcript indicating your own ability to use listening skills, you may want to arrange your transcript in a similar fashion.

The client in this case is a 20-year-old man who is in conflict with his boss at work. You will find him relatively verbal. For the most part, it requires a verbal, cooperative client to work through a complete interview using only listening skills.

Stage 1. Rapport/Structuring

Counselor/Client Statement	*Skill Classification and Comments*
Susan: Bob, do you mind if we tape this interview? It's for a class exercise in interviewing. I'll be making a transcript of the session, which the professor will read. Okay? And if you wish, we can turn the recorder off at any time. I'll show you the transcript if you are interested. If you decide later you don't want me to use this material, I won't and will start again.	Closed question followed by structuring information. It is critical that you obtain client permission before taping, and offer personal control over the material. As a beginner or student you cannot legally control confidentiality, but it is nonetheless your responsibility to protect your client.
Bob: Sounds fine; I do have something to talk about.	Bob seems at ease and relaxed. As the taping was presented casually, he is not concerned about its presence. Rapport is well on the way.
Susan: So, how's it going?	Open question, almost social in nature, designed to give maximum personal room to the client.
Bob: Pretty good, except for the boss. He's pretty awful.	Bob indicates clearly through his nonverbal behavior that he is ready to go. Already, Susan and he have some body mirroring. Therefore, Susan decides to move immediately to Stage 2. With some clients, several interviews may be required to reach this level of rapport.

Stage 2. Gathering information, defining the problem, and identifying assets

Susan: Could you tell me about it?	Open question, oriented toward obtaining a general outline of the problem.
Bob: Well, he's impossible.	Instead of the expected general outline, Bob gives a brief answer.

Susan:	Impossible?	Encourage.
Bob:	Yeah, really impossible. It seems that no matter what I do he is on me, always looking over my shoulder. I don't think he trusts me.	Clients often elaborate on the specific meaning of a problem if you use the encourager.
Susan:	Could you give me a more specific example of what he is doing to indicate he doesn't trust you?	Open question eliciting concreteness. Bob is a bit vague in his discussion.
Bob:	Well, maybe it isn't trust. Like last week, I had this difficult customer who was lipping off to me. He had a complaint about a shirt he had just bought. I don't like that type of thing, so I just started talking back. No one can do *that* to me! And of course the boss didn't like it and chewed me out. It wasn't fair.	As we make events concrete through specific examples, we can understand more fully what is going on in the client's life and mind. The underlying meaning of trust and the relationship with the boss is changing.
Susan:	As I hear it, sounds as though this guy gave you a bad time and it made you angry—and then the boss came in.	Paraphrase and reflection of feeling. Represents Level-3 empathy, as Susan's response is relatively similar to what Bob said. As she does not include the important dimension of fairness, some might call it a Level-2 response.
Bob:	Right! It really made me angry. I have never liked anyone telling me what to do. I left my last job because the boss was doing the same thing.	
Susan:	So your last boss wasn't fair either?	Paraphrase. Note that Susan has brought back Bob's key word *fair.* This would be a Level-3 empathic response. In addition, Susan's vocal tone and body language communicate warmth and respect. She is nonjudgmental as she listens.

(The interview continues to explore Bob's conflict with customers, his boss, and past supervisors. There appears to be a pattern of conflict with authority figures over the past several years. This is a common pattern among young males in their early careers in society. After a detailed discussion of the specific conflict situation and several other examples of the pattern, Susan decides to conduct a positive asset search.)

Susan:	Bob, we've been talking for awhile about difficulties at work. I'd like to know some things that have gone well for you there. Could you tell me about something you feel good about?	Paraphrase/structuring/open question.
Bob:	Yeah; I work hard. They always say I'm a good worker. I feel good about that.	Bob's increasingly tense body language starts to relax with the introduction of the positive asset search. He talks more slowly.
Susan:	Sounds like it makes you feel good about yourself to work hard.	Reflection of feeling, emphasis on positive regard, Level-3 empathy.
Bob:	Yeah. For example, . . .	

(Bob continues to talk about his accomplishments. In this way Susan learns some of the positives Bob has in his past and not just his problems. She has used the basic listening sequence to help Bob feel better about himself. Susan also learns that Bob has several important assets to help him resolve his own problems— among them, determination and willingness to work hard.)

Stage 3. Determining outcomes

Susan:	Bob, given all the things you've talked about, what would an ideal solution for you be? How would you like things to be?	Open question. The addition of a new possibility for the client represents additive empathy, a Level-4 response, as it enables Bob to think of something new.
Bob:	Gee, I guess I'd like things to be smoother, easier, and less full of conflict. I come home so tired and angry.	
Susan:	I hear that. It's taking a lot out of you. Tell me more specifically how things might be better.	Paraphrase, open question oriented toward concreteness.
Bob:	I'd just like less hassle. I know what I'm doing, but somehow that isn't helping. I'd just like to be able to resolve these conflicts without always having to give in.	
Susan:	Give in?	Encourage.

(In the goal-setting process, you will often find yourself changing the problem definition. Here Susan learns another dimension of Bob's conflict with others. Subsequent use of the basic listening sequence brings out this pattern with several customers and employees.)

Susan: So, Bob, I hear two things in terms of goals. One that you'd like less hassle, but another, equally important, is that you like not to have to give in. Have I heard you correctly?

Summary. Most likely this is a Level-4 summary, as Susan has helped Bob clarify his problem even though no resolution is yet in sight. Note the care and time Susan has given to the problem-definition and goal-setting stages.

Bob: You're right on, but what am I going to do about it?

Stage 4. Exploring alternatives and confronting client incongruity

Susan: So, Bob, on the one hand I've heard you have a long-term pattern of conflict not only with supervisors and bosses, but also with customers who give you a bad time. Clearly, you are a good worker and like to do a good job. On the other hand, I heard just as loud and clear you desire to have less hassle and not to have to give in to others all the time. Given all this, what occurs to you that you can do about it?

Major summary of the entire interview to this point. Susan, in this Level-4 response, has distilled and clarified what the client has said. While her words are interchangeable with those of Bob and *appear* to represent Level-3 empathy, the clarity of the interview was brought about largely by her own skills in listening. She remains nonjudgmental and appears to be very congruent with the client in terms of both words and body language.

Bob: Well, the first thing that occurs to me is that if I am a good worker—and I'm not dumb—perhaps I can take these conflicts as another chance to do well.

Many times clients can use their already existing positive assets to solve their own problems.

Susan: Uh-hummm . . .

Encourage. Susan's body language and vocal tone are supportive as well.

Bob: I could see this as a problem to be solved. I think I've been fighting it too much. I think I've let the boss and the customers control me too much. I think what I'd like to do the next time a customer comes in and complains is not say a word and simply fill out the refund certificate. Why should I take on the world?

Susan:	So one thing you can do is keep quiet. Sounds as if you are thinking you could maintain control in your own way by doing so, and you would not be giving in.	Paraphrase. Level-4 empathy, as Susan is using Bob's key words and feelings from earlier in the interview to reinforce his present thinking.
Bob:	Yeah, that's what I'll do, keep quiet.	
Susan:	Sounds like a good beginning, but I'm sure you can think of other things as well. What are some other things you could do, especially at those times when you simply can't be quiet? Can you brainstorm more ideas?	Open question.

(Clients are often too willing to seize the first idea that comes up. It may not be the best thing for them. Here it is helpful to use a variety of questions and listening skills to draw out the client further. With Bob, some ideas came easily but others more slowly. Eventually, he was able to generate two other useful suggestions: (1) to talk frankly with his boss about the continuing problem and seek his advice; and (2) to plan an exercise program after work to help blow off steam and energy. In addition, Bob began to realize that his problem with his boss was but one example of a continuing problem. He and Susan discussed the possibility of talking more or visiting a professional therapist. Bob decided he'd like to talk with Susan a bit more. A contract was made: if the situation did not improve within 2 weeks, Bob would seek professional help.)

Stage 5.   Generalization and transfer of learning

Susan:	So we've talked a great deal about the issue and you've decided that the most useful idea of all is to talk with your boss. But the big question is "Will you do it?"	Paraphrase, open question.
Bob:	Sure, I'll do it. The first time the boss seems relaxed.	
Susan:	As you've described him, Bob, that may be a long wait. Could you set up a specific plan so we can talk about it the next time we meet?	Paraphrase, open question. To generalize from the interview, it is important to encourage specific and concrete action in your client.
Bob:	I suppose you're right. Okay, occasionally he and I drink coffee in the late afternoon at Rooster's. I'll bring it up with him tomorrow.	
Susan:	What, specifically, are you going to say?	Open question, again eliciting concreteness.

Bob: I think it would be smart to tell him that I like working there, but am concerned about how to handle difficult customers. I think I'll ask his advice and how he does it. In some ways, it worries me; I don't want to give in to the boss.

Bob is able to plan something that might work. With other clients, you may find it helpful to plan role-plays, give advice, and lead the generalization plan more. You will also note that Bob is still concerned about "giving in."

Susan: Would you like to talk about giving in more the next time we meet? Maybe through your talk with him we can figure out how to deal with that. Sounds like a good contract, Bob: you'll talk with your boss and we'll meet later this week or next week.

Open question, structuring.

It would be possible to have specified the follow-up contract even more precisely, but this would most likely entail the use of influencing skills, prescribing homework, and so forth. Susan presented an especially important response during Stage 5 when she asked what Bob was going to do specifically. Again, you'll find that concreteness is very important in assisting clients to make and act on decisions.

▲ Summary

The five-stage structure of the interview has been demonstrated in the preceding example, showing that it is indeed possible to integrate all the skills and concepts of this book presented thus far into a meaningful, well-formed session. You may find it difficult to work through the systematic five-stage interview and not use advice and influencing skills, yet it can be done. It is a useful format to use with individuals who are verbal and anxious to solve their own problems. You will also find this decisional structure useful with resistant clients who want to make their own decisions. By acting as a mirror and asking questions, we can encourage many of our clients to find their own directions.

Theoretically and philosophically, this interview using only listening skills is close to that of Carl Rogers's person-centered therapy (Rogers, 1957). Rogers developed guidelines for the "necessary and sufficient conditions of therapeutic personality change," and the empathic constructs described in this chapter are derived from his thinking. Rogers traditionally has been opposed to the use of questions but more recently appears to have modified his position. Implicit in your ability to conduct an interview without information, advice, and influencing skills is a respect for the person's ability to find her or his own unique direction. In conducting an interview using only attending, observation, and the basic listening sequence, you are approaching a very person-centered approach to counseling and interviewing.

Box 7-1. Key Points

Basic listening sequence	These are the skills of questioning, encouraging paraphrasing, reflection of feeling, and summarizing, which make up the BLS. The basic listening sequence is useful in many different interview settings and in defining problems and outcomes in the interview.
Positive asset search	Clients grow from their strengths. Time should be given in every interview to identify positive assets and capabilities that may be used to solve problems and generate future development.
Empathy	Empathy means experiencing the client's world as if *you* were the client. Requires attending skills and using the *important* words of the client, but distilling and shortening the main ideas.
Additive empathy	The interviewer may *add* meaning and feelings beyond those originally expressed by the client. If done ineffectively, it may *subtract* from the client's experience. Empathy is best assessed by the client's reaction to a statement, not by a simple rating of the interviewer's comments.
Positive regard	This means selecting positive aspects of client experience and selectively attending to positive aspects of client statements.
Respect and warmth	Respect and warmth are attitudinal dimensions usually shown through nonverbal means—smiling, touching, and a respectful tone of voice—even when differences in values are apparent between interviewer and client.
Concreteness	Being specific rather than vague in interviewing statements constitutes concreteness.
Immediacy	An interviewer statement may be in the present, past, or future tense. Present-tense statements tend to be the most powerful. Immediacy is also viewed as the immediate "I – you" talk between interviewer and client.
Nonjudgmental attitude	Suspend your own opinions and attitudes and assume a value neutrality with regard to your clients.
Authenticity and congruence	These are the opposite of incongruity and discrepancies. The interviewer is congruent with the client and authentically himself or herself in their relationship.
Five stages of the interview	*Stage 1:* Rapport and structuring ("Hello.") *Stage 2:* Gathering information and defining the problem ("What's the problem?") *Stage 3:* Determining outcomes ("What do you want to happen?") *Stage 4:* Exploring alternatives and client incongruities ("What are we going to do about it?") *Stage 5:* Generalization and transfer of learning ("Will you do it?")

▲ Practice Exercises and Self-Assessment

Mastery of the skills of this chapter is a complex process that you will want to work on over an extended period of time. Some basic exercises for the individual and systematic group practice in each skill area follow.

Basic Listening Sequence

Exercise 1. Illustrating how the BLS functions in different settings

Imagine that you are role-playing a counseling interview and are playing the counselor. Write counseling leads as they might be used to help a client solve the problem "I don't have a job for the summer." In this case you will have to imagine that the client has responded. Write responses that represent the BLS.

Open question: _____

_____

Closed question: _____

_____

Encourager: _____

Paraphrase: _____

_____

Reflection of feeling: _____

_____

Summary: _____

_____

_____

_____

Now imagine you are a manager talking with an employee who has been late with a critical assignment. Your task is to use the BLS to find out what the employee's explanation is before you take action.

Open question: _____

_____

Closed question: _____

_____

Encourager: _____

Paraphrase: _____

_____

Reflection of feeling: _____

_____

Summary: _____

_____

_____

Finally, imagine yourself as a physician talking with a patient who has come in with a severe headache. Your first task in diagnosis is to find out the patient's view of the illness. Again, write BLS interviewing leads that might be helpful in obtaining that diagnosis.

Open question: _____

_____

Closed question: _____

_____

Encourager: _____

Paraphrase: _____

_____

Reflection of feeling: _____

_____

Summary: _____

_____

_____

Exercise 2: Systematic group practice in the BLS

Step 1. Divide into groups.

Step 2. Select a group leader.

Step 3. Assign roles for the first practice session.

▲ Role-played client
▲ Interviewer
▲ Observer 1
▲ Observer 2

Step 4. Planning.   The task the interviewer should state is to draw out the problem using the BLS and to summarize the problem at the end. You should note that this is the second stage of the interview structure (defining the problem and gathering data).

The suggested topics for practicing the BLS are as follows:

A problem in vocational choice, past or present

Difficulty in making a major decision, such as purchasing a new car, moving, or changing jobs

Role-playing a manager determining why an employee failed to complete an assignment correctly

Role-playing a social worker during a home visit

Consulting with a teacher about a child with discipline difficulties

Step 5. Conduct a 5-minute practice session using the BLS

Step 6. Review the practice session and provide feedback for 10 minutes.

Step 7. Rotate roles.

Basic Listening Sequence Feedback Sheet [1]

_____ (Date)

_____   _____
(Name of Interviewer)   (Name of Person Completing Form)

Instructions: Observers 1 and 2 will attempt to record the statements of the interviewer as accurately as possible. They will then record the skill category of the interviewer's statements.

Statement of interviewer		Skills					
		Open question	Closed question	Encourager	Paraphrase	Reflection of feeling	Summary
1.							
2.							
3.							
4.							
5.							
6.							
7.							
8.							
9.							
10.							

Did the interviewer (1) draw out a general picture of the problem? (2) get the main facts? (3) elicit key client feelings? and (4) provide a more coherent summary of the client's concern or positive asset?

[1]The structure of this form was suggested by Robert Marx.

Positive Asset Search

Exercise 1. The positive asset search as manifested in two types of interview

You are role-playing a counseling interview. Write counseling leads, using the BLS to draw out the client's positive assets and strengths.

In a vocational interview, the client says, "Yes, I am really confused about my future. One side of me wants to continue a major in psychology, while the other—thinking about the future—wants to change to business." Use the BLS to draw out this client's positive assets. In some cases, you will have to imagine client responses to your first question.

Open question: _____

_____

Closed question: _____

_____

Encourager: _____

Paraphrase: _____

_____

Reflection of feeling: _____

_____

Summary: _____

_____

_____

You are counseling a couple considering divorce. The husband says, "Somehow the magic seems to be lost. I still care for Jo, but we argue and argue—even over small things." Use the positive asset search to bring out strengths and resources in the couple on which they may draw to find a positive resolution to their problems. In marriage counseling in particular, many counselors err by failing to note the strengths and positives that originally brought the couple together.

Open question: _____

_____

Closed question: _____

_____

Encourager: _____

Paraphrase: _____

_____

Reflection of feeling: _____

_____

Summary: _____

_____

_____

Exercise 2. The positive asset search in daily life

Use the BLS to draw out a positive asset of a friend or family member. This can be particularly helpful to them when they face a troubling issue or concern. Reminding people that they have strengths helps them solve problems on their own. Report your results here.

_____

_____

_____

_____

_____

_____

_____

_____

_____

_____

_____

_____

_____

_____

Exercise 3. Systematic group practice in the positive asset search

Step 1. Divide into groups.

Step 2. Select a group leader.

Step 3. Assign roles for first practice session.

▲ Role-played client
▲ Interviewer
▲ Observer 1
▲ Observer 2

Step 4. Planning.   State the goals for the practice session. The task of the interviewer is to draw out the positive assets or strengths of the clients by using the BLS and to summarize them accurately at the end of the practice session. Special attention should be given to the feelings and emotions of the client about the positive assets.

The client can plan to talk about a positive life experience or success. This may be a skill, a special interest, or a successful handling of a difficult personal issue.

Observers should note the skills of the interviewer and the reactions of the clients, both verbal and nonverbal.

Step 5. Conduct a 5-minute practice session using the BLS.

Step 6. Review the practice session and provide feedback for 10 minutes.

Step 7. Rotate roles.

Positive Asset Feedback Sheet

_____ (Date)

_____   _____
(Name of Interviewer)   (Name of Person Completing Form)

Instructions: Observer 1 will record the statements of the interviewer as accurately as possible so that an ongoing log of the session is available to facilitate discussion. Observer 2 will rate key nonverbal and verbal reactions of the clients.

Statements of the interviewer:

1. _____
2. _____
3. _____
4. _____
5. _____
6. _____
7. _____
8. _____
9. _____
10. _____
11. _____
12. _____
13. _____
14. _____
15. _____
16. _____
17. _____
18. _____
19. _____

(continued)

Positive Asset Feedback Sheet (continued)

20. _____

21. _____

22. _____

Observation of client's nonverbal and verbal reactions:

1. _____

2. _____

3. _____

4. _____

5. _____

6. _____

7. _____

8. _____

9. _____

10. _____

11. _____

12. _____

13. _____

14. _____

15. _____

16. _____

17. _____

18. _____

19. _____

20. _____

21. _____

22. _____

Empathy

Exercise 1. Writing helping statements representing the five levels of empathy

"I'm really anxious. I got caught by the Internal Revenue Service for not declaring all of my income. I object to paying money for causes I don't believe in, like the money spent on war. Before, I always tried to be straight, but I think I may have overdone it this time!"

Write statements below representing the five levels of empathic response to the client concern above. These statements can employ any skill, but paraphrasing and reflection of feeling are perhaps the clearest and easiest statements to write.

Level 1 (subtractive): _____

_____

Level 2 (slightly subtractive): _____

_____

Level 3 (interchangeable response): _____

_____

Level 4 (slightly additive): _____

_____

Level 5 (additive): _____

_____

"My boy has gone to college, and I miss him terribly. We got along just fine and did so many things together. But now he doesn't write very often. I'm glad he is doing well . . . but what about me?"

Again, write statements representing the five levels of empathic responding.

Level 1 (subtractive): _____

_____

Level 2 (slightly subtractive): _____

_____

Level 3 (interchangeable response): _____

_____

Level 4 (slightly additive): _____

_____

Level 5 (additive): _____

_____

Exercise 2. Defining empathic dimensions

Definitions of the several empathic dimensions are presented earlier in this chapter under "Empathy: Qualitative Aspects of Skill Usage." Return to those pages and in the space below write a definition, in your own words, of each concept and provide at least one example from your observations of interviews.

Positive regard: _____

_____

_____

_____

Respect and warmth: _____

_____

_____

_____

_____

Concreteness: _____

_____

_____

_____

_____

Immediacy: _____

_____

_____

_____

_____

Nonjudgmental attitude: _____

_____

_____

_____

Authenticity and congruence: _____

_____

_____

_____

_____

Exercise 3. Rating interview behavior on empathic dimensions

Any systematic group practice exercise from this chapter or the whole book may be used. Alternatively, you may wish to rate an audiotape, videotape, transcript, or live interview on empathic responding. Provide specific and behavioral evidence for your conclusions, using the Empathy Feedback Sheet.

Empathy Feedback Sheet

_____ (Date)

_____   _____
(Name of Interviewer)   (Name of Person Completing Form)

Instructions: Observers are to (1) view an interview or segment of an interview, rating the empathic responding on a 5-point scale, and (2) provide specific behavioral evidence for their decisions.

	Level 1 (subtractive)	Level 2	Level 3 (interchangeable)	Level 4	Level 5 (additive)
1. Overall empathy rating					
2. Positive regard					
3. Respect and warmth					
4. Concreteness					
5. Immediacy					
6. Nonjudgmental attitude					
7. Authenticity and congruence					
8. Other observations					

(continued)

Empathy Feedback Sheet (continued)

Provide specific behavioral evidence in the space provided to justify your rating of empathic behaviors on the chart.

1. _____
_____

2. _____
_____

3. _____
_____

4. _____
_____

5. _____
_____

6. _____
_____

7. _____
_____

8. _____
_____

Structuring the Interview Using Only Attending Skills

Using the following model, role play a vocational interview in a practice session. The client should role play a real (current or past) vocational indecision issue or imagine a graduating high school senior who can't decide whether to work or go to college or an individual analyzing his or her career. Use the following sequence in your practice session:

1. Develop rapport in your own style with the client. Follow this with *structuring* the session by saying something like, "What we are going to do in this session is first discuss your issues of vocational choice, then we'll discuss some outcomes you'd like to see happen, followed by exploration in more detail of the alternatives you face. Finally, we'll talk about how anything you learn today can be used after you leave the interview. Is that okay?"

2. Gather information, define the problem, and identify assets. Use the basic listening sequence to define the problem from the client's point of view. Be sure to identify at least one client asset that may be helpful in solving the problem.

3. Determine outcomes. Again, use the basic listening sequence and determine where the client would like to go. Keep in mind that with some clients this stage should precede Stage 2.

4. Explore alternatives. Summarize the real and the ideal world (from 2 and 3 above) for the client. Brainstorm with the client alternatives that might be helpful to resolve the problem. With the client, establish priorities for the alternatives. Discuss and *examine discrepancies* as appropriate to the situation.

5. Generalization. After establishing priorities, ask the client what specific activities might be engaged in to follow through on the alternatives generated. Note the list of possibilities to assist generalization in the chapter.

Practicing the structure of the interview requires at least a half-hour per person, and an hour is preferable for developing the interview and later debriefing. As such, specific plans for meeting in pairs for a significant period of time are required. Alternatively, groups of four may meet for half a day to conduct practice sessions. In a class situation the full hour should be given to the person practicing interview structuring.

Structuring the Interview Feedback Sheet

_____ (Date)

_____   _____
(Name of Interviewer)   (Name of Person Completing Form)

Instructions: The interviewer will conduct a brief vocational counseling interview of 15 to 20 minutes using only attending skills. The observer will summarize the interview below in terms of each stage completed.

1. _Stage 1: Rapport and structuring._ Nature of rapport? Enough established before interview continued to next stage? Did interviewer provide structuring?

2. _Stage 2: Gathering information, defining the problem, and identifying assets._ Problem defined using only listening skills? Was at least one positive supportive asset of the client examined?

3. _Stage 3: Determining outcomes._ Specific outcome or goal outlined for the client through use of listening skills?

4. _Stage 4: Exploring alternatives and confronting incongruity._ Was interviewer able to assist client in generating new ideas through use of listening skills _only_?

(continued)

Structuring the Interview Feedback Sheet (continued)

5. *Stage 5: Generalization.* Specific plans for taking ideas home made and contracted for? Systematic plan of action for follow-up?

6. General comments on interview and skill usage:

Self-Assessment and Follow-Up

Several important concepts with four sets of practice exercises have been presented in this chapter. The concepts and levels of mastery are summarized below and listed on the form that follows. Check those areas for which you have demonstrated mastery. Provide evidence in the form of tapes, transcripts, or observations to prove that you have mastered the concepts. Space is provided for brief summaries of evidence.

The concepts and skills to be evaluated are as follows:

1. *Basic listening sequence:* Ability to use BLS in a variety of interviews with a variety of problems. You can help the client define the problem and define ideal outcomes from his or her frame of reference.
2. *Positive assets search:* Ability to use the BLS to draw out client assets and strengths.
3. *Empathy:* Ability to rate and classify empathy in a variety of interviews and demonstrate the several concepts with clients.
4. *Structuring the interview:* Ability to work systematically through the interview's five suggested stages using only listening skills. The ultimate measure of active mastery is whether or not your client does something different to achieve his or her goals and desired outcomes.

As a reminder, here are definitions of the mastery levels:

1. *Identification:* Ability to define the concept and identify it through observation
2. *Basic mastery:* Ability to use the skill in a role-played interview
3. *Active mastery:* Ability to use attending skills intentionally to facilitate or discourage client talk
4. *Teaching mastery:* Ability to teach others

Concept	Mastery Level				Brief Evidence of Mastery
	Identification	Basic	Active	Teaching	
Basic listening sequence					
Positive assets search					
Empathy					
Structuring the interview					

The concepts of this chapter are critical to your ability to integrate skills in the actual interview. Examine your mastery level summary and then define below specific goals for improving your interviewing efficiency over the next 3 months.

_____

_____

_____

_____

_____

_____

_____

▲ References

Blanchard, K., & Johnson, S. (1981). *The one-minute manager.* San Diego, Calif.: Blanchard-Johnson.

Carkhuff, R. (1969). *Helping and human relations* (Vols. 1 & 2). New York: Holt, Rinehart & Winston.

Egan, G. (1986). *The skilled helper* (3rd ed.). Monterey, Calif.: Brooks/Cole.

Ivey, A., & Authier, J. (1978). *Microcounseling* (2nd ed.). Springfield, Ill.: Charles C Thomas.

Rogers, C. (1957). The necessary and sufficient conditions of therapeutic personality change. *Journal of Consulting Psychology, 21,* 95–103.

Rogers, C. (1961). *On becoming a person.* Boston: Houghton Mifflin.

Advanced Skills and Concepts

If you are able to conduct a full, well-formed five-stage interview solely using listening skills, you are prepared to add advanced skills and concepts to your repertoire. However, listening forms the foundation of effective helping, and the early skills are critical for interviewing success.

This section begins in Chapter 8 with an examination of the skill of confrontation, which many consider the most important agent of change in the interview. Confrontation builds on your present ability to observe discrepancies in the client, but adds an attempt to facilitate your client's resolving those discrepancies with new thoughts and behaviors. This resolution of discrepancies results in client developmental change, which has been described as the aim of effective interviewing, counseling, and psychotherapy. Following an effective confrontation, you will find it possible to assess your client's developmental change and progress. This important chapter also emphasizes that clients present varying developmental levels and issues in the interview. It is your task to assess their overall developmental level and offer interventions, appropriate to those levels, that will lead to change.

Chapter 9, on focusing, extends the concept of confrontation and illustrates how to ensure that you have made a comprehensive examination of your client's issues. Too many counselors and interviewers focus too narrowly on their clients and miss issues important to their development.

Reflection of meaning is presented in Chapter 10. There you will examine the relationship between and among behaviors, thoughts, feelings, and their underlying meaning structure. You will find this skill complex and rich; it should provide you with a deeper understanding of each client's issues and history.

The final chapter of this section discusses seven skills and strategies of interpersonal influence. Skills such as directives, logical consequences, feedback, and interpretation are explored with specific suggestions for facilitating client developmental change.

The sum and substance of this section focuses on taking a more active stance with clients, helping them to move on via the addition of your own knowledge and input. The listening and observing skills of the first section provide the foundation for these more action-oriented skills and strategies.

At a mastery level of competence in the skills of this section, you may aim to do the following:

1. Master the art of confrontation and the ability to assess your client's developmental level of response to that confrontation

2. Adjust your counseling style and skills to meet the developmental needs of each unique client
3. Demonstrate the ability to change focus in the interview and to facilitate client exploration of the full complexities of a problem
4. Use the skill of reflection of meaning to help clients move to deeper levels of self-exploration and self-understanding
5. Use an array of influencing skills and strategies to assist client developmental progress, particularly when the more reflective listening skills fail to produce change and understanding

If you are a beginning counseling and interviewing student, do not expect to achieve active mastery of all the concepts in this section in your first course. Confrontation, for example, is a complex skill—one on which even the most experienced counselor or therapist can always improve. Furthermore, assessing developmental-level responses to your confrontation is a concept new to the helping field and is likely to be challenging even for experienced interviewers.

Thus, it is suggested that you first attempt the two basic levels of mastery: identification and basic mastery. Gradually, with this solid base, you can move to the predictability and skill in the interview required for active mastery. The effective counselor is always in process—always changing and growing in response to new challenges.

8 Confrontation and Development

How can confrontation and developmental concepts help you and your clients?

Major function

Development is the aim of interviewing, counseling, and therapy. Your task is to facilitate individuals moving beyond their problems to realize their full potential as human beings. While all counseling skills are concerned with development, it is the confrontation of discrepancies that acts as the lever for the activation of human potential.

Secondary functions

Knowledge and skill in these concepts result in the following:

▲ An increased ability to point out incongruity, discrepancies, or mixed messages in behavior, thought, feelings, or meanings and the ability to increase client talk with a view toward explanation and/or resolution of discrepancies
▲ The ability to assess clients' developmental levels and to choose appropriate microskills and confrontations to meet the specific needs of the unique client before you
▲ The ability to use confrontation in combination with other skills to promote and facilitate human development

---

▲ Introduction

Intentionality is not just a goal for interviewers: it is also a goal for clients. A client comes to an interview "stuck"—having either no alternatives for solving a problem or a limited range of possibilities. The task of the interviewer is to eliminate stuckness and substitute intentionality. *Stuckness* is an inelegant but highly descriptive term coined by Fritz Perls in 1969 to describe the opposite of intentionality. Other words that represent the same condition include *immobility, blocks, repetition compulsion, inability to achieve goals, lack of understanding, limited behavioral repertoire, limited life script, impasse,* and *lack of motivation.* Stuckness may also be defined as an inability to reconcile discrepancies and incongruity. In short, clients often come to the interview because they are stuck for a variety of reasons and seek intentionality.

The attending, observing, and listening skills of Sections I and II of this book, used effectively in a well-formed interview, help many clients to resolve their developmental impasses. However, a client has to be at a fairly high developmental level, with verbal skills of self-analysis, to be able to benefit fully from a helping approach using primarily listening skills.

Development as manifested in interviewing and counseling may be described as the resolution of incongruity, the working through of an impasse or developmental delay, and the process of transformation and change by which clients learn to manage their own lives.

Confrontation may be briefly defined as noting discrepancies in the client and feeding them back via the attending skills (or magnifying and directing them via the influencing skills). A specific sequence for noting and working with stuckness, discrepancies, and incongruity will be presented here.

▲ Instructional Reading

Confrontation

Confrontation is the most powerful of the microskills, but it rests solidly on effective listening and observing. It is actually a complex of skills that often results in a client's examination of core issues. When client discrepancies, mixed messages, and conflicts are confronted skillfully and nonjudgmentally, clients are encouraged to talk in more detail and to resolve their problems and issues.

Confrontation involves two major steps. The first, identifying mixed messages, conflict, and incongruity, has been discussed under client observation, but will be repeated here for emphasis. The second step is pointing out these issues clearly to clients and helping them work through the conflict to resolution. Therefore, the skills of questioning, client observation, reflective listening, and feedback loom large in effective confrontation.

Confrontational effectiveness can be measured by placing the client's response (denial, acceptance, and so on) along the continuum of the Confrontation Impact Scale. If your confrontation is not accepted by your client, you will want to move to other skills such as focusing, reflection of meaning, and the influencing skills and strategies discussed in later chapters. All of these advanced skills, however, also have the underlying goal of facilitating client development through the resolution of incongruities. For now, let's examine the two steps of confrontation.

Step 1: Identifying incongruities and mixed messages

When a person gives a clear, unambiguous message, he or she may be said to be congruent, integrated, and whole. You know where that person "is at." By contrast, when a person conveys a double message or says one thing verbally and something else nonverbally, the person may be said to be incongruent, contradictory, and conveying mixed messages (Ivey & Litterer, 1979, p. 99).

The question is how to identify incongruity. This is best done through client observation, questioning, and reflective listening. For example:

Client: I think I should get a raise.

Counselor: Could you tell me the reasons you think you deserve more money?

Client: I've been here a long time, and lots of people make more than I do. It doesn't seem fair, especially with the rising cost of living.

Counselor: Earlier, you said you like to take it easy when you are on the job whenever you can. You try to come in late when you feel you can get away with it. How does that square with your desire for a raise?

Client: Well, from that point of view, perhaps I'll have to work a little harder if I am going to get what I deserve, or think I deserve.

Needless to say, it isn't always that easy. This interviewer asked a client a question to elaborate on wishes and followed with a paraphrase of a previous discussion that contradicted the client's wishes. The final question ("How does that square with your desire for a raise?") prompts the confrontation.

A confrontation is actually a process or series of stages leading toward the identification and discussion of discrepancies. When the discrepancy is specifically identified by pointing out the incongruity or mixed message, the client often sees the issue and resolves the matter there and then. More likely, however, more extensive discussion involving reflective listening and influencing skills may be required to fully resolve the incongruity.

Several types of incongruity and mixed messages can be identified. Important among them are inconsistencies. The list below has been described in Chapter 3 in the discussion of observation skills. This time, however, think about each type of incongruity as representing a developmental impasse or some form of client stuckness. Development is change and movement, whereas immobility, stuckness, and polarization represent the lack of development. Your task as an interviewer is to free the client for developmental movement and change.

As you read each of the following examples, give specific attention to the mixed emotions and feelings underlying each of the issues. Incongruity can appear in the following ways:

Between two statements.   An example might be a client who says at one point that he or she cares very much for his or her spouse, but later in the interview directly contradicts that statement. This client may be considered "developmentally arrested" and has made neither a commitment to the relationship nor a commitment to leave. The confrontation and working through of these mixed feelings is critical for further development in the marriage. Working through may result in the active recognition of the mixed feelings and *deciding* to live with them as they are—or the *decision* to act in one way or the other and live effectively with that decision. In either form, the impasse is removed and the client has been freed for further development.

Between what one says and what one does.   A client may express sincere interest in taking vocational tests to clarify future plans but fail to show up for the tests time and time again. You will often have clients whose development in the interview and in relationship to you is marred by this kind of mixed message. At this point, you might wish to confront the discrepancies in this client so that the developmental process that is counseling could continue.

Between statements and nonverbal behavior.   A client may say he or she enjoys coming to counseling or a job interview, but the person's face may be tight and tense and the hands shaking. When a client expresses incongruity so clearly in the interview, a gentle and supportive confrontation may facilitate decision and action.

Between two nonverbal behaviors.   Teeth may be clenched while the client smiles. Depending on the developmental level of the client and the nature of the relationship, you may decide either to ignore this behavior or to use active confrontation.

Between statements and the context.   A client may say he or she is going to resolve a family problem when it is clear that the client has neither the power nor the money to bring about the resolution. An individual may blame him- or herself for not finding a job when the nation has a high rate of unemployment. Confrontations of this type of incongruity help clients become aware of real world external factors controlling them. In a sense, the confrontation becomes an interpretation, a reframing of the context. Client development that has been stuck in irrelevant self-blame can be facilitated by an awareness of the broader context.

Between two or more people.   This incongruity may exist between a husband and wife or between a counselor and client, for example. "He says this . . . and you say this . . . ": the direct confrontation of differences is critical to working through the many developmental snags that can arise in marriage or any other type of interpersonal relationship. Negotiation between and among people is based on effective confrontation.

Thus, the first step in effective confrontation is noting distinctions and differences. At times, you will find it helpful to magnify those differences so that incongruities that seem minor to the participants are seen more clearly. Once they are clearly identified, it is your task to facilitate the client's working through the developmental delay, arrest, or stuckness indicated by the incongruities.

Step 2: Working toward the resolution of incongruity and mixed messages

As noted earlier, simply labeling the incongruity through a nonjudgmental confrontation may be enough to resolve a situation. More likely, however, incongruity will remain a problem to be resolved. Keep in mind that it is important to focus on the elements of incongruity, rather than on the person, as the problem. Confrontation is too often thought of as blaming a person for his or her faults; rather, the issue is facing the incongruity squarely through such measures as the following:

1. Identify the incongruity clearly. Using reflective listening skills, summarize it for the client. Often the simple question "How do you put these two together?" will lead a client to self-confrontation and resolution.

2. Through the use of questioning and other listening skills, draw out the specifics of the conflict or mixed messages. *One at a time,* give attention to each part of the mixed message, contradiction, or conflict. If two people are involved, attempt to have the client examine both points of view. It is important at this stage to be nonjudgmental and nonevaluative—aim for facts. Allow your nonjudgmental stance to be reflected in your tone of voice and body language.

3. Periodically summarize the several dimensions of the incongruity. The model confrontation statement, "On the one hand . . . , but on the other hand . . . " appears to be particularly useful in summarizing incongruity. Variations include "You say . . . but you do . . . ," "I see . . . at one time, and at another time I see . . . ," and "Your words say . . . , but your actions say. . . . " Follow this with a check-out (for example, "How does that sound to you?"). When you point out incongruities as in these examples, the client is being "pinned to the wall" with specific facts. As a result, the importance of being nonjudgmental and including the check-out as a final part of the confrontation cannot be overstressed.

4. If necessary, provide feedback giving your opinions and observations about the discrepancies. You may wish to use influencing skills such as directives, logical consequences, and others (see Chapter 11) to facilitate resolution.

If the incongruity is not resolved by this process, it may be necessary to say, "You see it that way, I see it this way . . . we'll have to go at it again." Don't give up on positions you believe are correct, but allow your point of view to be modified by input from the client. Many clients are unaware of their mixed messages and discrepancies; pointing them out gently but firmly can be extremely beneficial to them. Finally, a wide variety of attending and influencing skills may be used to follow up and elaborate on confrontations.

The Confrontation Impact Scale

When you confront clients or provide them with a powerful intervention, you will find they may have a variety of responses. Ideally, they will respond actively to your confrontation, generate new ideas, and move forward. On the other hand, they may ignore or deny the fact that you have confronted them. Most often, however, the confrontation will be acknowledged and absorbed as part of a larger process of change.

It is possible to assess the direct impact on your confrontation on your client by using the Confrontation Impact Scale (CIS). For example, the effectiveness of a confrontation of mixed messages about a divorce may be measured on this 5-point scale:

1. *Denial.* The individual may deny that an incongruity or mixed message exists or fail to hear that it is there. ("I'm not angry about the divorce. It happens. I don't feel anything in particular.")

2. *Partial examination.* The individual may work on a part of the discrepancy but fail to consider the other dimensions of the mixed message. ("I care, I really care. How can I make it alone?" Note that the client fails to deal with issues of anger and frustration.)

3. *Full examination, but no change.* The client may engage the confrontation fairly completely, but make no resolution. Much of counseling operates at this level or at Level 2. Until the client can examine incongruity, stuckness, and mixed messages accurately, developmental change will be most difficult. ("I guess I do have mixed feelings about it. I certainly do care about the marriage. We've spent years together. But I sure am angry about what has happened.")

4. *Decision to live with incongruity.* It is possible for a confrontation to be considered successful if the person decides to accept the discrepancy as it is. Not all incongruity can be resolved. This acceptance of things as they are is a higher level of client thinking. ("Yes, there's not a lot I can do about it. I've just got to accept it as it is. In some ways, I'm glad we are splitting up, but in others I'll always be sad about the loss.")

5. *Development of new, larger and more inclusive constructs, patterns, or behaviors.* A confrontation is most successful when the client recognizes the discrepancy, works on it, and generates new thought patterns or behaviors to cope with and perhaps resolve the incongruity. ("I like the plan we've worked out. You've helped me see that mixed feelings and thoughts are part of every relationship. I've been expecting too much. I'm having dinner tonight with my spouse and we are going to have to develop a new way of thinking about the meaning of the relationship.")

You will find that virtually every helping lead you use, whether a question, reflection of feeling, or directive (whether it contains a planned confrontation or not), leads to client reactions that can be placed along this 5-point scale. You will find clients denying your question or encourage at times, while at other times they will recognize it. When things are going well, you will find clients transforming their concepts into new ideas, thoughts, and plans for action in their daily lives: it is these Level-5 responses that you seek for clients. Although developmental change is more rare and difficult than we would like, confrontation can speed and facilitate such progression.

During the process of counseling, you will find the Confrontation Impact Scale a helpful informal measuring tool to keep in mind, allowing you to track your client's reactions to you and your interventions. When you are off track, you will find clients responding at Level 2. When your clients seek to avoid your confrontation, you will likewise find them subtly avoiding the full issues. Your task is to recognize what is happening and to seek to keep the client at the minimum level of responding that allows them to acknowledge conflict and incongruity. Over time, clients will move toward Levels 4 and 5, but you will often find this movement to be slow.

Not only can you use this scale for direct client observation, but also for classifying larger portions of your interview. For example, you may expect clients to function at Level 1 or 2 early in the interview. If things are going well, you should expect a Level-3 response through most of the rest of the interview. If some new action is decided upon by the end of the interview, or some new awareness or insight is discovered, it represents the important developmental shift to Levels 4 and 5, which you are seeking.

You will find that the "Example Interview" in Chapter 12 provides examples of scoring the CIS. The client there exemplifies what typically happens: specifically, starting at Level 2 at the beginning of the problem discussion, followed by extensive Level-3 examination, and finally at the end approaching a Level-5 new response.

The Assessment of Developmental Level[1]

The general concept of intentionality is helpful as we think about the clients we serve in the interview. As clients progress developmentally, their level of intentional living rises. However, intentionality is complex and needs more amplification, since each client has different needs. Drawing on Piaget's thinking, Ivey (1986) suggests four basic levels of client development, ranging from low to high. It is important to match your interviewing style and your specific confrontations with each client's overall developmental level.

It is critical to understand, however, that each of us and each of your clients is a mixture of many developmental levels. You will find the most sophisticated and intellectual client denying certain problems at times and needing careful environmental structuring. Younger people or clients who may seem naive and inexperienced may suddenly bloom with more understanding than you thought possible. *It is neither possible nor wise to label any one client as being totally at one of the four developmental levels.* Rather, development implies movement and change. If you are a culturally sensitive and effective interviewer, counselor, or therapist, you will observe the individual in front of you in virtually constant change and movement.

The four developmental levels as they relate to the goal of intentionality are as follows:

Level D-1: Preoperational

Intentionality is lacking. The client is stuck with no alternatives or, at best, a limited range of possibilities. The client lacks skills and may need to be told what to do. The client may have a major discrepancy of which he or she is unaware.

---

[1]The material presented in this section is an adaptation of a more complex model presented in *Developmental Therapy: Theory into Practice* (Ivey, 1986). While the general framework here is similar to that of developmental therapy, some language and concepts have been changed for instructional purposes.

You will find that adolescent and adult clients present problems that can be conceptualized in Piaget's terms, which were originally designed for children. Developmental therapy's position is that all of us repeat and recycle developmental problems and opportunities again and again. If you find these concepts useful, you may wish to study the more complex models presented in Ivey (1986).

The use of the word "preoperational" here is different from the way Piaget used it and is best considered a metaphor. The word is quite descriptive of clients who come to counseling and therapy. They are indeed *preoperational* in that they are not able to operate on their environment. Thus, the term used here depicts problems frequently presented by clients as well as a more general cognitive state.

These clients are "preoperational" in that they may not be able to operate on their environment effectively. They may indulge in magical, irrational thinking. At least some preoperational thought and behavioral patterns may be found among virtually all clients who come to counseling and therapy.

Examples of clients at this developmental level include the following:

▲ A new employee on the job with extremely limited experience.
▲ A highly disturbed psychiatric inpatient.
▲ Students learning a new subject field.
▲ A client who may be at a higher developmental level in other areas but who is constantly repeating old, stuck behavior or thought patterns in the area of concern. This could be a lawyer who comes for help feeling like a total failure despite considerable success, or it could be a student whose academic performance is not up to his or her ability level. *Many very able and "normal" clients exhibit some patterns of magical thinking or lack of development when they come to the interview.* Your task is to confront these important incongruities.

Level D-2: Concrete operations

Some degree of intentionality is present. The client may understand some incongruities but be unaware of others. The client is often stuck on several issues, having skills but not always being able to use them. The client may understand his or her problem but be unable to "concretely operate" on the issues. Examples of such clients are as follows:

▲ An employee who has been promoted to a new job, only part of which he or she understands and has experienced before.
▲ Most neurotic patients or clients.
▲ Most clients who come in for counseling. They may function well in general but be stuck in certain areas of their lives (for example, lack of vocational information, inability to conduct a job search, inability to assert themselves, lack of communication with their spouses).

Level D-3: Self-directed formal operations

The client has intentionality but has not developed as fully as possible. The client requires assistance in finding his or her own way but needs only limited help from others. The formal operational client is able to separate self from situation and think about actions and thoughts. This may be contrasted with the concrete operational or preoperational client, who is so embedded in the problem that all he or she wants to do is get help in solving it. Examples of clients at this developmental level include the following:

▲ The employee who generally is a self-starter and does satisfactory work but is stuck on a particular issue.
▲ Clients who seek to better their already solid performance and can present their problems and concerns quite clearly. Such clients may be said to exhibit the "YAVIS" traits (young, attractive, verbal, intelligent, successful) and are particularly amenable to counseling.

To conduct a successful interview with a client using only listening skills generally requires an individual at the formal operational level. Thus, you may be beginning to realize that despite the importance of the basic listening skills, you may need more than listening to help many clients.

Level D-4: Mutual or dialectic

The client operates with intentionality and is able to generate a wide range of alternatives and choose sensibly from them. If interviewing assistance is needed, it tends to be brief or focused on self-learning. You will find that this type of client often wants to engage you in a dialogue or dialectic in which client and counselor work together as co-equals in the search for problem definition. You may find yourself learning as much from these clients as they learn from you. They are not only able to analyze themselves, but also to analyze their complex thinking processes and the environmental factors in the situation. Here are some examples:

▲ Employees who are self-starters and who operate well on their own. These employees may want to share their ideas and learn with you as well as from you. A hierarchy in terms of knowledge is inapplicable here.
▲ "YAVIS" clients seeking self-development.
▲ Clients who have resolved many problems in counseling and therapy but want to explore further and examine the process in general.
▲ Clients working through the process of transference (feelings and thoughts from the past projected onto the counselor or therapist) toward the latter part of the interview series.

As a general rule, clients at the lower developmental levels require more influencing skills and environmental structuring than do those at higher levels. For example, clients at the D-1 level often need to be told what to do (although they still require attending skills to help them discover their hidden potential). Clients at the D-2 level are ready for more interactive interviewing; a balance of attending and influencing skills is generally most appropriate for them. At D-3, clients are self-starters and may need only a minimal number of influencing skills. Such clients often respond best to attending skills that help them clarify their own thoughts, feelings, and meanings. D-4 clients can usually solve their own problems. They may come for interviewer support and guidance only when they require assistance on a specific issue, which they usually define clearly. They may desire mutuality as they seek and learn to work with others in a search not only for solutions to problems, but also for new problems to be solved.

It is important to remember that this is only a rough schema. Clients at all developmental levels can profit from confrontation and directives and from relationship-oriented attending skills. Some counseling and therapy theories argue that all clients should be treated in the same manner. However, data are beginning to support the idea that matching your style of interviewing with client problems and personal style may be beneficial (Berzins, 1977). Clearly, not all people are the same, so we should not expect them to respond uniformly to our interviewing behaviors. You can benefit the greatest number of clients by being flexible and having several alternatives available to them.

Assessing Your Clients' Developmental Levels

How can you determine the developmental level of your clients so that you can match your style with their individual needs and special problems? Critical to this assessment is your ability to attend to the client, to use the BLS, and to observe client verbal and nonverbal behavior. Following are some specific suggestions for determining the developmental level of clients:

Assume a new client is at the D-2 concrete operations level

Here a balance of attending and influencing skills is appropriate. If the client appears to be more independent and a self-starter, assume a D-3 formal operations level and use more attending skills. If the client appears puzzled and you note incongruities, move back to D-1 preoperational assumptions and actions and offer more support, perhaps even control.

Use observation skills to note client attending behaviors

If you are using too many influencing skills or your interviewing style is too directive (at least to the client's mind), clients will tend to avert their eyes (perhaps even raising them to the ceiling), frown, increase their speech rate and volume, and shift their body language (for instance, sitting forward in an aggressive fashion, sitting back with arms folded, jiggling legs, or drumming the chair impatiently). With clients who show these nonverbal behaviors, it is probably best to shift to increased use of attending skills—to a more formal operational, listening style of counseling.

On the other hand, if your style is too advanced, you may observe that clients are listening too intently; their eyes will tend to be downcast (or looking directly at you, seeking information); their bodies will be slumped and discouraged; and their voices lowered. With such clients, you may need to become somewhat more structured and take greater control of the interview environment.

Your client observation skills tell you when you are mismatching your counseling style or statement with the client's felt need. Though the above rules are true perhaps only 80% of the time, they do provide useful guidelines for when to shift your style. Clients seeking more from you will tend to show the "eyes-down" pattern; that may be the time to shift to more influencing skills and greater interview control or to confront the client with your own desire not to influence and control at that time. If the client shows the "avoidance" pattern and says "But . . . ," it is probably time to return to attending skills and the basic listening sequence. When in doubt, the general rule is to attend and ask open questions.

Note client incongruities

A large number of verbal and nonverbal incongruities in the client's behavior or life is often a sign of a lower developmental level. If the client is unaware of or denies incongruity, assume a lower developmental level. If the client has only a few incongruities and is able to state them clearly, assume a higher developmental level and a need for more attending skills.

Use the BLS to draw out client problems and obtain data for assessment

Keep the 5-point Confrontation Impact Scale (CIS) in your head. When you find a client denying that a problem exists, you most likely have a client at the magical, preoperational D-1 level. Clients at the concrete operational D-2 level are characteristically able to work with part of the discrepancy, but will need coaching to work things through. At the formal operational D-3 level, you will find that clients are able to describe their conflict clearly and will often easily achieve a Level-3 score on the CIS in response to your questions and confrontations. Mutual-oriented D-4 clients will be harder to identify. They may be "all over the map," but underlying their fluctuations will usually be a desire to work with you to identify and solve problems.

In terms of problem solution and change, Levels 4 and 5 of the CIS can be characteristic of any client, regardless of where they are developmentally when they start counseling. In achieving these higher levels of understanding, acceptance, and change, most clients can be observed gradually shifting and moving their developmental level in front of you due to your effective use of skills and theory. It is through the interaction with you as helper that developmental movement can occur—and your sensitive use of confrontation based on listening skills will be the key to facilitating this client movement.

Use the *who, what, where, why, when,* and *how* sequence to obtain an overall assessment

Use client observation skills and focusing (see Chapter 9) to note client reaction and to obtain as complete a picture of the situation as possible. Again, each client you face is a complex of many developmental levels. The lawyer cited earlier, for example, may be preoperational in terms of his ideas about failure, but very able to meet the concrete operations of the law court, and capable of D-3 and D-4 self-directed/formal thinking as he discusses a case with colleagues. Through questioning and assessment, then, you will find your client to be a mixture of many developmental levels, although one may predominate.

Note client "I statements"

Low-developmental-level clients will tend to say "I can't . . . ," "I won't . . . ," "I'm not able . . . ," "I'm not interested . . . ," and "I'm out of control. . . ." Higher-developmental-level clients tend to say "I can . . . ," "I will . . . ," and "I'm able. . . . " One goal of effective interviewing is to change client "I statements" from low developmental levels to higher levels.

Note client feelings and adjective descriptors

Lower-developmental-level client feelings tend to be ambivalent and confused— or clients may avoid feelings completely. They may also act inappropriately (for example, laughing while talking about a sad event) and/or show a preponderance of negative feelings about self and others. Higher-developmental-level clients will be able to describe their feelings accurately, and their feelings will be relevant to the situation.

Lower-level development may be shown by adjective descriptors and feelings that indicate passivity, negative evaluation, and impotency (*hopeless, bad, discouraged* and the like) as opposed to higher-level activity, positive evaluation, and potency (such as *glad, satisfied, making a difference*). At the end of therapy, clients will use more positive adjective and feeling descriptors. You may want to return to the discussion of feelings in Chapter 6; there you will find highly specific indicators of changes in developmental level and self-concept through the process of interviewing, counseling, and therapy.

Assess cultural and other factors

Lower-developmental-level clients in middle-class cultures tend to propose an external locus of control ("They are responsible for my problems") versus an internal locus ("I am responsible for my behavior"). Lower-developmental-level clients may also have an exclusively one-dimensional time perspective (for instance, only thinking in the past), whereas higher-level clients will speak in past, present, and future time dimensions. Lower developmental levels tend to be populated with dependent personalities; clients at higher developmental levels may demonstrate more independence.

Remember, too, that what makes for a high developmental level in one group may be considered low in another. For example, Westerners value independence, activity, and a strongly assertive personality. Among many Eastern peoples, the opposite may represent a highly developed individual. The Japanese, for example, often value dependence over independence and may even consider the overly independent individual rude and uncouth. Value and personality differences among different peoples must be considered in assessing developmental level.

All of these assessment possibilities are rough guidelines. However, if you find a client operating on a demonstrated lower level in several of the areas defined here, you may expect that your overall diagnosis is relatively correct.

Summary of Counseling Styles and Goals for Developmental Levels

The developmental-level concept can help you think about how counseling styles might change as a person grows in understanding. A deeply disturbed psychiatric patient, for example, is low in virtually all developmental skills and needs to be told what to do. At this stage listening doesn't work; highly directive intervention, such as medication, may be most appropriate. However, as the client develops, it may be possible to institute assertiveness training or a combination of techniques leading to sufficient intentionality to make release from the hospital possible.

A new employee in industry may require direction and teaching in the early stages (D-1). If all goes well, a participative, "coaching" style may be the most appropriate (D-2). If the employee develops well and shows creativity (D-3), the best approach may be using supportive attending skills and, minimally, influencing skills. If the employee becomes truly self-sufficient (D-4), the manager needs to intervene only occasionally by maintaining contact (attending behavior) and client observation skills.

One goal of interviewing and counseling, then, could be defined as moving the client to a higher level of intentionality. A successful interviewing or counseling series should ideally lead in the following directions:

From	To
Low developmental level and intentionality	High developmental level and greater intentionality
Incongruous verbal and nonverbal behavior	Congruent and genuine verbal and nonverbal behavior
Negative "I statements" ("I can't")	Positive "I statements" ("I can")
Negative or mixed, confused, and inappropriate emotions	Positive emotions appropriate to the context and acceptance of necessary "negative" feelings as real (such as sadness after a major loss)
Passive, impotent, and negative evaluative descriptors	Active, potent, and positive evaluative descriptors
External locus of control	Internal locus of control
Narrow time dimension	Ability to live in the past, present, and future
Dependence	Independence

These interviewing and counseling goals are culturally based and typical of White, middle-class, North American values. It has been demonstrated, for example, that dependency and an external locus of control are often characteristic of a healthy Asian personality (Sue, 1981). As mentioned earlier, different cultural groups have vastly different patterns of verbal and nonverbal communication. All the suggestions here for developing intentionality are culture-specific and would need adaptation when applied to people of different cultures and backgrounds. Some other research on cultural differences includes that of Hall (1959), Ivey, Ivey, and Simek-Downing (1987), and Marsella and Pedersen (1981).

Further, it should again be noted that clients exhibit different developmental levels as they talk about different topics or issues. The interviewer must use client observation skills to note gradual and/or sudden changes in client developmental level and move to a new style as necessary. For example, you may be working with a client who shows little understanding of the vocational world (D-2) and readily accepts your advice and suggestions of a coaching nature. The topic may then shift to feelings and values about religion, for which the client is operating at a self-directed D-3 level. A change to a client-directed counselor or interviewing style is appropriate.

In any case, you will find that noting client attending behavior patterns will be the most helpful indicator of how a client is responding to you. If you have not matched the client's developmental level satisfactorily, you will note it in the client's eye contact, body language, and verbal tracking patterns.

It is critical to remember that developmental level is task-specific. That is, a client may be at D-3 in terms of work and community leadership, but operating at D-1 or D-2 in terms of personal satisfaction or family relationships. Effective diagnosis and assessment of developmental level requires flexibility. Virtually every client is a mixture of developmental levels.

The following paragraphs describe a conceptual model for matching interviewer style with client needs.

A Conceptual Model for Interviewer Style Usage

Figure 8-1 illustrates the use of attending and influencing skills (or interviewer style) in relation to clients' developmental levels. We can posit four basic styles to match those levels:

Style 1: Environmental structuring

The interviewer directs the session, using influencing skills extensively. This is most appropriate for clients at level D-1. Examples of Style-1 interviewing are seen in medical inpatient psychiatry, correctional work, traditional one-to-one instruction or teaching, and working with a new, inexperienced employee.

There are a number of environmental-structuring therapies and techniques that are highly useful to many clients. Directive psychiatry and counseling are characteristic: here the counselor or interviewer "takes over" for the needy client and makes necessary decisions. In cases of trauma such as rape or child abuse, the counselor has the responsibility of taking action to help the individual. Children are functionally dependent and may require you to take direct action, not only with them, but also with the family. With clients who have less severe problems, directive techniques such as relaxation training, structuring the environment for behavior (for example, working with a hyperactive child), and body-oriented therapies such as dance and movement therapy may be appropriate.

Style 2: Coaching/concrete operations

The interviewer balances attending and influencing skills and works with the client in a participative manner. The interviewer knows things that the client doesn't and is willing to share them. This style is most appropriate for developmental level D-2. Examples are vocational counseling, assertiveness training, cognitive behavior modification, and reality therapy. The interviewer takes the present developmental abilities of the client and helps the client improve on them.

Style 3: Client-directed/formal operational

The interviewer supports the client's search primarily through use of the attending skills. Nondirective and modern Rogerian counseling styles typify this approach. At a more advanced level of formal operational thinking, techniques of Frankl's logotherapy and psychoanalytic methods may be used.

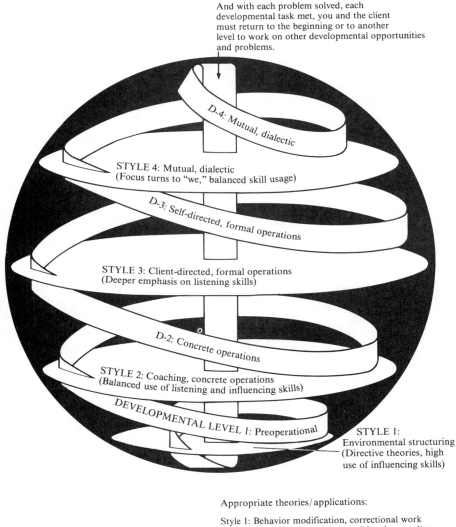

And with each problem solved, each
developmental task met, you and the client
must return to the beginning or to another
level to work on other developmental opportunities
and problems.

D-4: Mutual, dialectic

STYLE 4: Mutual, dialectic
(Focus turns to "we," balanced skill usage)

D-3: Self-directed, formal operations

STYLE 3: Client-directed, formal operations
(Deeper emphasis on listening skills)

D-2: Concrete operations

STYLE 2: Coaching, concrete operations
(Balanced use of listening and influencing skills)

DEVELOPMENTAL LEVEL 1: Preoperational

STYLE 1:
Environmental structuring
(Directive theories, high
use of influencing skills)

Appropriate theories/applications:

Style 1: Behavior modification, correctional work
Style 2: Assertiveness training, decisional counseling,
        reality therapy, rational-emotive therapy
Style 3: Person-centered therapy, logotherapy,
        psychodynamic therapy
Style 4: Feminist therapy, modern encounter groups,
        issues of transference, "I-you" talk between
        counselor and client

Figure 8-1.   Developmental level and counseling style [The developmental
sphere was originally drawn by Lois T. Grady and is adapted here with her permission. A more detailed version of the sphere may be found in Ivey (1986).]

Style 4: Mutual/dialectic

The interviewer may let self-starters alone to develop their own goals and methods. The manager who leaves a mature employee alone is using this style. The classical psychoanalyst who works with patients "on the couch" also leaves the direction of the session to the client.

Feminist counseling and therapy is a prime example of this orientation. The feminist therapist emphasizes working with the client as a co-equal. At times the feminist therapist may provide strong direction (Style 1), assertiveness training (Style 2), or listening (Style 3); but ultimately the goal is a co-constructed view of the world in which client and therapist learn together. Needless to say, it can be argued that most counseling and therapy theory have this goal in mind, at least implicitly, but nowhere has this been articulated more completely than in feminist orientations (Ballou & Gabalac, 1984; Gilligan, 1982).

The model in Figure 8-1 illustrates the need to match interviewer style with client developmental level. At the same time, remember that this is a general framework: an example of a client operating at multiple levels may illustrate the complexity of our clients.

An older woman entering the job market for the first time may be operating at a low level (D-1) vocationally and not have even the most elementary job-seeking skills. At the same time, she may have had wide experience in volunteer work and be a successful homemaker and counselor to her children and neighborhood families. In these areas of her life, she may be at a D-3 or D-4 level. Thus, in a single interview it may be necessary to move through several different interview styles, depending on the issue discussed. For the purposes of vocational counseling it may be best to begin with the coaching/consulting style for a D-2 client. On specific vocational issues an environmental-structuring, information-giving style may be needed.

As the client develops more confidence, knowledge, and experience, successful counseling will help him or her move in vocational expertise from D-1 to D-2 and higher levels. You'll find you can change your counseling style as the client grows. The cycle suggested here starts with attending to find out where the client is developmentally, then moves to a telling style, and continues to change from that point on in response to the client's reaction and movement.

Style-shift counseling is the term Anderson (1982) uses to describe the need to change counseling style in response to the development of the client. Many high school coaches, for example, are strong in Styles 1 and 2: they can direct and assist young athletes to develop and strengthen the concrete operations of sports. However, many of these same coaches try to "hang on" to their directive style when the young athlete matures and needs less direction, and they may even interfere with the development of their athletes.

And so it is in interviewing and counseling: too many interviewers try to "hang on" to an old style that worked with the client—they fail to move and grow with the client. If you find through observation that your interviewing style is no longer working as it did before, shift your style to meet the new developmental needs of your client.

In the course of vocational counseling, the homemaker we talked about earlier may speak of difficulties with her children. In this area she may present a different level of development (such as D-3), and a basically client-directed listening approach to this problem may be more appropriate.

Together, the concepts of interviewing style, client development, and differential use of attending and influencing skills form a "roadmap" that suggests which skill may be most useful to a client in a given situation.

As indicated by the list in Figure 8-1, different counseling and interviewing theories have general traits that appear to accord with different client needs. For example, the modern Rogerian and listening approaches to counseling are perhaps best suited for higher-developmental-level clients. Most clients, however, come to counseling for information and to solve problems for which they lack internal resources—they are D-2 clients. Thus, in most practical, day-to-day situations, Style 2 (coaching) interviewing and counseling is most common. Examples of Style-2 interviewing include vocational decisional counseling, rational-emotive therapy, assertiveness training, and reality therapy. However, all of these theories at times can work with clients on other developmental levels.

Remember: interviewing and counseling are for the client, not for the interviewer or counselor. Quality use of attending and influencing skills requires matching interviewing styles with the client's developmental level.

▲ Example Interview

The following interview excerpt is designed to show you how confrontation can help you assess developmental level and how you can shift your counseling style to meet different developmental needs. This excerpt has been edited down from a longer interview, and the conversation simplified to clearly exemplify the concepts described in this chapter. You will want to read this segment several times and study it carefully. At this point, aim for understanding. With experience and practice, these concepts will be useful and important to you in your interviewing practice.

As you will note, this type of analysis is complex; a lot happens in any counseling session. Four main points are reviewed *simultaneously* in the interview: (1) assessment of client development level, (2) use of the Confrontation Impact Scale, (3) examination of counselor style, and (4) use of confrontation and other microskills. With study and practice, you will find it possible to hold these concepts, as well as many others, in mind as you enter the complex world of the interview.

Sam: I'm having a terrible time with my wife right now. She's working for the first time and we've been having lots of arguments. She isn't fixing meals like she used to and isn't watching over the kids. I don't know what to do. (Developmental assessment: D-1, due to client verbalizations of inability. The client seems preoperational in terms of action. At the same time, it may be noted that he is able to describe the situation fairly clearly and so might be generally considered a D-2 client.)

Hal: So on one hand she's working and has lots of new things to do, but on the other hand, you expect her to continue with all the old things, and you feel pretty confused about it. (Style assessment: Style 3, due to reflective listening style. Implicit in this is an expectation that Sam will be able to resolve his problems with his present knowledge. This is an example of style mismatching.)

Sam: You damn betcha she's expected to do what she's always done—I'm not confused about that. (Developmental assessment: On the CIS, this statement would be rated as Level 1 because the client has *denied* the confrontation. The client's developmental level as D-1 is verified. It is necessary for Hal to shift his style to meet client needs.)

Hal: I see. You're not confused: you really don't like what's going on. Could you give me a specific example of what's happening—something that goes on between you when she gets home? (Style assessment: The paraphrase joins Sam "where he is" as Hal accepts Sam's view of things and unwillingness to work on the contradiction. Hal is attempting to see the world as Sam sees it and thus must enter Sam's world, which at present is D-1. But Hal is not satisfied with that—in asking the classic open question seeking concreteness, he is moving Sam from preopertional venting and inaction to concrete descriptions of events, characteristic of Style 2. If Hal is successful, Sam will move to D-2 concrete operations in the next statement.)

Sam: (sighs, pauses) Yeah, that's right, I don't like what's going on. Like last night, Mary was so tired that she just laid on the sofa—she didn't get around to fixing dinner 'til half an hour late. I was hungry and tired myself. We had a big argument. This has been going on for 3 weeks now. (Developmental assessment: CIS Level 2, as Sam is able to talk about part of the contradiction originally posed by Hal's confrontation. Sam might be described here in his response as partially D-2 concrete operations, as he is describing the situation concretely and specifically, but is also still preoperational on other parts of the conflict. For example, he does not seem aware of how his wife feels; he seems insensitive to the fact that his wife is working and is expected to do everything she did in the past for him.)

Hal: I see. That gives me a clearer picture. She's working all day, you both come home exhausted, and, Sam, you would like to be taken care of like you used to be. Do you think Mary physically can work and take care of you like she used to? (Style assessment: Style 2 coaching/concrete operations. Hal's implicit confrontation is now more concrete: "On one hand Mary is working and is exhausted, on the other hand you expect her to continue to take care of you.")

Sam: I guess I hadn't thought of it that way before. If Mary is working, she isn't going to be physically able to do what she did. But where does that leave me? (Developmental assessment: CIS Level 5, as Sam is able for the first time to see that Mary can't continue as she has in the past. His "If . . . then . . . " statement is characteristic of late concrete operational thinking. You may note that he is still thinking primarily of himself. To move to formal thinking and D-3,

Sam would have to be able to take Mary's perspective (for example, "I can see how Mary would feel—she must be too tired to do anything"). Ideally, the counselor would like to see the client move to this level of thinking, but it isn't always possible. As such, practical, workable compromises in counseling style and goals may have to be made.)

Hal: Yes, where does that leave you? Sam, let me tell you about my experience. My wife started working and I, too, expected her to continue to do the housework, take care of the kids, do the shopping, and fix the meals. She went to work because we needed the money to make a down payment on a small house. Today's couples just seem to need two incomes to make it.

Well, what I found was that my wife couldn't work unless I helped around the house. I had to decide which was more important—getting the house for all of us or maintaining our traditional roles at home.

What I've done is share some of the household work with her. I don't like it, but it seems like it's got to be done. I've taken over the shopping and now I pick the kids up at day care, too. How would that square with you? Do you want your wife to work, and, if so, are you willing to help her? (Style assessment: Style 2 coaching/concrete operations. Hal is operating like a coach. He is speaking up directly with his ideas, but he is also allowing the client to react to them. Clearly, Hal is trying to get Sam's thinking and behavior to move. His last statement contains an important implicit confrontation: "On the one hand your wife is working and if she continues, she'll need some help; on the other hand, perhaps you don't want her to work—what is your reaction to this?")

Sam: Uhhh . . . we need the money. I've missed the last two car payments. It was my idea that Mary go to work. But isn't housework "women's work"? (Developmental assessment: CIS Level 3, in that Sam is now facing up to the contradiction he is posing. He has not yet synthesized his desire for his wife to work with his helping her, but at least he is moving toward a more open attitude. Sam has tentatively moved to D-2 and early concrete operations in this thinking about his wife's working. As he acknowledges his part in the situation and the need for more money, he is beginning to come to a new synthesis for the problem—he is less incongruent and is taking beginning steps toward resolving his discrepancies. But, as he begins this developmental movement, note that a new preoperational problem appears: how can Sam help his wife when he considers housework "women's work"?)

Comment: For each developmental task completed in the interviewing process, it often seems that a new problem arises. Just as the counselor is beginning to facilitate client movement, a new obstacle ("women's work") arises. This new developmental block must be confronted, and once again the client needs to move from preoperational thinking and behavior to concrete operations and action.

The progress of this client to this point actually took the counselor half the session. Working through the concept of "women's work" and changing it developmentally to "work in the home that must be shared if the car payments are to be met" took the rest of the session.

Development-oriented counseling requires that you have the ability to enter the world of the client and see it from his or her perspective. It means that you yourself must be capable of formal operations and realizing that the same event may be viewed differently by different people. It will require that you respect and honor client positions with which you personally may disagree. But unless you are willing to shift your style and accurately hear the client, nothing is going to happen.

If the counselor in the above example had stayed solely with listening skills, it is possible that the client would have rejected counseling and left the interview, never to return. It is necessary that you be equipped with many skills and theories to meet the distinct needs of the unique individuals who come to you for assistance.

▲ Summary

This chapter has brought two important concepts together, those of confrontation and development. Clients will tend to stay where they are unless they are confronted in some manner. Through the process of listening carefully and reflecting back to the client what you hear, you will enable higher-developmental-level clients to think about themselves and their behavior and to confront themselves. The process of your active listening supports their own ability to look at and confront their own discrepancies.

With clients who suffer from more serious blocks, impasses, and stuckness, you will find that the increased use of environmental structuring and coaching/concrete operational methods is more helpful. Even the most sophisticated and advanced client will at times need assistance in concretely operating in the world. For example, you may find that some clients will gain all kinds of D-3 formal operational understandings about themselves; yet these insights and understandings are useless unless they are taken into daily practice and used seriously. For such clients, who often suffer from overintellectualization, you may find it necessary to shift your style to a lower-developmental orientation. While the high-level formal operations thinker may be conceptually advanced, he or she may be very limited in the world of action.

Box 8-1. Key Points

Why?	Development may be considered the primary aim of counseling. Clients come to us stuck and immobilized in their development processes. Through the use of microskills—confrontation in particular—we facilitate their developmental progress.
What?	*Confrontation* has been defined as noting one of the six (or more) types of incongruities and discrepancies, then feeding back or paraphrasing that discrepancy to the client. Our task is then to work through the resolution of the discrepancy.

(continued)

Box 8-1 (continued)

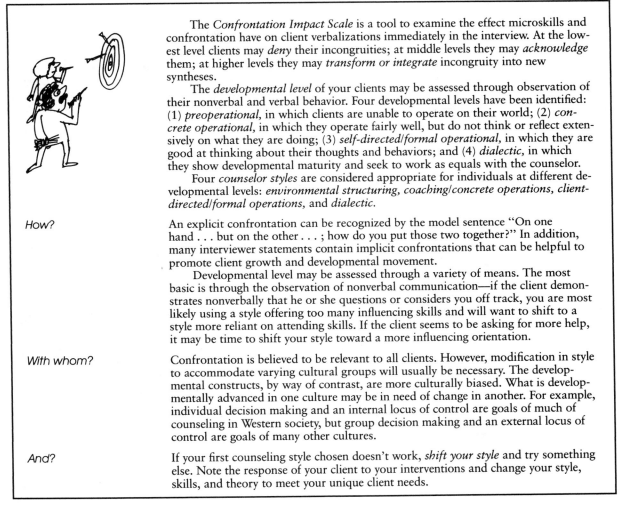

The *Confrontation Impact Scale* is a tool to examine the effect microskills and confrontation have on client verbalizations immediately in the interview. At the lowest level clients may *deny* their incongruities; at middle levels they may *acknowledge* them; at higher levels they may *transform or integrate* incongruity into new syntheses.

The *developmental level* of your clients may be assessed through observation of their nonverbal and verbal behavior. Four developmental levels have been identified: (1) *preoperational,* in which clients are unable to operate on their world; (2) *concrete operational,* in which they operate fairly well, but do not think or reflect extensively on what they are doing; (3) *self-directed/formal operational,* in which they are good at thinking about their thoughts and behaviors; and (4) *dialectic,* in which they show developmental maturity and seek to work as equals with the counselor.

Four *counselor styles* are considered appropriate for individuals at different developmental levels: *environmental structuring, coaching/concrete operations, client-directed/formal operations,* and *dialectic.*

How?   An explicit confrontation can be recognized by the model sentence "On one hand . . . but on the other . . . ; how do you put those two together?" In addition, many interviewer statements contain implicit confrontations that can be helpful to promote client growth and developmental movement.

Developmental level may be assessed through a variety of means. The most basic is through the observation of nonverbal communication—if the client demonstrates nonverbally that he or she questions or considers you off track, you are most likely using a style offering too many influencing skills and will want to shift to a style more reliant on attending skills. If the client seems to be asking for more help, it may be time to shift your style toward a more influencing orientation.

With whom?   Confrontation is believed to be relevant to all clients. However, modification in style to accommodate varying cultural groups will usually be necessary. The developmental constructs, by way of contrast, are more culturally biased. What is developmentally advanced in one culture may be in need of change in another. For example, individual decision making and an internal locus of control are goals of much of counseling in Western society, but group decision making and an external locus of control are goals of many other cultures.

And?   If your first counseling style chosen doesn't work, *shift your style* and try something else. Note the response of your client to your interventions and change your style, skills, and theory to meet your unique client needs.

▲ Practice Exercises and Self-Assessment

This chapter may be considered a transition point from which to continue your own personal development as a counselor and interviewer. It seeks to point out that every client you meet is a unique and distinct human being, just as you are a unique and distinct person yourself. If you are going to help others, you will need an array of skills and concepts so that you can understand and work with points of view different from your own.

Individual Practice in Confrontation

Exercise 1. Identification of incongruity

The six types of client discrepancies listed in the chapter on client observation skills have been discussed again for the first phase of the confrontation skill. If you have not completed the observation exercise for discrepancies (Exercise 8 of Chapter 4), complete it now before you go further. The ability to identify discrepancies through client observation skills is central to the use of confrontation.

Exercise 2. Practicing confrontation of incongruity

An employee comes in late for the fifth day in a row and says the following:

"Boss, I'm sorry, but there just isn't anything I can do. Usually I can make it, but not today."

A confrontation statement from the boss in this case might be this:

"Bob, on the one hand you say you aren't usually late. On the other hand, we both know you've been late all week. How do you put these two together?"

As already mentioned, critical in such statements is a nonjudgmental tone of voice and body language. Perhaps the most difficult aspect of a successful confrontation is not showing judgment through nonverbal displays of anger or frustration.

Using the model sentence "On the one hand . . . , but on the other hand . . . " provides a standard and useful format for the actual confrontation. Of course you may also use variations such as "You say . . . but you do . . . ," and remember to follow up the confrontation with a check-out.

Write confrontation statements for the following situations. Remember to include a check-out with the confrontation.

A client breaks eye contact, speaks slowly, and slumps in the chair while saying, "Yes, I really like the idea of getting to the library and getting the vocational information you suggest. Ah . . . I know it would be helpful for me."

_____

_____

_____

"Yes, my family is really important to me. I like to spend a lot of time with them. When I get this big project done, I'll stop working so much and start doing what I should. Not to worry."

_____

_____

_____

"I really want to go to State University, but I fear I don't have the money or grades to get there."

_____

_____

"My daughter and I don't get along well. I feel that I am really trying, but she doesn't respond. Only last week I bought her a present, but she just ignored it."

_____

_____

_____

Exercise 3. Practice with the Confrontation Impact Scale

Review the Confrontation Impact Scale described on page 175. Then write client responses to the following confrontations, representing each of the anchor points on the CIS.

Sam: How can you expect me to work around the house? That's women's work!

Hal: On one hand, you feel that work around the house is women's work, but on the other hand you expect your wife to help earn the daily bread _and_ do the housework as well. How do you put that together?

Write five different levels of response for Sam:

Level 1 (Denial): _____

_____

_____

Level 2 (Partial examination of incongruity): _____

_____

_____

Level 3 (Full examination, but no change): _____

_____

_____

Level 4 (Decision to live with incongruity): _____

_____

_____

(Note here that a decision to live with incongruity may not meet your own personal value structure, but it may be a satisfactory resolution to the client.)

Level 5 (Development of new, larger, more comprehensive constructs, patterns, or behaviors): _____

_____

_____

Client: I'm getting tired of talking with you. You always seem to think I'm taking the easy way out.

Counselor: Sounds as if you're telling me that on the one hand you want to change—that's why you started counseling—but on the other, now that it's getting close you want to leave. That seems similar to the way you handle your relationships with the opposite sex: when it gets close, you leave. How do you respond to that?

Level 1: _____

_____

_____

Level 2: _____

_____

_____

Level 3: _____

_____

_____

Level 4: _____

_____

_____

Level 5: _____

_____

_____

Systematic Group Practice in Confrontation

Step 1.   Divide into groups.

Step 2.   Select a group leader.

Step 3.   Assign roles for the first practice session.

▲ Role-played client
▲ Interviewer
▲ Observer 1, who will give special attention to classifying overall client developmental level and to identifying counselor style, using the Assessing Developmental Level Feedback Sheet

▲ Observer 2, who will rate each client statement using the Confrontation Feedback Sheet and, during a replay of an audio- or videorecording, will stop the tape after each client statement and rate it carefully, together with the others

Step 4. Planning.   State the goal of the session. The interviewer's task is to use the basic listening sequence to draw out a conflict in the client and then to confront this conflict or incongruity. Important will be your ability to observe and note discrepancies *on the spot* in the session and to feed them back to the client.

A useful topic for the role-played client is any issue about which he or she feels undecided or conflicted. One topic that most individuals feel conflicted about currently is the changing roles of men and women. If one is supportive of the change, then one feels conflicted about those who won't/don't change. If one wants to "keep things as they are," another form of conflict prevails.

Observers should use this time to examine the feedback sheets and plan their own interviews.

Step 5. Conduct a 5-minute practice session using confrontation skills as part of your listening and observation demonstration.

Step 6. Review the practice session using the skill.

Step 7. Rotate roles.

Some general reminders.   This exercise is an attempt to integrate many of the skills and concepts used thus far in this book. Allow sufficient time for thinking through and planning this practice session.

Confrontation Feedback Sheet

_____ (Date)

_____   _____
(Name of Interviewer)   (Name of Person Completing Form)

Instructions: Summarize the main words of the client insofar as possible so that the response of the client to each counselor lead may be noted. Give special attention to client response to explicit and implicit confrontations by the counselor.

Confrontation Impact Scale rating form	Level				
	1	2	3	4	5
	Denial	_Partial examination_	_Full examination; no change_	_Decision to live with incongruity_	_Development of new constructs_
1. _____					
2. _____					
3. _____					
4. _____					
5. _____					
6. _____					
7. _____					
8. _____					
9. _____					
10. _____					
11. _____					
12. _____					
13. _____					
14. _____					

Individual Practice in Assessing Developmental Levels

A number of specific ways have been suggested in this chapter to help identify the developmental level of the client. Following are some brief client statements for which you are to (1) identify the probable developmental level of each client and (2) indicate the most appropriate style of interviewing, in the space provided.

"I'm sure what you are saying is correct. You're the expert. But I've worked by myself for a long time with a lot of success, and I think I know most of the answers." (Eyes upward and looking away, arms crossed over chest, foot jiggling. You as interviewer are aware that the client or subordinate's past performance has been superior.)

Level and recommended style: _____

"I can't solve my problems. . . . I just sit and mope, and I've done that now for 6 months. I just feel like a limp dishrag." (Eyes downcast, leaning forward as if asking for something. Your observations of this client suggest that he or she hasn't been able to do anything for a period of time.)

Level and recommended style: _____

"I am really getting into this vocational plan we are developing. I think it might just get me the job I want. What do we do next?" (Direct eye contact, leaning forward, open posture. This behavior is congruent with the rest of the interviewing sessions you have engaged in in a participatory, coaching fashion.)

Level and recommended style: _____

"I've thought about it a lot and have some good ideas, but I need someone to listen and help me sort things through." (Direct eye contact, leaning forward, smooth, assured vocal tones. Your experience suggests this client has been able to work things out with minimal help.)

Level and recommended style: _____

"Always in the past I've been able to solve problems with my boss. But the techniques I've used in the past don't seem to work anymore, and I think I'm stuck. He seems to be going after me. What do you suggest?" (Leaning forward, open body posture, hesitant vocal tone, eye contact variable. This is a veteran employee who has previously been virtually on her own.)

Level and recommended style: _____

"I feel so dependent on my husband. How could he leave me? I thought we had a good marriage. I've never handled the bills or the income tax. I don't know what job I can get. What should I do?" (Variable eye contact, slumped in chair, worried tone, and rapid speech. Although disturbed now, this client has personal strengths and resources. She has done community and volunteer work at a high level.)

Level and recommended style: _____

"I'd like to tackle that new job. It looks like a blast. I know I can handle it."
(Direct eye contact, congruent body language. You are aware, however, that
this client has a history of failing to complete assignments and overestimating
his ability. The client has resisted suggestions from you in the past.)

Level and recommended style: _____

Systematic Group Practice in Assessing Developmental Level

Exercise 1. Identifying developmental level and counseling style

This exercise is a variation on the old parlor game of charades. Each member of
the group role-plays a client before the group. The group as a whole interviews
the client, using the BLS. After the group has had 3 minutes to interview the
client, they discuss the interview and determine the developmental level and most
appropriate interviewing style. The positive asset search will be helpful in determining developmental level as well. Use the Assessing Developmental Level Feedback Sheet that follows.

Exercise 2. Matching and mismatching interviewing styles

Step 1. Divide into groups.

Step 2. Select a group leader.

Step 3. Assign roles for the first practice session.
▲ Role-played client
▲ Interviewer
▲ Observer 1
▲ Observer 2

Step 4. Planning.   The "Individual Practice" preceding this section presents
several brief scenarios. Have different members of the group role-play those
clients, with accompanying verbal and nonverbal behaviors. State the goals for
the session. The interviewer's task is first to match interviewing style with client
developmental level and use the appropriate balance of attending and influencing
skills. After completing this task successfully, change abruptly to another interviewing style and note what happens to the client's verbal and nonverbal
behavior.

***Step 5. Conduct a 3-minute practice session with a matched style and then
3 minutes with a mismatched style.***

Step 6. Review the practice session and provide feedback for 9 minutes.

Step 7. Rotate roles.

Assessing Developmental Level Feedback Sheet

_____ (Date)

_____   _____
(Name of Interviewer)   (Name of Person Completing Form)

Instructions: Complete the form below.

1. What behavior patterns do you observe? What developmental level is represented by the client?

   Attending behavior patterns _____

   Discrepant verbal or nonverbal behavior _____

   Nature of "I statements" _____

   Nature of feeling words and emotions _____

   Nature of descriptors (activity, potency, and evaluation) _____

   External versus internal locus of control _____

   Apparent overall developmental level (D-1, D-2, D-3, D-4) _____

   Cite evidence in terms of observable behavior to justify your conclusion, below.

2. What counseling style is the interviewer using? Check one or more styles below.

   _____ Style 1: Environmental Structuring

   _____ Style 2: Coaching/Concrete Operations

   _____ Style 3: Client-Directed/Formal Operations

   _____ Style 4: Dialectic/Mutual

   Cite your evidence in terms of interviewing behavior (skill usage and techniques):

3. What happens to the client when interviewing style is deliberately mismatched?

Self-Assessment and Follow-Up

Confrontation and its special relationship to development are key aspects of mastery of the concepts of intentional interviewing and counseling. The following self-assessment exercises are designed to organize your learning and plan your future work in helping.

1. What one message stands out most for you from this chapter?

Which of the many constructs and ideas are most meaningful to you? Selecting your own issues is critical if you are to become fully intentional. The position of this text should be clear: there are many ways to be an effective helper. But each way must be *authentic* for each counselor, interviewer, or therapist.

_____

_____

_____

_____

_____

2. Mastery of confrontation and development

Provide evidence of your mastery of these concepts with accompanying notes, transcripts, tapes, or case studies.

_____

_____

Identification.   You will be able to identify, through observation, incongruities in the client and note the use of confrontation in conjunction with other skills. You will also be able to identify the developmental level of clients and the basic styles used by counselors.

_____   Ability to observe incongruities manifested by a client in the interview.

_____

_____

_____   Ability to classify and write counselor statements for the presence or absence of elements of confrontation.

_____

_____

_____   Ability to identify client developmental level through observation.

_____

_____

_____ Ability to identify and classify counseling and interviewing style through observation.

_____

_____

Basic mastery.   You will be able to demonstrate confrontation skills in a role-played interview and in practice sessions demonstrate your ability to engage in the four different counseling and interviewing styles.

_____ Ability to demonstrate confrontation skills in a role-played and/or real interview.

_____

_____ Ability to demonstrate the four counseling and interviewing styles in a role-played and/or real interview.

_____

_____

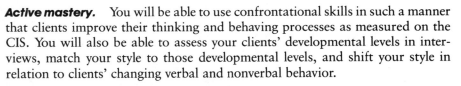

Active mastery.   You will be able to use confrontational skills in such a manner that clients improve their thinking and behaving processes as measured on the CIS. You will also be able to assess your clients' developmental levels in interviews, match your style to those developmental levels, and shift your style in relation to clients' changing verbal and nonverbal behavior.

_____ Ability to help clients change their manner of talking about a problem as a result of confrontation. This may be measured formally by the CIS or by others' observation.

_____ Ability to move clients from discussion of issues at the lower levels of the CIS at beginning of discussion of a problem to talking about the issue at higher developmental levels by the end of the interview or when the topic is exhausted.

_____ Ability to identify client responses inferred from the CIS on the spot in the interview and change counseling intervention to meet those responses.

_____ Ability to identify client developmental level in the interview and shift interview style to meet that level.

_____ Ability to operate in an interview demonstrating all four counseling styles.

_____ Ability to "let go" of one style and shift style to meet the needs of clients as they develop in relation to you.

Teaching mastery.   Are you able to teach developmental and confrontation concepts to clients and other persons? These concepts are generally intended more for counselors and interviewers than for clients. However, you will find developmental concepts useful in assisting self-directed formal operational thinkers: for example, to realize that their young children simply do not think

as they do. In addition, you will find that the "bull in the china shop" personality or those given to judging others excessively can benefit from instruction in the gentler confrontation skills. Present evidence of your teaching mastery here.

_____

_____

_____

What one single goal would you set for yourself with regard to the skill of confrontation and the concepts of development?

_____

_____

_____

▲ References

Anderson, T. (1982). *Style-shift counseling*. Abbotsford, British Columbia: Interpersonal Effectiveness.

Ballou, M., & Gabalac, N. (1984). *A feminist position on mental health*. Springfield, Ill.: Charles C Thomas.

Berzins, J. (1977). Therapist-patient matching. In A. Gurman & A. Razin (Eds.), *Effective psychotherapy*. New York: Pergamon Press.

Gilligan, C. (1982). *In a different voice*. Cambridge, Mass.: Harvard University Press.

Hall, E. (1959). *The silent language*. New York: Fawcett.

Ivey, A. (1986). *Developmental therapy: Theory into practice*. San Francisco: Jossey-Bass.

Ivey, A., & Litterer, J. (1979). *Face to face: Communication skills for management*. North Amherst, Mass.: Amherst Consulting Group.

Ivey, A., Ivey, M., & Simek-Downing, L. (1987). *Counseling and psychotherapy: Integrating skills, theory, and practice*. Englewood Cliffs, N.J.: Prentice-Hall.

Marsella, A., & Pedersen, P. (1981). *Cross-cultural counseling and psychotherapy*. New York: Pergamon Press.

Sue, D. (1981). *Counseling the culturally different*. New York: Wiley.

9 Focusing: Tuning in with Clients and Directing Conversational Flow

---

How can focusing help you and your clients?

Major function	Focusing is a skill that enables you to direct client conversational flow to the areas you want. For those who seek neither to impede nor to direct client talk, awareness of focusing and its power will allow you to reduce your unconscious direction of client conversation.
Secondary functions	Knowledge and skill in focusing result in the following:

▲ Broadening your own and the client's perspective on a problem by examining an issue from alternative points of view. Focusing often results in increased cognitive complexity and the realization that many of life's decisions are more difficult than may at first be supposed.
▲ Increasing your ability to open or close client talk according to the needs of a specific interview.
▲ Through helping your client to focus on important issues, facilitating his or her confrontation of critical issues.

▲ Introduction

FOCUSING

Focusing is perhaps best described through an example.

"I just had a terrible argument with the manager. She thinks I don't know what I'm doing. My sales record has been good, at least as good as other people around here."

This client statement could occur in a therapy session, a vocational counseling interview, an on-the-job performance appraisal, or a variety of interpersonal situations. The question is how the counselor can best respond.

By now you know the answer is that the interviewer has a virtually infinite set of ways to respond to this person. You could attend or not attend; you could ask a variety of questions; you could reflect feelings; you could confront—any of these responses might be helpful, and each leads the client in a different direction.

Focusing is a skill to add to the microskills discussed thus far. Focusing adds precision to client observation and the microskills through selective attention to certain aspects of client talk. People tend to talk about what others will listen to or reinforce. There are many possible ways of focusing clients; two examples are the following:

1. *Focus on the client:* "*Sandy, you* sound upset. Could *you* tell me more about your feelings?" (reflection of feeling, open question)
2. *Focus on the main theme or problem:* "*Terrible argument?*" (encourager) "Could you tell me about your *sales record?*" (open question)

You can see that focusing on the person could lead Sandy to talk more about personal issues, whereas focusing on the main theme or problem encourages discussion of about what happened and the facts of the situation. In both cases, listening skills combine with focusing to lead the client in very different directions. Which of the two alternatives is correct? Both may be useful in obtaining a complete summary of the situation; at the same time, either could be overused.

Four additional areas of focus will be presented in this chapter:

3. *Focus on others:* manager, other salespeople
4. *Focus on mutual issues or group:* the interviewer-and-client relationship or the entire management team
5. *Focus on interviewer:* through a self-disclosure or "I statement"
6. *Focus on cultural/environmental/contextual issues:* broader issues often not readily apparent, such as racial or sexual issues, company policy, economic trends, and the like

This chapter emphasizes focus as a way to ensure a complete assessment of the problem presented by a client and to understand conversational flow in the interview.

Counselors can confront and facilitate client awareness through focusing. Many clients tend to see their situations rather simplistically and repetitively, constantly talking about other people and failing to note their own involvement in the problem or the broader contextual issues. Some counselors would even argue that a goal of successful interviewing and counseling is to confront and facilitate client awareness of the world's complexity. In other cases, clients are fully aware—even painfully aware—of the complexity that surrounds them, and are unable to focus on any single issue. In both cases the interviewer's ability to help the client focus is critical.

The following transcript illustrates how the focusing skill is used in practice.

▲ Example Interview

Gilbert:	Well, Paul, could you tell me what you have on your mind this morning?
Paul:	Yeah, Gilbert, I'm really pleased that Ann is accepted to college. But I think, oh my gosh, that's a terrible amount of tuition I have to come up with.
Gilbert:	Uh-huh . . . how are you feeling about that? (Open question, oriented to feeling. The focus is on the *client*.)

Paul: Well, like I say, I'm really pleased. But gosh, that's really some responsibility there. I want to do as much as I can. With the economy not doing so well, I'm not sure I can get it all together.

Gilbert: Is Ann aware of the problem of the cost of going to school? (Closed question. The focus is on *others*.)

Paul: Well, she's earned a fair amount of money. But I don't think she really understands how much money we have to put together. We've always had enough. She just sort of seems to sit there and expect me to come up with it. That's a little troubling.

Gilbert: Uh-huh . . . well, are there any loans available through some of the area's federal agencies, some private foundations? (Closed question. The focus is on the *environmental context,* larger issues that may surround the problem.)

Paul: I hadn't thought about that. I think I could write the university and ask. I read in the paper that there is some kind of loan program. But isn't it true that there is a possibility of the government cutting back on those programs and maybe even eliminating those things?

Gilbert: Well, I tell you, I had an experience with sending my own kid to school recently and I understand that, ah, that Jamie's financial support, ah . . . was going to be cut assuming she stayed another year. So that could be a problem. But this financial thing seems to have you in a bit of a quandary. (The focus in this self-disclosure is on the *interviewer.* The paraphrase and reflection of feeling at the end of the self-disclosure wisely focuses on the *main theme or problem*—that is, finances. Self-disclosures are often helpful, but for the most part they should be kept brief.)

Paul: Yeah, I'm concerned about how I'm going to meet all those needs. It kind of scares me.

Gilbert: In what way, Paul? (open question, focus on client)

Paul: Well, I just feel a great need to solve the problem, and I'm just sitting here looking at the books and I don't see any extra money. I suspect what I'm going to have to do is cut back.

Gilbert: Tell me a bit more about the finances as you see them. (open question; focus is on the main theme or problem)

Paul: Well, I've got $1500 in the savings bank. I don't see how I can save much between now and September. Tuition and room and board are more than $4000 and Ann has about $750. That leaves us a bit short.

Gilbert: Before we go any further, Paul, let me summarize some of the factors we've been talking about. *You're* concerned and worried and feel quite responsible for *Ann's* education. A loan might help, but the *economic situation* is such that it is a question mark. *I* feel that, myself, helping a daughter through college. *Finances* are really bugging you. Now the question seems to be, what can *we* do together to help solve the problem? Is there anything that *we* have done so far that impresses you as helpful or stands out? (In this summarization Gilbert goes through the several focus dimensions and adds the critical dimension *we,* or *mutual* focus, to the problem.)

Paul: One thing that stands out for me is your mentioning that I feel responsible. I know from past counseling I've been in that I tend to take more responsibility for an issue than I need to. I sometimes make decisions for other people without listening to them. I may be creating part of the problem myself.

Gilbert: Paul, I sense you taking the responsibility for taking responsibility. You're not alone. There's me, who is interested in helping you work things through; Ann, who undoubtedly, as I have heard you talk about her, wants to do her full share; and the college and government may help out, too. (Interpretation focusing first on the *client,* then moving again to a multiple *we* focus in an effort to enable the client to understand that he is not as alone in this matter as he thinks he is.)

Paul: Maybe we can work this through. I appreciate your reminding me. Sometimes I make myself alone when I don't need to be. I need to think through the possibility of working with others. Your listening to me and sharing makes me feel less alone and by myself. I don't feel as alone as I did.

Comment: The concepts of focusing here are used to illustrate that many problems are simultaneously more complex and less complex than we often think (see Box 9-1). In individualistic Western society we often place responsibility on the individual. The individual accepts this responsibility for problem solving and fails to realize that an entire system of interrelationships is involved in solving any problem or issue. A "we" focus as a core concept, as opposed to an "I" focus, may help individuals accept themselves as part of a system in addition to taking individual initiative and responsibility.

Box 9-1.   Focus Analysis for Interview with Paul

Main issue as presented	Large tuition bill to be paid[1]
Client focus	Paul and pronoun *you*
Main theme/problem focus	Tuition bill and finances
Others focus	Ann
Mutual group, "we" focus	Client-interviewer relationship—"we"
Interviewer focus	Gilbert

(continued)

[1]Note that the interviewer can focus on all of these issues plus many others, or simply focus on the main theme or problem or just on the individual's feelings and attitudes. Focus analysis provides a map of possible issues that need to be considered in any important decision.

Box 9-1 (continued)

Cultural/ environmental/ contextual focus	A variety of issues, some of which are outlined below: ▲ Federal agencies/private foundations ▲ Government cutbacks/general economic conditions ▲ Financial background and resources ▲ Timing and preparation of application forms ▲ College desired ▲ Ethnic or religious background ▲ Family experience with college (for instance, first family member to attend)

▲ Instructional Reading

Six areas of focus analysis have been identified. Within each, more complexity can be found. Beginning counselors and interviewers should generally start responding to the individual client before them. Research and experience have shown that simply learning to respond to the individual and his or her perceptions of the world is most basic. When responding to clients, using personal pronouns (*you, your*) and names is critical.

To begin this section, we will present a case concerning the heavily loaded emotional issue of abortion. Your task is to practice differentiating between individual and problem/main-theme focuses by using a variety of microskills.

"I just had an abortion."

Client focus: _____

Problem/main-theme focus: _____

This is an easy example. Too many beginners focus on the main theme or problem ("Tell me more about the abortion"), which may result in a voyeuristic interview in which many facts are obtained but little is learned about the client. An extremely important task is finding out how the client felt about the abortion and now feels about herself. ("Could you share some of your personal feelings about this?")

Through each of the following examples note how you can use the concept of confrontation to facilitate focusing and the development of awareness.

"I just had an abortion and I feel pretty awful. They treated me terribly, and I felt just like a piece of meat. Bob won't have anything to do with me. My parents don't know."

Client focus: _____

Problem/main-theme focus: _____

Focusing on the feelings and thoughts of the woman would clearly be an individual or client focus. However, the woman exists in relation to a problem, and a main-theme focus ("You feel a lot of things about the abortion . . . let's sort them out.") opens the issue even further.

At this point it becomes apparent that significant others (Bob, her parents, the physician and nurses) are important in the problem. Another focus area, then, is on others. Use the space below to make three alternative focus responses:

Focus on others (Bob): _____

Focus on others (parents): _____

Focus on others (physician and nurses): _____ _____

_____

If you focus on Bob solely, issues involving the parents or feelings toward the physician and nurses are temporarily lost. It is important to keep all significant others in mind in the process of problem resolution and problem examination, perhaps saving questions or other listening skills for a later point. For a full understanding of the abortion experience, all of these relationships (and probably others) need to be explored. In turn, the client will probably have personal feelings and thoughts toward each of these people, so it may be necessary to focus again on the client.

The client may continue her discussion as follows:

"I feel everyone is just judging me. They all seem to be condemning me. I even feel a little frightened of you."

A mutual focus often emphasizes the "we" in a relationship. Use the following space for a mutual-focus statement.

Focus on mutual issues: _____

_____

_____

_____

One possibility here is "Right now, *we* have an issue. Can *we* work together to help you? What are some of your thoughts and feelings about how *we* are doing?" The emphasis is on the relationship between counselor and client. Two people are working on an issue, and the client accepts partial ownership of the problem. Some counseling theories would argue against this relational approach. Among most people in Western cultures, emphasizing the distinction between "you" (client focus) and "me" (interviewer focus) would perhaps be more common. Among some Asian and Southern European peoples, the "we" focus may be especially appropriate: *We* are going to solve this problem." The "we" focus provides a sharing of responsibility, which is often reassuring to the client regardless of his or her background.

Another type of mutual focus is on the group. In this case, "we" could be extended to include the client, the counselor, Bob, the parents, and perhaps even the physician and nurses, for as long as the client has a problem, all the significant others have problems as well. A typical approach in counseling and management problem solving in this country is to fix the blame on a specific individual. A relational "we" approach assumes that the group, or the dyad, or the community takes responsibility for the problem. With a "we" focus, responsibility is shared, and common efforts are made toward resolution. A smoothly working encounter or therapy group often emphasizes "we" in this manner, as does the effective management or production team in industry. The well-known Japanese quality workmanship stems from a basic "we" orientation in that society. Family therapy and systems thinking, too, often operate from a "we" basis.

Another type of focus is for the interviewer to refer to himself or herself. For our example, what would a focus on the interviewer be?

Interviewer focus: _____

An interviewer focus could be a self-disclosure of feelings and thoughts about the client or situation: for example, "*I* feel concerned and sad over what happened; *I* want to help" or "*I*, too, had an abortion . . . *my* experience was . . . " or perhaps even some personal advice. Opinions vary on the appropriateness of interviewer or counselor involvement, but increasingly the value and power of such statements are being recognized. They must not be overused, however, or the client may end up doing therapy with the counselor.

Perhaps the most complex and confusing focus dimension is that of cultural/environmental/contextual issues. Some topics within those broad areas are listed below, along with possible responses to the client.

▲ Moral/religious issues: "What is your church's position on abortion?"
▲ Legal issues: "Abortion is illegal in this state. How have you dealt with the issue?"
▲ Women's issues: "A support group for women concerned with abortion is just starting. Would you like to attend?"
▲ Economic issues: "You were saying you didn't know how to pay for the operation . . . "
▲ Health issues: "How have you been eating and sleeping lately? Do you feel after-effects?"
▲ Educational/career issues: "How long were you out of school/work?"
▲ Ethnic/cultural issues: "What is the meaning of abortion among people in your family/church/neighborhood?"

Any one of these issues, plus many others, could be important to any client. With some clients all of these areas might need to be explored for satisfactory problem resolution. The counselor or interviewer who is able to conceptualize a client problem broadly can introduce many valuable aspects of the problem or situation. Note that much of cultural/environmental/contextual focusing depends on the interviewer bringing in concepts from his or her own knowledge and not simply following ideas presented by the client.

It would now be useful for you to write responses to the following individuals' statements, using a variety of focus possibilities. Note that the cultural/environmental/contextual focus has been presented first. It is helpful for the counselor or interviewer to be aware of many of these issues before responding—and while responding—to the client at other levels.

"I'm having a terrible time with Sam. He's fouling up the whole department. Like last week he got confused over budgets and cost us plenty! I know he's the boss's favorite and had a good record before he came here, but he's no hot shot. He just gives me a pain. I wish I were rid of him."

Brainstorm the many possible cultural/environmental/contextual issues that might be related to this problem:

_____

_____

_____

_____

_____

_____

_____

_____

_____

_____

_____

Now write several alternative counselor statements that focus the problem in different ways:

Client: _____

_____

Problem/main theme: _____

_____

Others: _____

_____

Mutual or group: _____

_____

Interviewer: _____

_____

Cultural/environmental/contextual: _____

_____

Box 9-2.   Key Points

Why?	Client problems and issues have many dimensions. It is tempting to accept problems as presented and oversimplify the complexity of life. Focusing helps interviewer and client develop an awareness of the many factors related to an issue as well as to organize thinking. Focusing can help a confused client zero in on important dimensions. Thus, focusing can be used to either open or tighten discussion.
What?	There are six types of focuses. The one you select determines what the client is likely to talk about next, but each offers considerable room for further examination of client issues. As a counselor or interviewer, you may do the following:

▲ *Focus on the client:* "Bill, you were saying last time that *you* are concerned about *your* future . . . "

▲ *Focus on the main theme or problem:* "Tell me more about your *getting fired.* What happened?"

▲ *Focus on others:* "So *Howard Jones* and you didn't get along. I'd like to know a little more about Howard . . . "

▲ *Focus on mutual issues or group:* "*We* will work on this. How can *you and I (our group)* work together most effectively?"

▲ *Focus on interviewer:* "*My* experience with Howard was . . . "

▲ *Focus on cultural/environmental context:* "It's a time of *high unemployment.* Given that, what types of jobs in the *economy* appeal to you?"

How?	Focusing is consciously added to the basic microskills of attending, questioning, paraphrasing, and so on. Careful observation of clients will lead to the most appropriate focus. In assessment and problem definition it is often helpful to consciously and deliberately assist the client to explore issues by focusing on all dimensions, one at a time.
With whom?	Focusing will be useful with all clients. With most North American clients the goal is often to help them focus on themselves (client focus), but with many other people, particularly those of a Southern European or Asian background, the "we" focus may be more appropriate. The goal of much North American counseling and therapy is individual self-actualization, whereas among other cultures it may be the development of harmony with others. Deliberate focusing is especially helpful in problem definition and assessment, in which clients are assisted to see the full complexity of their problem. Moving from focus to focus can help increase your clients' cognitive complexity and their awareness of the many interconnecting issues in making important decisions. With some clients who may be scattered in their thinking, a unitary focus may be wise.
And?	Focus is most often multiple. It is helpful to look at an individual, the problem, and the main theme. Cultural issues may undergird the resolution. Thus, counseling leads with multiple focuses are appropriate.

▲ Practice Exercises and Self-Assessment

This chapter has presented several practice exercises within the instructional reading; therefore, the number of exercises in this section will be reduced to two, followed by the usual "Self-Assessment and Follow-Up" section.

Individual Practice

Exercise 1. Writing alternative focus statements

A 35-year-old client comes to you to talk about an impending divorce hearing. He says the following:

"I'm really lost right now. I can't get along with Eleanor. I miss the kids terribly. My lawyer is demanding an arm and a leg for his fee, and I don't feel I can trust him. I resent what has happened over the years, and my work with a men's consciousness-raising group has clarified things for me, but only partially. How can I get through the next two weeks?"

Fill in the client's main issue as you see it and complete the blanks for the several alternative focus categories in the spaces that follow. Be sure to brainstorm a number of cultural/environmental/contextual situations; refer to page 209 to help you develop that list.

Main issue as presented: _____

_____

_____

_____

Client focus: _____

_____

Problem/main theme focus: _____

_____

Others focus: _____

_____

Mutual, group, "we" focus: _____

_____

Interviewer focus: _____

_____

_____

Cultural/environmental/contextual focus: _____

_____

Now write below alternative focus statements, as indicated.

Reflection of feeling focusing on the client:

_____

_____

Open question focusing on the problem/main theme:

_____

_____

Closed question focusing on others:

_____

_____

Reassurance statement focusing on "we":

_____

_____

Self-disclosure statement focusing on yourself, the interviewer:

_____

_____

Paraphrase focusing on a cultural/environmental/contextual issue:

_____

_____

An imaginary summary (assuming a longer interview) in which you demonstrate a mixed focus, with all six types in one summary:

_____

_____

_____

_____

_____

_____

Systematic Group Practice

Step 1. Divide into groups.

Step 2. Select a group leader.

Step 3. Assign roles for the first practice session.

▲ Role-played client
▲ Interviewer
▲ Observer 1, who will give special attention to focus of the client
▲ Observer 2, who will give special attention to focus of the interviewer

Step 4. Planning.   Establish clear goals for the session. The task of the interviewer in this case is to go through all six types of focus, systematically outlining the client's issue. If the task is completed successfully, a broader outline of issues related to the client's concern should be available.

A most useful topic for this role-play is a decision you have to make. This could range from a vocational decision to a problem on the job to a family decision such as a vacation or large purchase. At this point in group practice, real personal issues may be discussed. However, it is still possible to role-play a friend or some other situation that you know well.

Observers should take this time to examine the feedback sheet and plan their own interviews.

Step 5. Conduct a 5-minute practice session using the focusing skill.

Step 6. Review the practice session and provide feedback for 10 minutes.
Give special attention to the interviewer's achievement of goals and determine the mastery competencies demonstrated.

Step 7. Rotate roles.

Some general reminders.   Be sure to cover all types of focus; many practice sessions explore only the first three. In some practice sessions three members of the group all talk with the same client, and each interviewer uses a different focus.

Focus Feedback Sheet

_____ (Date)

_____   _____
(Name of Interviewer)   (Name of Person Completing Form)

Instructions: Observer 1 will give special attention to the client and Observer 2 to the interviewer. Note the correspondence between interviewer and client statements. In the space provided, record the main words used. Classify each statement by checking a box.

Main words	Client						Interviewer					
	Client (self)	Main theme/problem	Others	Mutual/group/"we"	Interviewer	Cultural/environmental/contextual	Client	Main theme/problem	Others	Mutual/group/"we"	Interviewer (self)	Cultural/environmental/contextual
1. _____												
2. _____												
3. _____												
4. _____												
5. _____												
6. _____												
7. _____												
8. _____												
9. _____												
10. _____												
11. _____												
12. _____												
13. _____												
14. _____												

(continued)

Focus Feedback Sheet (continued)

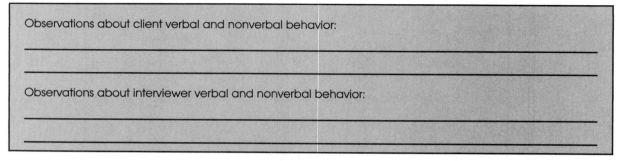

Observations about client verbal and nonverbal behavior:

_____

_____

Observations about interviewer verbal and nonverbal behavior:

_____

_____

Self-Assessment and Follow-Up

1. The interviewer's ability to focus the session in many different ways offers considerable possibilities for controlling and managing the session.

This control can be used to help clients be sure they explore many broad issues relating to their concerns. At the same time, the question of control raises important professional and ethical issues in interviewing practice. Important among these is who should be responsible for the direction of the interview. Some argue that focusing makes an implicit issue more explicit and frees the interviewer to help the client even more. Others argue that any form of control in the interview should be avoided. What is your position on this important issue?

_____

_____

_____

2. Mastery of focusing skills

What specific competencies have you mastered with regard to focusing? At what level? Use the following categories to assess your understanding and skills. Give evidence of your mastery level in the space provided or via supplementary materials such as video- or audiotapes.

Identification. You will be able to identify six types of focus as they are demonstrated by interviewers and clients. You will note their impact on the conversational flow of the interview.

_____   Ability to identify focus statements of the interviewer.

_____

_____

_____ Ability to note the impact of focus statements in terms of client conversational flow.

_____

_____

_____ Ability to write alternative focus responses to a single client statement.

_____

_____

Basic mastery. You will be able to use the six focus types in a role-played interview and in your daily life.

_____ Ability to demonstrate use of focus types in a role-played interview.

_____

_____

_____ Ability to use focusing in daily life situations.

_____

_____

Active mastery. You will be able to use the six types of focus in the interview, and clients will change the direction of their conversation as you change focus. You will also be able to maintain the same focus as your client, if you choose (that is, no topic jumping). You will be able to combine this skill with earlier skills in this program (such as reflection of feeling and questioning) and use each skill with alternative focuses.

Check below those skills you have mastered and provide evidence via actual interview documentation (transcripts, tapes, and so on).

_____ My clients change the direction of their conversation as I change focus.
_____ I maintain the same focus as my clients.
_____ During the interview I can observe focus changes in the client's conversation and change the focus back to the original one if it is beneficial to the client.
_____ I can combine this skill with skills learned earlier. Particularly, I can use focusing together with confrontation to expand client development.
_____ I am able to use multiple-focus strategies for complex issues facing a client.

Teaching mastery. I am able to teach focusing to clients and other persons. The impact of teaching is measured by the achievement of students, given the above criteria.

_____

_____

3. Given the many possibilities for further mastery of this skill as outlined above, what single goal might you set for yourself at this point?

_____

_____

_____

_____

_____

10 Eliciting and Reflecting Meaning: Helping Clients Explore Values and Beliefs[1]

How can reflection of meaning help you and your clients?

Major function

Two people may both have had a vacation on the beach. But whereas one talks about the glorious sun and the wonderful experience, the second talks about the sunburn and the problems that occurred. They have experienced the same event, but it *means* something different to each of them. A couple making love experience the same overt behavioral phenomenon. But internally, at the meaning level, to one person the act means a reaffirmation of commitment while to the other it signals time to break off, as the relationship is getting too close.

Reflection of meaning is concerned with finding the deeply held thoughts and feelings (meanings) underlying life experience. If you use reflection of meaning, you may expect clients to search into deeper aspects of their life experience.

Secondary functions

Knowledge and skill in reflection of meaning result in the following:

▲ Facilitating clients' interpretation of their own experiences. Reflection of feeling and the skill of interpretation are closely related to this skill. However, clients can use reflection of meaning to interpret for themselves what their experience means.
▲ Assisting clients to explore their values and goals in life.
▲ Understanding deeper aspects of client experience.

▲ Introduction

He who has a why *to live can bear with almost any* how.

Nietzsche

Consider the following statement: "I just got divorced, and I have plenty to do." What does this statement mean? The words are clear and explicit, but different people saying those same words may have very different meanings. For example, for client A this means feelings of guilt and the need to restructure life through psychotherapy; for client B it means anger and the need for revenge; for client C it means that new housing must be found and new child-care arrangements developed for simple survival; and for client D it may mean a turn to a more

---

[1] Conversations with Otto Payton of the Medical College of Virginia were important in the development of this skill for the microtraining framework. The initial stimulus came from a meeting in the summer of 1979 with Viktor Frankl, whose logotherapy offers a critical and central ingredient missing from much current theory. This chapter is dedicated to Viktor Frankl.

playful, hedonistic life. The same words mean different things to different people. Our task in this chapter is to learn how to assist clients in finding the meanings that underlie their feelings, thoughts, and actions.

Meaning may be described as the "motor" of human development, a key motivating agent. While all four clients above need to solve the overt, explicit problem of divorce, their routes toward problem solution will vary because each one has a different underlying structure of meaning impelling behavior. Your task in using the skill of reflection of meaning is to cut through the surface statements and find the underlying meaning structure. Knowing and clarifying deeply felt meanings can change many overt behaviors simultaneously, for meaning and purpose may be described as very basic to human experience.

Two levels of speech and action may be identified. Thus far, we have been working primarily with *explicit*, observable levels. Attending, questioning, encouraging, paraphrasing, and summarizing all focus on reacting specifically to what a client says and does. In using reflection of feeling it is necessary to distinguish the concepts of implicit and explicit feelings. We know that our feelings may sometimes run deeper than our own awareness of them. As deep as, and sometimes deeper than, feelings run meanings, which provide basic organizing constructs for our lives. The skill of noting and reflecting meaning often operates at an *implicit* level.

It is important, at this point, to consider the relationship of reflection of meaning to other skills, such as paraphrasing and encouraging. Figure 10-1 provides a pictorial representation of meaning and its relation to behaviors, thoughts, and feelings. The following points are important in relating the figure and its concepts to your own practice.

1. All four dimensions are operating simultaneously and constantly in any individual or group. We are systems, and any change in one part of the system affects the total.

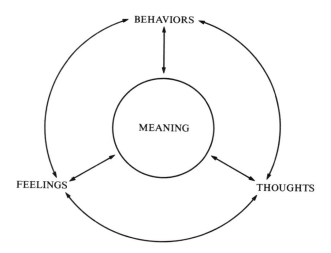

Figure 10-1. Pictorial representation of the relations among behaviors, thoughts, feelings, and meaning

2. As a rough rule, paraphrases speak to thoughts, reflections of feelings to feelings, attending behavior and client observation to behaviors, and reflection of meaning to meaning. Additionally, different helping methods and theories view different areas of the model as most important.

3. In using these skills, we attempt to break down the complex behavior of the client into component parts. It is possible that attacking only one dimension (for instance, thoughts through paraphrasing) will lead to a change in client behavior, which in turn affects changes in feelings and meaning. *A change in any one part of the system may result in a change in other parts as well.* Even though, for practical purposes, we divide the client and the counseling interview into component parts, we cannot escape the interaction of those parts.

4. For many clients meaning is the central issue, and it is here that the most profound change may occur. For other clients, however, change in thoughts (rational-emotive therapy, cognitive-behavior modification) may be most helpful. Still others may change behavior (behavior modification, reality therapy) or work on feelings (Rogerian, encounter therapy). Meaning-oriented therapies include psychoanalysis, logotherapy, and certain types of cognitive-behavior modification.

5. A multimodal approach (Lazarus, 1976) may involve using all the skills and concepts in an effort to maximize change and personal growth.

To obtain some sense of the distinctions among the several concepts, let us review them in terms of the experience of divorce:

▲ *Behaviorally,* the person undergoing divorce is doing many things. He or she is consulting with a lawyer, perhaps arguing with the spouse on the telephone, finding new housing, *doing* many things. You will find the words *do, doing,* and *acting* characteristic of the behavioral mode.

▲ *Feelings* are the emotions occurring in the individual while he or she is acting. For example, the client engaging in the behavior of finding new housing may feel sad, angry, or glad—perhaps all three and more. The words *emotion, affect,* and *feelings* and the many feeling words you generated in Chapter 6 exemplified this mode.

▲ *Thoughts* are internal messages occurring in the person's mind that occur simultaneously with the behavior and feeling. For example, the client searching for a house may have many different thoughts constantly running through his or her mind: "I'm guilty, I shouldn't have had that affair" or "How can I afford decent housing?" or "I wonder what the kids are doing now?" or even "I'm a bad person." Many such almost random thoughts run through our minds constantly as we go through our daily routines. Sometimes a client gets stuck on one repeating type of destructive thought pattern (for example, "I'm a bad person"). In such cases, cognitive techniques such as thought-stopping can be useful.

▲ *Meaning* is closely allied to feelings and thoughts and may be considered an important driving force of behavior. However, the meaning level represents a clustering or grouping of thoughts and feelings into a more coherent whole. Meanings may be described as the underlying, major constructs that we use to organize our experience: our thoughts, feelings, and behavior. Meaning is manifested by more overt and directly observable thoughts, feelings, and behavior. Key words associated with meaning are *values, beliefs, unconscious motivators* (things that impel our behavior, of which we are not presently aware), and *making sense of things*.

The world around us is often complex and confusing. We process the data of the world (for instance, what divorce means to us) through our auditory, visual, and kinesthetic patterns. Some of those patterns of organization come from society and culture, others come from parents and close friends, and some are totally unique to us. Some theorists suggest we use a form of *inner speech* in which we "talk" to ourselves and make sense of things. All of us seem to have some system of ordering meaning, concepts, and judgments, but with varying degrees of clarity.

Counseling can help individuals clarify underlying meanings. It is, of course, helpful to assist a client explore a divorce or the death of a significant person through questioning, paraphrasing, and reflecting feeling. But the thoughts and feelings are not usually worked through until they are organized into some meaningful value pattern, which often provides *reasons* for what happened. "Death, I guess, is part of life." "I can't help missing him, but at least I know he's in heaven." "I guess my extreme reaction is partly because I feel guilty and afraid of dying myself." These are just three examples of organized meaning systems' responses to the idea of death.

Noting and reflecting meaning may at times be a difficult skill, yet, used sparingly and effectively, it can help clients find themselves and their direction more clearly.

In practice, the eliciting and reflection of meaning looks and sounds very much like questioning, a reflection of feeling, or a paraphrase. However, it is distinctly different in tone or purpose. You will often find the reflection of meaning following a "meaning probe" or question ("What does that mean to you?") or an encourager focusing on an important single key word ("Divorce . . . "). The reflection of meaning is structured like the reflection of feeling with the exception that "You feel . . . " becomes "You mean. . . . " The reflection of meaning then paraphrases the important ideas of meaning expressed by the client. The skill is particularly important in cognitive-behavior modification, existential approaches to counseling, and logotherapy. The following transcript illustrates the skill in action.

▲ Example Interview

In the following interview the client is talking about his feelings about a past divorce.

Jay: So, Carl, you're thinking about the divorce again . . . (encourager-restatement)

Carl: Yeah, that divorce has really thrown me for a loop, I tell ya. I really cared a lot about Dolores and . . . ah . . . we got along well together. But there was something missing.

Jay: Uh-huh . . . something missing? (Single-word or short-phrase encourager. Note that clients often talk about what these words mean in more depth. Encouragers appear to be closely related to meaning, in many cases.)

Carl: Uh-huh, we just never really shared something very basic. You know . . . it was like the relationship didn't have enough depth to go anywhere. We liked each other, we amused one another, but beyond that . . . I don't know . . .

Jay: I think I can feel that. Uh . . . as I listen, there seem to be a lot of different things going on. What sense do you make of it? (A mild self-disclosure is followed by an open question searching for Carl's meaning in the situation.)

Carl: Well, in a way, it seems like the relationship was somewhat shallow. When we got married, there just wasn't much . . . ah . . . depth there that I had hoped for in a meaningful relationship.

Jay: Mm-hmmm . . . you seem to be talking in terms of shallow versus meaningful relationships. What does a meaningful relationship feel like to you? (Encourager followed by a reflection of meaning. Note that Carl's personal constructs for discussing his past relationship center on the word *shallow* and the contrast *meaningful*. This polarity is probably one of Carl's significant meanings around which he organizes much of his experience. The open question is designed to further the exploration of meaning.)

Carl: Well, I guess . . . ah . . . that's a good question. I guess for me, in order to be married, there has to be some real, you know, some real caring beyond just on a daily basis. It has to be something that goes right to the soul. You know, you're really connected to your partner in a very powerful way.

Jay: So, connections, soul, deeper aspects strike you as really important. (Reflection of meaning. Note that this reflection is also very close to a paraphrase, and Jay uses Carl's *main words*. The distinction centers around issues of meaning. A reflection of meaning could be described as a special type of paraphrase.)

Carl: That's right. If I'm married to somebody, I have to be more than just a roommate. There has to be some reason for me to really want to stay married, and I think with her . . . ah . . . those connections and that depth were missing, and we didn't miss each other that much. We liked each other, you know, but when one of us was gone, it just didn't seem to matter whether we were here or there.

Jay: So there are some really good feelings about a relationship that is meaningful even when the other person is gone. That relationship didn't have that. It didn't have those values for you. (Reflection of meaning plus some reflection of feeling. Note that Jay has added the word *values* to the discussion. In reflection of meaning it is likely that the counselor or interviewer will add words such as *meaning, understanding, sense,* and *values*. Such words seem to produce a very different discussion and lead the client to interpret experience from her or his own frame of reference. A reflection of meaning comes from the client's frame of reference. An interpretation is derived from the counselor's frame of reference or theoretical ideology.)

Carl: Uh-huh.

Jay: Ah . . . could you fantasize how you might play out those thoughts, feelings, and meanings in another relationship (open question oriented to meaning)

Carl: Well, I guess it's important for me to have some independence from a person, but I'd like that independence such that, when we were apart, we'd still be thinking of the other one.

Jay: Um-humm.

Carl: In other words, I don't want a relationship in which we are always tagging along together. You know, the extreme of that is where you don't care enough whether you are together or not. That isn't intimate enough. I guess what it boils down to is that I really want the intimacy in a marriage. My fantasy is to have a very independent partner whom I care very much about and who cares very much about me, and we can both live our lives and be individuals and have that bonding and that connectedness.

Jay: Let's see if I can put together what you're saying. The key words seem to be independent with intimacy and caring. It's those concepts that can produce bonding and connectedness, as you say, whether you are together or not.

Comment: This reflection of meaning becomes almost a summarization of meaning. Note that the key words and constructs have come from the client in response to questions about meaning and value. A logical place to move from this point is to further exploration of meaning or, more specifically, to actions in life the client could take to actualize these deeply felt meanings. The counseling would seek to bring behavior into accord with thoughts. Current relationships could be explored for how well they achieve the client's important meanings as well as for behaviors that illustrate or do not illustrate the meaning in action. Meaning often operates at a deep level and determines what people think and do. Incongruities and discrepancies between meanings and actions can be very troublesome to many clients. Further, meanings themselves can conflict within the client's world.

▲ Instructional Reading

The most direct way to determine what a situation or a relationship means to a client is to ask a question. Skilled questioning can uncover underlying, implicit meanings. To elicit meaning and start the more self-analytic and reflective process of meaning making, three key elements must be present:

1. The behaviors, thoughts, and feelings need to have been made explicit and clear through attending behavior, client observation, and the BLS. A general understanding of the client is essential as a first step.

2. Questions where content is oriented toward meaning may be asked. For example:

"What does this *mean* to you?"
"What *sense* do you make of it?"
"What *values* underlie your actions?"

"*Why is that important* (or unimportant) to you?"

"Could you give me examples of some *values that are important in your life decisions*? How have those *values been implemented* in your life?"

"What are some of the *reasons* you think that happened?"

"Which of your *personal values* support/oppose that behavior/thought/feeling?"

"*Why?*" (by itself, used carefully)

3. A reflection of meaning in which the key meaning and value words of the client are reflected. It is very important to use the exact, key words of the client for the major ideas. Your task is reflecting meaning, values, and the way a client makes sense of the world. It is his or her own unique system—not yours. A reflection of meaning is structured similarly to a paraphrase or reflection of feeling (see the examples below).

Once the implicit meaning is brought forward, it is relatively easy to reflect meaning. Simply change "You feel . . . " to "You mean. . . . " Other variations could include "You value . . . ," "You care . . . ," "Your reasons are . . . ," or "Your intention was. . . . " Distinguishing between a reflection of meaning and a paraphrase or reflection of feeling may at times be most difficult. Often the skilled counselor will blend the three skills together. For practice, however, it is useful to separate out meaning responses and develop an understanding of their import and power in the interview. Noting the key words that relate to meaning (*meaning, value, reasons, intent, cause,* and the like) will help distinguish reflection of meaning from other skills.

Reflection of meaning becomes vastly more complicated when meanings or values conflict. Just as clients may express mixed and confused feelings about an issue, so may explicitly or implicitly conflicting values underlie their statements. A client may feel forced to choose between loyalty to family and loyalty to spouse, for instance. Underlying meanings of love for both parties may be complicated by a value of dependence fostered by the family and the independence represented by the spouse. In making a decision, it may be more important for the client to sort out these felt meaning constructs than the more overt facts and feelings associated with the decision.

For example, a young person may be experiencing a value conflict over vocational choice. The facts may be paraphrased accurately and the feelings about each choice duly noted, yet the underlying *meaning* of the choice may be most important. The counselor can ask "What does each choice mean for you? What do you make of each?" The client's answers provide the opportunity for the counselor to reflect back the meaning, eventually leading to a decision that not only involves facts and feelings but also values and meaning.

Reflection of meaning and interpretation. Reflection of meaning may be confused with interpretation, an advanced skill of interpersonal influence. In an interpretation the counselor supplies the client with a new frame of reference or understanding. The words and meanings may be elicited from the client, but they are the counselor's impressions. Reflection of meaning, by contrast, focuses on the client's frame of reference, even if the meanings and values are unclear. Through questioning and reflection, clients search for deeper ideas underlying their statements and behaviors and learn to reinterpret their experience from their own frame of reference.

Now that we have defined reflection of meaning, the remainder of this instructional reading will focus on the place of this skill in different theoretical frameworks. Many counseling and therapy theories give attention to issues of meaning. The following are a few examples of how this skill undergirds the helping process.

Reflection of Meaning and Logotherapy

If one person were to be identified with meaning and the therapeutic process, that individual would have to be Viktor Frankl, the originator of logotherapy. Frankl (1959) has pointed out the importance of a life philosophy that enables us to transcend suffering and find meaning in our existence; he argues that our greatest human need is for a core of meaning and purpose in life.

Logotherapists search for meaning underlying behavior and action. Dereflection and modification of underlying attitudes are specific techniques that logotherapy uses to uncover meaning. Many clients "hyperreflect" (think about something too much) on the negative meaning of events in their lives and may overeat, drink to excess, or wallow in depression. They are constantly attributing a negative meaning to life. The direct reflection of meaning may encourage such clients to continue these negative thoughts and behavior patterns. Dereflection, by contrast, seeks to help clients discover "the multitude of values that lie beyond their own weak selves" (Lukas, 1980, p. 30). The goal is to help clients think of things *other* than the negative issue and to find alternative positive meaning in the same event. The questions listed at the beginning of "Instructional Reading" represent first steps to help clients dereflect and change their attitudes. The following abbreviated example illustrates this approach.

Client: I just can't stop abusing my child. I feel helpless.

Counselor: I understand that; we've talked about it in some detail. Could you explore with me for awhile some of the things you have valued and enjoyed in the past? Or that you still like even now?

(Client and counselor explore via reflection of feeling and questions a range of activities that have been satisfying. The counselor particularly attends to positive values during the process.)

Counselor: (reflecting meaning) So what is truly most meaningful to you is having some time to be yourself and to be alone. You seem to have found that you can feel best and can come out and be with others if you have time to explore what is most important to you. Let's carry that on further.

The dereflection process has only begun, but positive steps have been initiated. At issue here is finding something positive in a negative situation. This does not deny the negative aspects but seeks to find something positive in each individual from which a more positive approach to the problem may be developed. At a later point the issue of child abuse may be approached once again with a positive action plan. (A modified exercise in dereflection may be found in the Exercises at the end of this chapter.)

Reflection of Meaning and Person-Centered Therapy

Carl Rogers's person-centered therapy (Rogers, 1961) is often characterized as predominantly paraphrasing and reflection of feeling, at least in the early stages. However, *meaning* plays perhaps an even more important part in his overall thinking and conceptualization. The following brief excerpt illustrates how the use of reflection of meaning and reflection of feeling are closely intertwined:

Client: . . . I have all the symptoms of the fear.

Therapist: Fear is a very scary thing. Is that what you mean? (Note reflection of feeling, followed by a meaning check-out.)

Client: Mm-hm. (long pause)

Therapist: Do you want to say any more about what you mean by that? That it really does give you symptoms of fear?

This pattern of encouraging, listening to the client, and searching for deeper meanings is quite similar to the reflection of meaning discussed in this chapter. Reflection of feeling, by contrast, would work more directly with the emotions themselves. Meaning is a deeper concept and area for talk.

Reflection of Meaning and Cognitive-Behavioral Approaches

Cognitive-behavior therapy (Beck, 1976; Meichenbaum, 1977) has become an important area for the practice of counseling. Cognitive-behavioral theorists talk in depth about cognitive structures and internal dialogue. They are interested in overt behavior, but also want to explore the underlying processes (or "inner speech") that monitor and guide more observable behavior.

The typical cognitive-behavioral approach directs clients to specific activities to change or alter thought sequences and meaning—for example, thought-stopping, guided imagery, implosion, and other techniques. Moreover, cognitive-behavioral therapists add an additional armament of influencing skills and strategies to their work. They seek to move clients more rapidly into new patterns of cognition and meaning.

Counselor: So the reason you gamble is to avoid your own deeper feelings of self-doubt and worthlessness? Your inner speech and repeating statements to yourself seem to be "I'm no good; I'm worthless." Right?

Client: Yeah, those ideas keep running through my mind. The excitement of the race track helps me forget . . . for awhile . . .

Counselor: Stay with that feeling now. . . . Magnify that feeling of worthlessness . . . think about it. What comes to your mind?

Client:	My father . . . he always said I'd turn out worthless. I guess he was right.
Counselor:	He was right? Who's living your life—you or your father? Whose thoughts are you living?
Client:	I guess I'm living up to his expectations.
Counselor:	Down to his expectations, you mean—what self-image do you want? Right now, say to yourself, "This is my life . . . my decision. . . . "

This is but one example of the many techniques a directive cognitive-behaviorist might use to facilitate a client's change of meaning. At issue is finding the underlying thought and meaning structures that motivate life experience and then actively changing them to more positive frames of reference. The cognitive-behaviorist does not just reflect meaning, but actively works to help clients find more useful, positive meanings in their lives.

▲ Summary

Eliciting and reflecting meaning is a complex skill that requires you to enter the sense-making system of the client. Full exploration of life meaning requires a self-directed, verbal client (Developmental Level 3). The skill complex is most often associated with a client-directed, formal operations interviewing style. However, all of us are engaged in the process of meaning making and trying to make sense of a confusing world. With clients who are at preoperational and concrete operational levels, you will still find that eliciting and reflecting meaning is useful. However, these clients will not be able to see patterns in their thinking or be as self-directed and reflective as those who think at a more complex level. You may find that the more directive approach to meaning taken by the cognitive-behavioral orientation is more useful with this group.

Meanings are organizing constructs that are at the core of our being. You will find that exercises with this skill, if completed in depth, will result in a more comprehensive understanding of your client than is possible with most other skills. Mastering the art of understanding meaning will take more time than other skills. The exercises in this chapter are designed to assist you along the path toward this goal.

Box 10-1.   Key Points

Why?	Meaning organizes life experience and often serves as a metaphor from which clients generate words, sentences, and behaviors. Clients faced with complex life decisions may make them on the basis of meaning, values, and reasons rather than on objective facts or on feelings. However, these meanings and values are often unclear to the client.

(continued)

Box 10-1 (continued)

What?	Meanings may be identified through noting and observing client words and constructs that describe their values and attitudes toward important issues and people. As meaning is often implicit, it is helpful to ask questions that help clients explore and clarify meaning. For example:

"What does this *mean* to you?"
"What *sense* do you make of it?"
"What *values* underlie your actions?"
"*Why* is that important to you?"
"*Why?*" (by itself, used carefully)
"What was your *intention* when you did that?"

How?   Meanings are reflected through the following process:

1. Beginning with a sentence stem like the following: "You mean . . . ," "Could it mean that you . . . ," "Sounds like you value . . . ," or "One of the underlying reasons/intentions of your actions was. . . ."
2. Using the client's own words that describe the most important aspect of the meaning. This helps ensure that you stay within the client's frame of reference rather than using your own interpretation.
3. Adding a paraphrase of the client's longer statements that captures the essence of what has been said but, again, operates primarily from the client's frame of reference.
4. Closing with a check-out such as "Is that close?" or "Am I hearing you correctly?" may be helpful.

Meanings may be more complex in situations in which two values or two meanings collide. The use of questions, reflection of feelings, and so on may be required to help clients sort through meaning and value conflicts.

With whom?   Reflections of meaning are generally for more verbal clients and may be found more in counseling and therapy than in general interviewing. It is a temptation to reflect negative meanings back to troubled clients—the task with such clients, however, is to help them find positive meanings. This may be done through questioning about situations in the client's past in which positive feelings existed and searching there for meanings that may be contrasted with the negative view. There may be no positive meaning immediately apparent, especially for a victim of trauma. (But the simple fact of *survival* is positive meaning.) A well-timed reflection of meaning may help many clients facing extreme difficulty. It can help clarify cultural and individual differences, *if* the client is willing to share them.

And?   Reflection of meaning is a skill basic to logotherapy and person-centered therapy and is an alternative that may be useful in cognitive-behavioral counseling. The skill has implications for other theories as well.

▲ Practice Exercises and Self-Assessment

The concepts of this chapter build on previous work. If you have solid attending and client observation skills, can use questions effectively, and demonstrate effective use of the encourager, paraphrase, and reflection of feeling, you are well prepared for the exercises that follow.

Individual Practice

Exercise 1. Identification of skills

Read the client statement below. Which of the following counselor responses are paraphrases (P), reflections of feeling (RF), or reflections of meaning (RM)?

"I feel very sad and lonely. I thought Bill was the one for me. . . . After my divorce I saw a lot of people, but no one special. Bill seemed to care for me and make it easy for me. Before that I had fun, particularly with Bob. But it seemed at the end to be just foolish, alienated sex. It appears Bill was it; we seemed so close."

——————— "You're really hurting and feeling sad right now."

——————— "Since the divorce you've seen a lot of people, but Bill provided the most of what you wanted."

——————— "Looks like the sense of peace, caring, ease, and closeness meant an awful lot to you."

——————— "You felt really close to Bill and now are sad and lonely."

——————— "Peace, caring, a special one mean a lot to you. Bill represented that to you. Bob seemed to mean mainly fun, but it ended up with feelings of alienation. Is that right?"

List possible single-word encouragers for the same client statement in the space below. You will find that the use of single-word encouragers, perhaps more than any other skill, leads your client to talk more deeply about the unique meanings underlying behavior and thought. A good general rule is to search carefully for key words, repeat them back, and *then* reflect meaning.

——————————————————   ——————————————————

——————————————————   ——————————————————

——————————————————   ——————————————————

——————————————————   ——————————————————

Exercise 2. Identifying client issues of meaning

Affective words in the preceding client statement include *sad* and *lonely*. Some other words and brief phrases in the client statement contain elements that suggest more may be found under the surface. The following are some key words that you may have listed under possible encouragers: *the one for me, care for me, easy for me, I had fun, foolish, alienated sex,* and *we seemed close.* The feeling words represent the client's emotions about the current situation; the other words represent the meanings she uses to represent the world. Specifically, the client has given us a map of how she constructs the world of her relationships with men.

To identify underlying meanings for yourself, talk with a client, or someone posing as a client, observing his or her key words—especially those that tend to be repeated in different situations. Use those key words as the basis of encouragers, paraphrasing, and questioning to elicit meaning. Needless to say, this should be done with considerable sensitivity to the "client" and his or her needs. Record the results of your experience with this important exercise here. You will want to record *patterns* of meaning making that seem to be basic and that may motivate many more surface behaviors, thoughts, and feelings.

Exercise 3. Questioning to elicit meanings

Assume a client comes to you and talks about an important issue in her or his life (for instance, divorce, death, retirement, a pregnant daughter). List five questions that might be useful in bringing out the meaning of the event.

1. _____

2. _____

3. _____

4. _____

5. _____

Exercise 4. Observation

Use the Feedback Sheet after the "Systematic Group Practice" to observe meaning issues as they are explored in a role-played or real interview. Another alternative is viewing a skilled talk-show host on TV and recording your observations on the Feedback Sheet.

Exercise 5. Practice of skills in other settings

During conversations with friends or in your own interviews, practice eliciting meaning through a combination of questioning and single-word encouragers, and then reflect the meaning back. You will often find that single-word encouragers lead people to talk about meaningful issues. Record your observations of the value of this practice here. What one thing stands out from your experience?

_____

_____

_____

_____

_____

_____

_____

_____

_____

Systematic Group Practice

Two group exercises are suggested here. The first focuses on the skill of eliciting and reflecting meaning, the second on the dereflection process as it might be used in logotherapy.

Exercise 1. Systematic group practice in eliciting and reflecting meaning

Step 1. Divide into practice groups.

Step 2. Select a group leader.

Step 3. Assign roles for the first practice session.

▲ Role-played client
▲ Interviewer
▲ Observer 1, who observes client descriptive words and key repeated words
▲ Observer 2, who notes interviewer behavior

Step 4. Planning.   For practice with this skill, it will be most helpful if the interview starts with the client completing one of the following model sentences. The interview will then follow along, exploring the attitudes, values, and meanings to the client underlying the sentence.

"My thoughts about divorce are . . . "
"My thoughts about death are . . . "
"My thoughts about moving from this area to another are . . . "
"The most important event of my life was . . . "

A few alternative topics are "My closest friend," "Someone who made me feel very angry (or happy)," and "A place where I feel very comfortable and happy." Again, a decision conflict or a conflict with another person may be a good topic.

Establish the goals for the practice session. The task of the interviewer in this case is to elicit meaning from the model sentence and help the role-played client find underlying meanings and values. The interviewer should search for key words in the client response and use those key words in questioning, encouraging, and reflection. A useful sequence of microskills for eliciting meaning from the model sentence is (1) the open question "Could you tell me more about that?"; (2) encouragers and paraphrases focusing on key words to help the client continue; (3) reflections of feeling to ensure that you are in touch with the client's emotions; (4) questions that relate specifically to meaning (see Box 10-1); and (5) reflecting the meaning of the event back to the client, using the framework outlined in this chapter. It is quite acceptable to have key questions and this sequence in your lap to refer to during the practice session.

Examine the basic and active mastery competencies in the "Self-Assessment and Follow-Up" section and plan your interview to achieve specific goals.

Observers should study the feedback sheet especially carefully.

Step 5.   Conduct a 5-minute practice session using the skill.

Step 6.   Review the practice session and provide feedback for 10 minutes.

The feedback forms are useful. It is often tempting to just talk, but you might forget to give the interviewer helpful and needed specific feedback. Take time to complete the forms before talking about the session. As always, give special attention to the mastery level achieved by the interviewer.

Step 7.   Rotate roles.   Remember to share time equally.

Some general reminders.   This skill can be used from a variety of theoretical perspectives. It may be useful to see if an explicit or implicit theory is observable in the interviewer's behavior.

Exercise 2. Systematic group practice in dereflection and attitude change

Follow the same steps as for Exercise 1. This exercise is intended to remind you of the power and importance of finding positive dimensions and meaning in negative situations. Your central aim here is to prevent and balance the excessive attention given to the negatives in life experience by helping people find positive dimensions and strengths in difficult, troubling situations.

The task of the role played-client is to talk about something negative in his or her life. For example:

An illness
A death
Loss of job or inability to find work

An accident
A divorce or other significant loss
Betrayal by a friend

The first task of the interviewer is to draw out the person's negative experience through eliciting and reflecting meaning (as in Exercise 1). Then, however, the interviewer is to draw out a positive dimension of the experience via questioning; for example, in discussing an illness—"Could you talk about some positive experiences or something you learned at the hospital?" "What situations have you learned to value more as a result of that experience?" "What do you value even more now as a result?" These positive value statements may be reflected back to check on the accuracy of the interviewer's understanding.

As a final step, the interviewer may summarize the negative experience and the positive meaning statements and feed them both back to the client via a summarization. (For instance, "You seem to feel that being ill and near death was your worst fright ever, but at the same time you seem to value your relationships with your children and family even more now. Does that make sense to you?") In this way the positive and negative elements in the situation may be joined in a new synthesis. Some clients find this experience useful in reframing their view, and their process of hyperreflection on the negative is balanced by the positive dimensions. This can often lead to new actions and behaviors.

Summarize here your findings about the concept of dereflection (or use the Feedback Sheet).

There is another, alternative way to approach the above exercise. At times you will have clients who fail to see the negative in a situation; they may deny the reality of what has happened to them. This is particularly true of the victims of childhood abuse, spousal abuse, rape, and of those who have been held hostage. To maintain their sanity, these individuals have had to find *only* positive things in their universe; they deny the negative. Bringing out the negative meaning in such events can be therapeutic. However, you should be aware of the danger in this use of dereflection and attitude change and proceed with caution, with the direction and support of your staff and supervisor. Do not practice the negative dereflection discussed here until you have had considerable knowledge and experience both with the field and with your individual client.

Reflecting Meaning Feedback Sheet

_____ (Date)

_____   _____
(Name of Interviewer)   (Name of Person Completing Form)

Instructions: Observer 1 completes the first part of this form, giving special attention to recording descriptive words the client associates with _meaning_ and to key repeated words. In the second part, Observer 2 notes the interviewer's use of the reflection of meaning skill, giving special attention to questions that appeared to elicit meaning issues.

Part One: Client Observation

Key words/phrases:

_____

_____

_____

What are the main meaning issues of the interview?

Part Two: Interviewer Observation

List questions and reflections of meaning used by the interviewer, continuing on a separate sheet as needed.

1. _____

2. _____

3. _____

4. _____

5. _____

6. _____

Comment on the effectiveness of the reflection of meaning skill.

Self-Assessment and Follow-Up

1. What did this chapter mean to you?

What constructs and ideas stood out for you personally?

_____

_____

_____

_____

_____

_____

2. Words and phrases have been given real prominence in this chapter.

Are you able to match your interviewer style with the main key words and phrases of the client? Can you tell which words are yours and which are the client's? As the interview progresses, who gradually adopts the other's main words—you or the client?

_____

_____

_____

_____

_____

3. Mastery of eliciting and reflecting meaning skills

What specific competencies have you mastered in this area? Give evidence in the space provided, in transcripts, or with audio- or videotapes.

Identification.   You will be able to differentiate this skill from the closely related skills of paraphrasing and reflection of feeling. You will be able to identify questioning sequences that facilitate client talk about meaning. You will be able to identify client words indicative of meaning issues.

_____   Ability to identify and classify the skills.

_____

_____

_____   Ability to identify and write questions that elicit meaning from clients.

_____

_____

————— Ability to note and record key client words indicative of meaning.

_____

_____

Basic mastery. You will be able to demonstrate the skills of eliciting and reflecting meaning in the interview. You will be able to demonstrate an elementary skill in dereflection.

————— Ability to elicit and reflect meaning in a role-played interview.

_____

_____

————— Ability to use dereflection and attitude change in a role-played interview.

_____

_____

Active mastery. You will be able to use questioning skill sequences and encouragers to bring out meaning issues and then reflect meaning accurately. You will be able to use the client's main words and constructs to define meaning rather than reframing in your own words (interpretation). You will not interpret, but rather, facilitate the client's interpretation of experience.

————— Are you able to use questions and encouragers to bring out meaning issues?
————— When you reflect meaning, are you able to use the client's main words and constructs rather than your own?
————— Are you able to reflect meaning in such a fashion that the client starts exploring meaning and value issues in more depth?
————— As necessary in the interview, are you able to switch the focus in the conversation from meaning to feeling (via reflection of feeling or questions oriented toward feeling) or to content (via paraphrase or questions oriented toward content)?
————— When a person is hyperreflecting on the negative meaning of an event or person, are you able to find something positive in that person or event and enable the client to dereflect by focusing upon the positive?

Teaching mastery. You will be able to teach eliciting and reflecting meaning to others. Generally speaking, this is a skill that is only appropriate to teach relatively advanced counselors and therapists in training. However, discussion of meaning issues with clients and helping them understand cognitively the distinctions among behaviors, thoughts, feelings, and underlying meanings may be helpful. This may be part of a larger treatment program for the client in

which you gradually help the client understand what is underlying his or her life. In this way clients may learn how to interpret their own experiences, in effect, learning how to reflect and examine their own meanings.

4. What place do you give this skill in your repertoire of helping skills?

Is this a skill you will want to use? In what way?

_____

_____

_____

_____

_____

▲ References

Beck, A. (1976). *Cognitive therapy and emotional disorders.* New York: International Universities Press.

Frankl, V. (1959). *Man's search for meaning.* New York: Simon and Schuster.

Gendlin, E. (1979). Experiential psychotherapy. In R. Corsini (ed.), *Current psychotherapies.* Itasca, Ill.: F. E. Peacock.

Kelly, G. (1955). *The psychology of personal constructs* (Vols. 1 & 2). New York: Norton.

Lazarus, A. (1976). *Multimodal behavior therapy.* New York: Springer-Verlag.

Lukas, E. (1980). Modification of attitudes. *International Forum for Logotherapy, 3,* 25–35.

Meichenbaum, D. (1977). *Cognitive-behavior modification.* New York: Plenum.

Rogers, C. (1961). *On becoming a person.* Boston: Houghton Mifflin.

11 Influencing Skills and Strategies: Taking Action for Client Benefit

How can influencing skills help you and your clients?

Seven skill and strategy areas of interpersonal influence are summarized in this chapter. A working definition of each area, along with its major function in the interview, is given below.

Skill and Definition	Major Function
Directives. Indicates clearly to a client what actions the interviewer wishes the client to take	To assist a client in understanding a task and helping to ensure action
Logical consequences. Presents the probable results of a client action, either negative or positive	To make clients aware of the impact of their actions and to facilitate their making a choice for the future
Self-disclosure. Shares your own thoughts and feelings with the client	To facilitate client self-disclosure and provide useful models for behavior change
Feedback. Provides accurate data on how the counselor or others view the client	To facilitate self-exploration and self-examination using data on how others view the client
Interpretation/reframe. Provides the client with an alternative frame of reference from which to view life situations	To facilitate the client's ability to reframe life situations and view them from alternative perspectives
Influencing summary. Provides the client with a brief summary of what the interviewer has said or thought during a session	To enable the client to pull together, remember, and understand the interviewer's influencing statements
Information/advice/instruction/opinion/suggestion. Presents information and ideas of the interviewer to the client	To bring new points of view and information to the client's attention

▲ Introduction

The most basic dimension of effective counseling and interviewing involves hearing clients out, seeing their point of view, feeling their world as they expe-

rience it. The interviewing skills discussed so far, if used effectively, may be all that are needed to produce developmental growth and change, since the several skills of attending provide the base for all interviewing in this culture.

Listening and attending are not always sufficient, however. Clients are not always developmentally ready for interviews based solely on listening. To assume a more coaching/concrete operational counseling style and to facilitate many self-directed/formal operational clients in their self-exploration, you will find that the skills and strategies of interpersonal influence are useful adjuncts. This chapter summarizes the influencing skills and their place in the interview. It is not the function of this book to treat them in detail; that would require a book in itself (Ivey & Gluckstern, 1983). If you are competent in the listening skills of the earlier chapters, it may be possible to add some of the influencing skills to your interviewing practice.

Counseling and interviewing may be described as a process of interpersonal influence. Whether you use elementary attending skills, questions, or directives telling clients what to do, you are always influencing the client. The earlier skills of listening influence clients indirectly through systematic but often unconscious patterns of questioning and other skills. *But the influencing skills attempt to influence the client directly and consciously.*

Recognizing our influence on clients, of course, carries with it important ethical and value issues. It is possible to use the tools of the interview in a manipulative fashion. The position of intentional interviewing is that all counseling skills, be they attending or influencing in nature, should be focused on the client's needs and wishes. Ethical practice demands respect for the client and an awareness of the power relationships inherent in the interview. Interviewers and counselors, by their position, have power over their clients, and they need to use this power responsibly for the client's benefit, not their own.

Common to all seven of the influencing skills presented here is a degree of confrontation and stimulation toward the development of new thoughts and actions. Through the use of a directive, interpretation, or feedback, your client will be confronted with an alternative point of view. This new view may clarify a client incongruity and facilitate the resolution of discrepancies. Thus, you may want to use the Confrontation Impact Scale (CIS) as a means to analyze the manner in which your influencing skill or strategy is received by your client.

The Strategies of Interpersonal Influence

Influencing skills such as directives, interpretation, and feedback usually are best given in the context of active listening to the client, being concrete and clear in your wording, and through observing and checking out with your client the impact of your intervention. The word *strategy* describes the influencing skill, as most often the effective use of interpersonal influence involves examining the context of the client, listening, and selecting developmentally appropriate and individually relevant influencing skills. When a directive doesn't work for the resistant client—who is perhaps at the D-1 preoperational level—you may find that a clear statement of logical consequences is a more effective strategy.

In sum, a strategic model is proposed (see Box 11-1) in which you (1) attend and listen to the client and are sure you understand where he or she is "coming from"; (2) assess that client for developmental level and select an intervention that is developmentally relevant; and (3) observe the consequence of your interviewing lead and move from that observation to your next step.

Box 11-1.   The 1-2-3 Pattern of Listening, Influencing, and Observing Client Reaction

1. Listen	In any interaction with clients it is critical that you use attending, observation, and listening skills to determine the client's definition and view of the world. How does the client see, hear, feel, and represent the world through "I statements" and key descriptors for content (paraphrasing), feelings (reflection of feeling), and meaning (encouragers and reflection of meaning)?
2. Assess and influence	An influencing skill is best used after you understand clients' impressions and representations of their experience. Assessment of client developmental level should be useful here. An interpretation, self-disclosure, feedback statement, or other influencing skill provides a new frame of reference or informational base from which clients may act.
3. Check out and observe consequences	Following the use of an influencing skill, use a check-out ("How does that seem?") and observe the consequences of your action. If either client verbal or nonverbal behavior, or both, becomes discrepant and you sense an increasing distance from you as an interviewer, return to the use of listening skills. Influencing skills, of necessity, remove you from being totally "with" clients. Consequently you must pay additional attention to your client observation skills when you attempt to use influencing skills. In determining what to do next, you will want to examine the impact of your intervention using the five levels of the CIS.

The degree of interpersonal influence desired in the interview varies from theory to theory. The word *influence* can be most upsetting to a Style-3 client-directed, formal operational counselor, whereas many proponents of behavior modification (Style 1) aim deliberately to change the client as much as possible. Most theories now seem to agree on extensive client involvement, but there is increasing evidence and acceptance of the need for changing counseling and interviewing style to meet the unique developmental needs of each client. The skills and strategies of listening and influencing can be used for greater or lesser interpersonal influence, depending on how the skill is used. Even paraphrasing can greatly influence the client and interview process.

It is possible to place the skills on a rough continuum of interpersonal influence. Figure 11-1 rates the attending skills and several of the influencing skills in terms of their influence in the interview. The task of the counselor is often to open client discussion of a topic and then to close this discussion when appropriate. When a client is overly talkative and becoming upset, it may be useful to ask a closed question and then change the focus by asking an open question on another topic, depending on the goal of the interview. When an interview is moving slowly, an interpretation or directive may add content and flow.

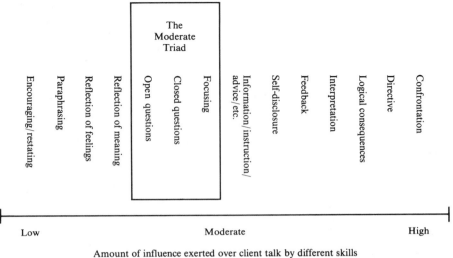

Amount of influence exerted over client talk by different skills
(All skills rest on a foundation of attending behavior and client observation.)

Figure 11-1. The interpersonal influence continuum

Basic to the flow of the interview and to facilitating client growth are quality attending behavior and client observation skills. The interviewer must establish contact and note the impact of that contact. These two achievements provide the essential information to determine what skill may be appropriate at what time. Attending behavior can encourage or discourage client talk for the client's benefit—client observation tells you when to change skills and focus.

The influencing skills are those in which the interviewer talks most and most strongly directs the session, while the listening skills allow the client to talk in greater depth and determine the direction of the session. This, of course, is an oversimplification. While it is generally accurate, keep in mind that an effective reflection of meaning or other listening skill may sometimes be more influential than a directive or confrontation. The timing and *how* you use the skill are ultimately most important.

Nonetheless, you may find it helpful to think of the interpersonal influence continuum from time to time during your interviews. If you feel that you are coming on too strong and the client is resisting, it may be wise to move to lower levels of influence. Similarly, if the client is bogged down, the careful use of an influencing skill may help organize things and move the interview along more smoothly.

Most important for the beginning interviewer are the *moderate triad* of skills: open and closed questions and focusing. Experience has shown that mastery of these skills is almost as important as attending behavior and client observation. If you can ask questions effectively and focus on varying topics, you have the ability to open and close almost any topic or issue your client presents. If a client has difficulty talking, an open question coupled with a slight change of focus may give her or him space to open up. If the topic seems inappropriate, a change of focus coupled with some closed questions will usually slow down the pace. This is particularly true when the client is more emotional than the interviewer feels able to handle. An open question may then be used to switch to another, less difficult topic. Later you can return to the difficult issue. You can achieve the same effects with the other skills, but the moderate triad are "swing" skills in terms of their influence and do not seem to disrupt the interview flow as much as do skills from either side of the triad.

The Framework for Skill Presentation: Illustrations of the Influencing Skills and Strategies

As this chapter presents so many skills and strategy areas, the following presentation is organized differently from most of the earlier chapters. It is suggested that you read this chapter slowly, digesting each separate skill and practicing each one before moving on and reading about the next skill area.

Each skill discussion will contain a brief transcript of how that skill might be used in an actual interview. The content of the interview will be consistent for all skills: a recurring problem of lack of assertiveness, the failure to express one's point of view, and the accompanying inability to obtain what one wants. Assertiveness training itself is a systematic strategy that will be reviewed in Chapter 13, but there are many ways to elaborate, understand, and perhaps even change the lack of assertiveness in a client.

In the example below, let us assume that Anne, the counselor, uses the BLS to obtain a general summary of Katie's inability to express herself. This transcript, of course, is abbreviated and edited for clarity.

Anne: Could you tell me what you'd like to talk about today?

Katie: I couldn't do it. I simply can't express myself. I've tried many times and I can't get people to listen to me. Whether it is the boss, my lover, or the man at the garage, they all seem to run over me.

Anne: Run over you?

Katie: Yeah, I keep finding that I'm so damned accommodating that I'm always trying to get along. People like me for going along with them, but I never get what I want. Smiles, yes, but delays and nothing. I'm disgusted with myself.

Anne: Sounds as if you are really angry and disgusted about your inability to get what you want.

Katie: Right, it just goes on and on . . . I never seem to change.

Anne: Could you give me a specific example of the last time you had these feelings of anger and disgust? What happened? What did you say? What did they do?

Katie: Well, I was at a garage. I had called in for an early morning appointment. They said come in at 8:00 and so I was there on time. I had to go to a meeting at 10:00. When I checked at 9:30, they hadn't even started yet. The guy smiled and said, "Sorry, girlie, we couldn't get to it." He was a real pig, but I just looked down and didn't say anything—even though I really wanted to scream. I made another appointment and my car still has that screwy, strange sound.

Anne: So, Katie, you seem to be saying that you are not getting what you want, and you are tired of being a doormat. The situation at the garage is one illustration of what you consider a pattern—something you repeat in various forms again and again by allowing others to walk over you. You're frustrated with others and disgusted with yourself for not acting more forcefully. Have I heard you correctly?

The BLS has been used here to draw out the central facts and feelings that describe the client's concern. While this client is obviously intellectually capable of thinking about herself and her situation, she is preoperational in terms of her ability to get what she wants. She needs to learn the concrete operations of assertiveness. Thus, she is primarily a D-2 client, but for this particular developmental task, she is clearly D-1—and in some aspects of self-reflection, she is probably D-3, self-directed/formal operational. There is also a part of Katie that should be able to work on a more mutual dialogue/dialectic basis in a framework of equality with the counselor. Katie is a typical client, in other words, operating at several levels simultaneously: preoperational in terms of assertiveness, capable of engaging in many, but not all, concrete operational functions in terms of acting in the world, and, as she is able to describe her situation so clearly, capable of self-reflection representing the third developmental level.

Let us now turn to the several skills and strategies of interpersonal influence and consider briefly how each might be of benefit to the client.

▲ Instructional Reading

For further study of the seven influencing skills and strategies discussed in the following pages, you can read Ivey and Gluckstern (1983), Ivey and Authier (1978), and Ivey, Ivey, and Simek-Downing (1987). Remember that each influencing skill exists within the strategy of (1) attending, (2) assessing developmental level and introducing intervention, and (3) assessing the impact on the client. Influencing skills tend not to be repeated as frequently in the interview as do our listening skills. You may use only one to three or four of these skills and strategies in a session, but you will want to use them carefully and skillfully.

Directives

When giving a directive, you simply tell the client what to do, what action to take, or what to say or think next. Many of those who take the position that interviewers should not direct their clients fail to address the fact that an interviewer often tells the client to take a test, to free-associate from a dream, to try a new behavior with a spouse or colleague, or to engage in some productive homework. Research has found that some effective interviewers couch as many as half of their leads in some form of directive. Rational-emotive therapists suggest homework assignments; behavioral counselors direct through assertiveness training; and even humanistically oriented counselors may at times tell their clients what to do (for instance, the Gestalt "hot-seat" exercise). Competent managers, physicians and nurses, and social workers do not hesitate to give directions to their clients.

Box 11-2 gives example directives for counselors to use. Each of these directives is worded as it might be given to the client, Katie, who lacks assertiveness. What is crucial is giving an *effective* directive. To give a directive that is likely to work, the following rules must be observed:

Box 11-2.   Example Directives Used by Counselors of Different Theoretical Orientations

	The several directives are described, then followed by illustrations of how that directive might be used with a person such as Katie, our earlier example.
Specific suggestions/ instructions for action	"I suggest you try . . . "
	"Katie, the next time you go to the garage, I'd like you to stand there in front of the counter, make direct eye contact with the shop head, and clearly and firmly tell him that you have a meeting at 10:00 and that you must be taken care of *now*. If he says there will be a delay, get him to make a firm time commitment. Then follow up with him firmly 15 minutes later."
	This type of clear directive is usually most effective with clients who don't have skills and need firm guidance—most likely too elementary a directive for Katie.
Paradoxical instructions	"Continue what you are doing . . . " "Do the problem behavior/thinking/action at least three times."
	"Katie, I want you to notice what you're doing in terms of lack of assertiveness. Next week, at least three times, I want you deliberately to give in to other people's demands. And, at the same time, I want you to notice carefully how you are behaving and how they react."
	With clients who refuse to follow suggestions and directives, a paradoxical directive may be useful both in developing awareness and promoting change. Katie could profit from more awareness of her own feelings and behavior.
Imagery	"Imagine you are back in the situation. Close your eyes and describe it precisely. What do you see, hear, feel?" "Describe your ideal day/job/life partner."
	"Katie, you seem a bit vague about the time you gave in to your parents. Close your eyes, visualize your parents . . . (pause) . . . now what are they saying to you? What are you saying to them? How do you feel in this process?"
	Imagery directives seem to be most appropriate for verbal, self-directed D-3 clients who are interested in different ways of self-exploration. Additionally, many children and young people like the freedom and creativity allowed in this type of directive.
Role-play enactment	"Now return to that situation and let's play it out." "Let's role-play it again, only change the one behavior we agreed to."
	With Katie, the counselor would use virtually the same words. Katie would be encouraged to take her part and play it out with the counselor taking the role of the shop manager. (Role-playing is an especially effective Style-2 concrete operations technique. It makes the client behavior clear and specific. Given that clarity, changes in concrete behavior become much easier to make. This is one of the most basic techniques used in assertiveness training.)

(continued)

Box 11-2 (continued)

Gestalt hot-seat	"Talk to your parent as if he or she were sitting in that chair. Now go to that chair and answer as your parent would."
	This technique is similar to a role-play, but the client plays both parts. The physical aspects of this technique often would help an individual such as Katie get in touch with preoperational feelings and emotions. Following this basically Style-1 intervention, it is often useful to move to Style 3 and help the client debrief what he or she felt or thought during the often dramatic individual role-play. Then you may return to a Style-2 intervention to help the client move to specific action.
Gestalt nonverbal	"I note that one of your hands is in a fist; the other is open. Have the two hands talk to one another."
	This is similar to the hot-seat. Katie would learn to be in touch with her nonverbal communication. Generally speaking, such interventions require a client at a higher developmental level, although the counseling style is environmental structuring: D-1.
Free association, as in psychodynamic transactional analysis	"Take that feeling and free-associate back to an early childhood experience . . . " " . . . to what is occurring now in your daily life." "Stay with that feeling, magnify it. Now, what flashed into your mind first?"
	This technique is for full formal operational clients who are self-directed. Katie might be expected to free-associate back to a specific childhood experience that helps explain her present behavior. Many of us are repeating old parent-child interactions in the present. Transactional analysis focuses on how we continue those childhood patterns in our adult life.
Positive reframing/ dereflection	"Identify a negative experience, thought, or feeling. Now identify something positive in that experience and focus on that dimension. Synthesize the two."
	"Katie, we've discussed the negative in the situation with your parents. What positives can you see in it? Relax . . . (pause) . . . let it flow . . . "
	This type of intervention may be expected to produce a sense of awareness—and possibly pride—in that it highlights Katie's interpersonal sensitivity, her caring, and her flexibility. In fact, it may be these very skills that have made Katie successful in many interpersonal situations. However, she fails to discriminate when to use the skills and when not to.
Relaxation	"Close your eyes and drift." "Tighten your forearm, very tight, now let it go."
	Katie may be especially tight and tense; relaxation training can be taught as a Style-1 environmental-structuring intervention. Once Katie is able to relax and be in control of her body, she will be better able to cope with the very real stresses she encounters daily.
Systematic desensitization	This involves (1) deep muscle relaxation; (2) construction of an anxiety hierarchy; and (3) matching objects of anxiety with relaxation. This is a more complex Style-1 counseling strategy and would be useful to Katie if she had a deep-seated anxiety problem with assertiveness. She would first learn deep muscle relaxation; then she and her counselor would list objects of anxiety from most tension-provoking to least. At the top of the anxiety hierarchy might be speaking up for one's rights to

(continued)

Box 11-2 (continued)

<table>
<tr><td></td><td>one's parents; less anxiety-provoking might be the garage situation. Other increasingly anxiety-free situations would be generated until a state of complete calm is imagined. You would lead the client in a carefully planned session or sessions to practice relaxation under stress.</td></tr>
<tr><td>Language choice</td><td>"Change 'should' to 'want to.'"<br>"Change 'can't' to 'won't.'"

"Katie, you say you can't do anything with the shop head. Change 'can't' to 'won't,' because you are in charge of your own behavior. . . . Good . . . now say that again."

Words such as can't imply that a situation is out of control; by having her change can't to won't, Katie is being forced to be in charge of her own behavior. This environmental-structuring D-1 approach may be particularly helpful with self-directed formal operational clients (Level 3) who are preoperational in terms of some of their thinking and behavior.</td></tr>
<tr><td>Meditation</td><td>"Be still. Focus on one point. Relax. Concentrate on breathing. Let all thoughts slip from your mind."

Katie may prefer training in meditation as a mode of relaxation. Teaching meditation is more characteristic of a Style-3 client-directed, formal operations approach.</td></tr>
<tr><td>Family therapy communications</td><td>"Don't talk to me . . . talk to him now."
"Change chairs with your wife and sit closer to your daughter . . ."

You may find it helpful to bring Katie's parents in for family counseling. Many of the directives used individually work well when adapted to family and group counseling.</td></tr>
<tr><td>Homework</td><td>"Practice this exercise next week and report on it in the next interview."

"Katie, next week I want you to try some of the skills we've worked on in the roleplay. Focus on your eye contact patterns—you've learned you tend to look down when there's the potential of conflict. Just this week, focus on this one dimension."

Data are increasingly clear that much learning during the interview is lost if it is not immediately transferred to daily life.</td></tr>
</table>

1. *Use appropriate body language, vocal tone, and eye contact.* Demonstrate effective attending. When you use influencing skills, your attending behaviors tend to be more assertive than when you are listening (for example, more direct eye contact, a stronger tone of voice, leaning forward, but not aggressively).

2. *Be clear and concrete in your verbal expression.* Know what you are going to say and say it clearly and explicitly. Compare the following:

Vague: "Go out and arrange for a test."

Concrete: "After you leave today, contact the testing office to take the Strong-Campbell Interest Blank. Complete it today, and they will have the results for us to discuss during our meeting next week."

Vague: "Relax."

Concrete: "Sit quietly . . . feel the back of the chair on your shoulders . . . tighten your right hand . . . hold it tight . . . now let it relax slowly . . ."

These examples all illustrate the importance of indicating clearly to your client what you want to have happen. Directives need to be authoritative and clear, but also stated in such a way that they are in tune with the needs of the client.

3. *Check out whether your directive was heard and contemplated.* Just because you think you are clear doesn't mean the client understands what you said. Explicitly or implicitly check out to make sure your directive is understood. This is particularly important when a series of directives have been given. For example, "Could you repeat back to me what I have just asked you to do?" or "I suggested three things for you to do for homework this coming week. Would you summarize them to me to make sure I've been clear?"

Undergirding directives, then, is an important pattern:

1. Understanding the client's frame of reference (usually gained through attending skills such as questioning and reflection of feeling)
2. Stating your position and directive clearly and concisely
3. Checking out whether the directive was understood and determining its impact on the client

This 1-2-3 pattern will repeat itself for each of the influencing skills.

Individual Practice in Directives

Exercise 1. What are the three major points suggested by the text for giving directives?

1. _____

2. _____

3. _____

Exercise 2. Which of the following directives are vague (V), and which are concrete (C)?

_____ "I want you to imagine you are talking to your mother."

_____ "Imagine your mother is sitting in that chair. Now talk to her as if she were really sitting there."

_____ "I'll introduce you to Joan, our secretary, and she will arrange for you to take the aptitude test we agreed on."

_____ "Try out that idea next week."

_____ "Here is some homework for you to do. Next week you are to ask five people how they spend their leisure time. This may give you some ideas for your own life and will also give you something specific to talk to people about. We'll talk about the results next week."

Exercise 3. Write below vague and specific directives for the following situations.

Be sure to include a check-out with your directives.

Tell a client to obtain information about vocations during the coming week.

Vague: _____

_____

Concrete: _____

_____

Direct a client to engage in relaxation training during the coming week.

Vague: _____

_____

Concrete: _____

_____

Direct a subordinate to write a memo for you.

Vague: _____

_____

Concrete: _____

_____

Logical Consequences

The process of learning in this culture is heavily based on the consequences of actions (Dreikurs & Grey, 1968). Client actions planned for the future are likely to have consequences in the client's life. For example, an individual may want to change jobs simply because the new one offers more pay. However, the change may disrupt family life through a move, which in turn may cause other problems. Alternatively, the same move may bring unforeseen positive consequences. Explaining to others the probable consequences of their behaviors, if done sparingly and carefully, may at times be helpful in the interview or counseling session.

Warnings are forms of logical consequences. They inform the other person of the negative possibilities involved in a decision or action and the consequences that may result. These types of logical consequences tend to reduce risk taking and produce conformity. They often center on *anticipation of punishment*. A teacher in a disciplinary situation wants and needs a certain minimum of conformity, as does a correctional officer. In interviews some clients plan very risky

actions without considering the full range of possible consequences. A client considering a divorce, dropping out of school, or "telling the boss off" may profit from being informed about the consequences of the action.

Encouraging risk taking and attempting new tasks is a more positive form of logical consequences. In the schoolroom some children conform too much and demonstrate little creativity. They have been so conditioned by threats and warnings and bad outcomes that they are afraid to move. In such situations the goal may be to encourage risk taking by pointing out positive outcomes of a possible decision or action. *Anticipation of rewards* is a form of logical consequences in which the individual may be asked to imagine the positive consequences and rewards of new behavior or actions. In interviews you may wish to encourage clients to be more assertive or to try some new action; anticipating positive outcomes may be helpful in this process.

Logical consequences may at first seem to be a type of coercion or moralizing, yet it is the rare human behavior that does not have its costs and benefits, and it is the counselor's task to help the client sort out those likelihoods while working toward a decision. You may do this through the attending skill of questioning or directly through sharing logical consequences. In providing a logical consequence response, consider the following suggestions:

1. Through attending skills, make sure you understand the situation and the way your clients understand it.
2. As clients move toward decisions, encourage thinking about possible positive and negative results of the decision. This is often done by questioning.
3. Provide clients with data on both the positive and negative consequences of any decision or action. If they think only in negative terms, help them think of positives. If they are thinking only in positives, prompt thinking in negatives.
4. As appropriate to the situation, provide clients with a summary of positive and negative consequences in a *nonjudgmental manner.* With many people this step is not needed; they will have made their own judgment and decision already.
5. Let clients decide what action to take in counseling situations. In teaching or management, on the other hand, you may decide at times and actually enforce the consequences.

In counseling, logical consequences tends to be a gentle skill used to help people sort through issues more completely. It also may be used in ranking alternatives when a complex decision is at hand. In management and teaching situations the same generally holds true. For disciplinary and reward issues, however, it is important to note that the power rests with the manager and teacher: they decide the *consequences.* In interviewing, the task is simply to assist the client in foreseeing consequences. In both management and teaching situations, letting the employee or student decide what action to take is critical. But, people who hold power over others need to *follow through with the consequences* they warned about earlier, or their power will be lost.

Individual Practice in Logical Consequences

Exercise 1. Using the five steps of the logical consequences skill, briefly indicate to the client, Katie, what the logical consequences would be for her of continuing with her behavior.

Summarize Katie's problem in your own words.

_____

_____

_____

Ask Katie specific questions about the positive and negative consequences of continuing her behavior.

Positives: _____

_____

Negatives: _____

_____

Provide Katie with your own feedback on the probable consequences of continuing her behavior.

_____

_____

_____

Summarize the differences between your feedback given above and that of Katie, who says she doesn't want to change (this implies the use of confrontation).

_____

_____

_____

_____

Encourage Katie to make her own decision.

_____

_____

_____

Exercise 2. Logical consequences using attending skills

Through questioning skills you can encourage clients to think through the possible consequences of their actions. ("What result might you anticipate if you did that?" "What results are you obtaining right now while you continue to engage in that behavior?") However, questioning and paraphrasing the situation may not always be enough to make the client fully aware of the logical consequences of actions. Write below, for the various types of clients and situations, logical consequences statements that might help the client understand the situation more fully.

A student who is contemplating taking drugs for the first time:

_____

_____

_____

A young woman contemplating an abortion:

_____

_____

_____

A student considering taking out a loan for college:

_____

_____

_____

An executive who has just been fired because of poor interpersonal relationships:

_____

_____

_____

A client who comes to you consistently late and who is often uncooperative:

_____

_____

_____

Self-Disclosure

Should you discuss your own personal observations, experiences, and ideas with the client? Self-disclosure on the part of the counselor or interviewer has been a highly controversial topic. Many theorists argue against sharing oneself openly, preferring a more distant, objective persona. However, more recently, humanistically oriented counselors have demonstrated the value of appropriate self-disclosure. It appears that self-disclosure can encourage client talk, create additional trust between counselor and client, and establish a more equal relationship in the interview. Nonetheless, not everyone agrees that this is a wise skill to include

among the counselor's techniques. Some express valid concerns about the counselor's monopolizing the interview or abusing the client's rights by encouraging openness too early; too, they point out that counseling and interviewing can operate successfully without any interviewer self-disclosure at all.

A self-disclosure consists of the following:

1. *Personal pronouns.* A counselor or interviewer self-disclosure inevitably involves "I statements" or self-reference using the pronouns *I, me,* and *my.*
2. *Verb for content or feeling or both.* "I think . . . ," "I feel . . . ," and "I have experienced . . . " all indicate some action on the part of the counselor.
3. *Object coupled with adverb and adjective descriptors.* "I feel happy about your being able to assert yourself more directly with your parents." "My experience of divorce was something like yours. I felt and I still feel. . . . "

Feeling words and expression of feeling are particularly important in self-disclosure. In essence, the structure of a self-disclosure is simple: it is "self-talk" from the counselor. Making self-talk relevant to the client is a more complex task involving the following issues, among others.

Genuineness. This is a vague term, but it can be made more concrete by emphasizing that the counselor must truly and honestly have had the experience and idea. This could be termed "genuineness in relation to self," an important beginning. But the self-disclosure must also be genuine in relation to the client. For example, a client may have performance anxiety about a part in a school play. The counselor may genuinely feel anxiety about giving a lecture before fifty people. The feelings may be the same or at least similar, but true genuineness demands a synchronicity of feeling. The counselor's experience in this case is probably too distant from that of the client. Self-disclosure should be fairly close to client experience; for instance, the counselor might relate a situation in which he or she felt similar performance anxiety in parallel circumstances at the same age.

Timeliness. If a client is talking smoothly about something, counseling self-disclosure is not necessary. However, if the client seems to want to talk about a topic but is having trouble, a slight leading self-disclosure by the counselor may be helpful. Too deep and involved a self-disclosure may frighten or distance the client.

Tense. The most powerful self-disclosures are usually made in the present tense ("Right now I feel _____ .") However, variations in tense can also be used to strengthen or soften the power of a self-disclosure. Consider the following:

Katie: I am feeling really angry about the way my parents sulk when I go out on my own. They really tick me off.

Counselor: (present tense) Right now, I like the way you are fighting. It makes me feel good to see you fighting for your rights.

Counselor: (past tense) I can see that you felt angry. I've always liked that. I've felt that way toward my parents, too.

Counselor: (future tense) I know you're going to make it in the future. I think anger is a good motivator.

Clearly, effective self-disclosure can be a complex skill, yet it can open the interview to new dimensions of sharing and helpfulness. In the example above, it may be useful for Katie to learn to express anger, but anger must also be managed. It is usually not helpful to unleash years of anger all at once. It will take a client at a fairly high developmental level to work though those angry feelings with some degree of insight and understanding.

Self-disclosure as a skill is most characteristic of Styles 3 and 4, in which the client and counselor assume more mutuality. However, more limited self-disclosures may be used sparingly with clients at preoperational and concrete operational developmental levels.

Individual Practice in Self-Disclosure

The structure of a self-disclosure consists of "I statements" made up of three dimensions: (1) the personal pronoun *I* in some form; (2) a verb such as *feel, think, have experienced*; and (3) a sentence objectively describing what you think or what happened.

Exercise 1. Writing self-disclosure statements

Imagine that a client comes to you with each of the problems below. For each problem write one effective and one ineffective self-disclosure. Before you begin, assume that you have already listened to the client carefully and that a self-disclosure indeed might be appropriate at this moment. Nonetheless, include a check-out with each statement.

"I just can't get along with men. They bug me terribly. They seem so macho and self-assured. I feel they are always looking down on me. How do you feel toward them?"

Effective: _____

_____

_____

Ineffective: _____

_____

_____

"I find myself afraid and insecure in large groups. It just doesn't feel right. What should I do?"

Effective: _____

_____

_____

_____

Ineffective: _____

_____

_____

_____

"I'm concerned about how you feel toward me. You remind me of my parents. Just how do you feel toward me?"

Effective: _____

_____

_____

Ineffective: _____

_____

_____

Feedback

Feedback is concerned with providing clients with clear data on their performance and/or on how others may view them. It may even involve self-disclosures on your part. As indicated earlier in the Guidelines for Effective Feedback (Box 2-2 in Chapter 2), feedback is centrally concerned with the following:

> To see ourselves as others see us,
> To hear how others hear us,
> And to be touched as we touch others . . .
> These are the goals of effective feedback.

Feedback to one another is important in the process of developing skills in counseling and interviewing. The guidelines given earlier for practicing effective feedback in small-group sessions are equally critical in counseling and interviewing:

1. *The client receiving feedback should be in charge.* Feedback is more likely to be successful if the client solicits it. However, at times you as interviewer will have to determine if the client is ready and able to hear accurate feedback. Only give as much feedback as the client can use at the moment.

2. *Feedback should focus on strengths and/or something the client can do something about.* It does little good to tell a client to change many things that are wrong. It is more effective to give feedback on positive qualities and build on strength. When you talk about negatives, they should be areas that the client can do something to change or can learn to accept as a part of reality.

3. *Feedback should be concrete and specific.* Just as with directives, it does little good to offer vague feedback. For example, "You aren't able to get along with the group" is not as helpful as "You had two arguments with Ginny that upset both of you, and now you are disagreeing strongly with Lois. What does this mean to you?"

4. *Feedback should be relatively nonjudgmental.* Critical to being nonjudgmental is accepting vocal qualities and body language. Too often feedback turns into evaluation: "You did a good job there" as compared to "I saw you relax and become more joyful as you became more assertive." Stick to the facts and specifics. Facts are friendly; judgments may or may not be.

5. *Feedback should be lean and precise.* Most people have many areas that could profit from change. However, most of us can change only one thing at a time and can hear only so much. Don't overwhelm the client. Select one or two things for feedback and save the rest for later.

6. *Check out how your feedback was received.* Just as in an effective directive, check to see how the other person reacts to feedback. "How do you react to that?" and "Does that sound close?" and "What does that mean to you?" are three examples that involve the client in feedback and will indicate whether or not you were heard and how useful your feedback was.

Again, note the 1-2-3 pattern: (1) attend to the client; (2) use the influencing skill appropriate to the developmental level of the client; and (3) check out how well the skill was received and how useful it was.

Note also that clarity and concreteness are just as important in effective feedback as they are in effective direction giving. Good advice and instruction both require the 1-2-3 pattern plus concreteness and clarity if they are to be meaningful to the client. These same principles apply to all the influencing skills.

Another type of feedback is more judgmental. *Praise* and certain types of *supportive statements* convey your positive judgment of the client. Negative judgments may be shown through *reprimands* and certain types of punishments. In judgmental feedback the interviewer takes a more active role.

Judgmental feedback is often considered inappropriate in counseling situations. However, management settings, correctional institutions, schools and universities, and other face-to-face settings often require judgmental feedback. Most often judgmental feedback involves an interviewer who has some power over the life of the client or other person. (Some would argue, in fact, that nonjudgmental feedback is impossible if the interviewer has any power over the client. Thus all feedback, to some extent, could be considered judgmental.)

The suggestions for judgmental types of feedback such as praise, support, reprimands, and punishments follow the same guidelines proposed earlier in this section. Such feedback tends to be more effective when the client is in charge as much as possible and when the feedback includes some emphasis on strengths as well as weaknesses, is concrete and specific, and is lean and precise. Judgmental feedback can be delivered in a tone of voice that is nonjudgmental and factual, thereby removing some of the sting. The check-out is particularly important in judgmental feedback. It provides the client with an opportunity to react, and the interviewer has some idea of how the feedback, positive or negative, was received.

You can see that the feedback skill typically involves the assumption of a self-directed, formal operational client who is able to think about self. At the dialectic level, feedback becomes especially important, although it may be helpful in small doses for clients at Levels 1 and 2 of development.

Individual Practice in Feedback

Exercise 1. What are the six guidelines for feedback?

Summarize them below in your own words.

1. _____

2. _____

3. _____

4. _____

5. _____

6. _____

Exercise 2. In business a manager may give an employee periodic feedback about work performance.

In an encounter group you may give someone else in the group your impression of his or her behavior. (Note how similar feedback and self-disclosure are in this case. However, feedback provides specific, concrete data about behavior, whereas a self-disclosure may consist mainly of subjective impressions.) In correctional institutions, schools, and other teaching situations, feedback may be used to praise or reprimand others.

Select three situations and summarize your perceptions of effective and ineffective feedback you have observed in the past.

_____

_____

_____

_____

_____

_____

_____

_____

_____

_____

_____

_____

_____

_____

Exercise 3. Self-disclosure types of feedback can be particularly powerful.

Sharing your own positive and negative reactions to the client is basic to this form of feedback. Self-disclosure as feedback involves authentic "I–you" talk. You share your impressions of another person. Used sparingly and effectively, it can be one of the most effective microskills.

How does this form of feedback compare with the criteria suggested in this section (nonjudgmental, concrete, and so on)?

_____

_____

_____

_____

_____

_____

_____

_____

Interpretation/Reframing

Though interpretations may vary in content depending on the theoretical orientation on which they draw, they all have one element in common: the interviewer presents the client with a new frame of reference through which to view the problem or concern and, hopefully, better understand and deal with the situation. Another term used increasingly in this context, and a term that describes the same process, is *reframing*. Interpretation should be contrasted with reflection of meaning, in which the interviewer assists the client to find new meanings and interpretations on his or her own.

Reflection of meaning may be necessary and helpful *before* you attempt an interpretation, however. Reflections of meaning often lead clients to their own new frames of reference as they examine their own world, making an interpretation unnecessary—but examining meaning may simply loosen up your clients' constructs and thinking and prepare them for your alternative frame of reference, your interpretation.

A client may be worried and upset over a troubling dream. Different theories of helping would interpret the dream differently, but each would provide a new frame of reference for understanding the dream. For example:

Client: I dreamed I was walking along cliffs with the sea raging below. I felt terribly frightened; I couldn't find my parents.

Counselor: (psychodynamic) You'd really like to get rid of your parents, but the thought is terrifying.

Counselor: (transactional analysis) I note you are looking to find or take care of your parents. This is very similar to what is going on in your life right now. They've just moved in with you, and you've said earlier they were like children and you were like the parent.

Counselor: (decisional) You've just entered college and it feels as if you might fall off the cliffs. You wish your parents were here to help you make practical decisions.

Which is the correct interpretation? Depending on the situation and context, any of these interpretations could be helpful or harmful. The value of the interpretation depends on the client's reaction to it. Each provides the client with a new, alternative way to consider the situation. In short, interpretation renames or redefines "reality" from a new point of view. By contrast, a reflection of meaning would use the questioning for meaning sequence and then ask the client what sense or meaning he or she obtained from the data.

Interpretation may be contrasted with reflection of feeling, reflection of meaning, and the paraphrase. In those three skills the interviewer remains in the client's *own* frame of reference. In interpretation the frame of reference comes from the counselor's personal and/or theoretical constructs. The following are examples of interpretation (reframing) paired with other skills.

Client: (he has a record of absenteeism) I really feel badly about missing so much work.

Interviewer: (reflection of feeling) You're really troubled and worried. (paraphrase/restatement) You've been missing a lot of work. (interpretation) You've missed a lot of work and you are aware of your boss's views on absenteeism. This makes you concerned about whether or not you'll be able to keep up with the job.

Client: (with agitation) My wife and I had a fight last night after watching this sexy movie. I tried to make love and she rejected me again.

Counselor: (reflection of feeling) You're upset and troubled. (paraphrase) You had a fight after the movie and were rejected again sexually. (interpretation) Sounds like your fear of rejection caused you to be rejected by your wife. Or (interpretation) Your wife only turns you on enough for sex given some outside stimulus, such as a movie. Or (interpretation) The feelings of rejection trouble you. Are those feelings similar to the dream you had last week?

In each of the above interpretations, the interviewer or counselor adds something beyond what the client has said. There are a multitude of interpretative responses that may be made to any client utterance, and they may vary according to the theory and personal experience of the counselor.

Interpretation has traditionally been viewed as a mystical activity in which the interviewer reaches into the depths of the client's personality to provide new insights. However, if we consider interpretation to be merely a new frame of reference, the concept becomes less formidable. Viewed in this light, the depth of a given interpretation refers to the magnitude of the discrepancy between the frame of reference from which the client is operating and the frame of reference supplied by the interviewer. For example, a client may report feeling overly upset when the boss makes a minor criticism. The interviewer, counselor, or therapist may have noted this as a constant pattern. Several interpretations could be made, with varying depth:

"You seem to react very strongly to virtually any criticism from your boss."
"You appear to have a pattern of difficulty with authority."
"You feel very unsure of yourself and need approval to validate your worth."
"Your boss represents your father, and you are repeating with him the same patterns that you experienced with your father's criticism."

Again, interpretations will vary according to the theoretical orientation of the interviewer. You may wish to examine the situations in this section and reframe them from various theoretical perspectives with your supervisor or a colleague. The successful interviewer has many alternative interpretations available and selects them according to the long-term and immediate needs of the client.

Interpretations are best given in the 1-2-3 pattern of attending carefully to the client, providing the interpretation, then checking out the client's reactions to the new frame of reference ("How does that idea come across to you?"). If an interpretation is unsuccessful, the interviewer can use data obtained from the check-out to develop another, more meaningful response.

Finally, it should be mentioned that reflection of meaning used in combination with questioning skills often enables clients to make their own interpretations and generate their own new frames of reference. A client working effectively with an interviewer using the skill of reflection of meaning is often better able to make interpretations than a skilled counselor.

Developmentally, interpretations at the so-called deeper levels are appropriate for clients at Levels 3 and 4, whereas more obvious, concrete interpretations are more suitable for Level-1 and -2 clients. Generally speaking, you will also find that more concrete and specific influencing skills are effective with Levels 1 and 2, while more abstract and varied influencing skills may be useful with formal operational and dialectic clients. However, always keep in mind the intellectualizing client who prefers to work in abstractions. Allowing yourself to maintain an abstract style with that client may be pleasant, but you will often find such individuals need more concrete approaches to reality. Their very ability to think about thinking and to be abstract has removed them from the real world. They remain in some ways as preoperational and unable to live and work in their environments as are many young children. *Higher developmental levels are not necessarily "higher."*

Katie: I've had a terrible time asserting myself. I always seem to be pleasing someone else.

Counselor: (interpretation using Style 1) Clearly, Katie, you have never learned how to get what you want. We've tried many things, gone through several interviews. Next time you go out, I will go with you, observe what happens, and prompt you if necessary. (This interpretation recognizes failure as failure, takes environmental control, and ends with a directive for action.)

Counselor: (interpretation using Style 2 coaching/concrete operations) On the basis of the role-play, Katie, I'd say you hadn't yet learned the skills of self-assertiveness. You've done a lot of thinking about things, but now we need some action. When someone says "no" to you, you crumble. You need to stand a bit straighter, use a firmer voice, and *look at* that difficult person.

Counselor: (interpretation using Style 3 client-directed, formal operations) Katie, your feelings seem very similar to the dream you had last week when your hands were tied. This would seem to go back to your patterns of childhood interaction with your parents.

Counselor: (interpretation using Style 4 dialectic) Katie, even with me, here and now, you seem to be lacking assertiveness. You seem to respond to me in a similar way as you do to the man at the garage and to your parents. Now, at this moment, how do you react to that interpretation and to me personally for saying it?

Any of these interpretations may be useful to Katie. The latter two facilitate personal understanding of the issue, but the matter of concrete action remains. All the insight in the world does not make individuals act on their thoughts and feelings.

Individual Practice in Interpretation/Reframing

Interpretations provide alternative frames of reference or meanings for events in a client's life. In the examples below, provide an attending response (question, reflection of feeling, or the like) and then write an interpretation. Include a check-out in your interpretation.

Exercise 1.

"I just can't seem to get along with men, they bug me terribly. They seem so macho and self-assured. I feel they are always looking down on me. How do you feel toward them?"

Listening response: _____

_____

Interpretation from a Freudian frame of reference: _____

_____

_____

Interpretation from a feminist frame of reference: _____

_____

_____

Interpretation from your own frame of reference in ways that are appropriate for the four client developmental levels:

1. Preoperational: _____

_____

2. Concrete operations: _____

_____

3. Self-directed/formal operations: _____

_____

4. Dialectic: _____

_____

Exercise 2.

"I'm thinking of trying some pot. Yeah, I'm only 13, but I've been around a lot. My parents really object to it. I can't see why they do. My friends are all into it and seem to be doing fine."

Listening response: _____

_____

Interpretation from a conservative frame of reference: _____

_____

_____

_____

_____

Interpretation from an occasional user's frame of reference:

_____

_____

Interpretation from your own frame of reference in ways that are appropriate for the four client developmental levels:

1. Preoperational: _____

_____

2. Concrete operations: _____

_____

3. Self-directed/formal operations: _____

_____

4. Dialectic: _____

_____

Influencing Summary

This skill needs to be mentioned only briefly. It is similar to the attending summary except that the counselor or interviewer summarizes the interview from her or his point of view. Special attention is often given to what the interviewer has suggested and commented on during the session. One brief example can illustrate this skill:

Counselor: Katie, so far in this session we've talked about your inability to control what happens in your relations with others. I've suggested that this stems from your relationship with your mother and from living in a sexist society. You learned your behavior through her model. I've suggested several alternative things for you to try during the week. One of them was to sit quietly in a meeting and simply observe what goes on between people. Another was to deliberately seek to have direct eye contact and be more assertive with the service head in the garage. Finally, I've suggested you consider joining an assertiveness training group being organized in your community. Does that sum it up? What are your reactions and plans?

An influencing summary of this type integrates the several strands of thought involved in an interviewer's intervention and provides an opportunity to obtain client feedback. No practice exercises are suggested for this skill, but this is not to deny its importance. It is suggested that you practice this skill in conjunction with other practice sessions in the influencing series.

Information/Advice/Instruction/Opinion/Suggestion

Influencing skills can be divided into an almost infinite array of specialized topics. Beware: excessive emphasis in this area may lead you to forget attending!

All of the above skills, in one form or another, are concerned with imparting information to the client. The task is to be clear, specific, and relevant to the client's world. There is no need to downplay the importance of these skills, for most forms of interviewing, counseling, and even therapy involve imparting information to clients. An important part of both transactional analysis and rational-emotive therapy, for example, is directly instructing clients in the content of their theories. Relaxation trainers often teach their clients how to relax at home. Instructional procedures in management, medicine, and other interviewing situations are equally or more important.

Providing helpful information consists of steps closely related to those already discussed under the influencing skills:

1. Attend to the client and be sure that he or she is ready for the information or advice.
2. Be clear, specific, concrete, and timely in your instructional procedures. The concepts already discussed under feedback, directives, and logical consequences may be especially helpful in preparing more complex programs of instruction.
3. Check out with the client that your ideas have been understood.

Psychological education—the direct instruction of clients in the skills of living—often uses these skills. Again, no practice exercises are suggested with them. However, as you teach the skills of interviewing to clients and others, you will be needing and using effective information giving and instruction. Many of the ideas about teaching clients and conducting workshops presented in the Appendix should be helpful to you in planning effective ways to impart information.

Box 11-3.   Key Points

1-2-3 pattern	In any interaction with a client, first attend and obtain the client's frame of reference, then assess developmental level and use your influencing skill, and finally add a check-out to obtain the reaction to your use of the skill.
Interpersonal influence continuum	The influencing and attending skills may be classified from low to high degrees of influence. Encouragers and paraphrasing are considered relatively low in influence, whereas confrontation and directives are high in influence.
Moderate triad	The "swing skills" of the interpersonal influence continuum are focusing and open and closed questions. They provide a framework for determining the topic of conversation while keeping a balance between influencing and attending skills.
Directives	Directives indicate clearly to a client what action to take. Central to an effective directive is (1) appropriate body language, vocal tone, and eye contact; (2) clear and concrete verbal expression; and (3) checking out that directive was heard.
Logical consequences	This skill involves indicating the probable results of a client's action, in five steps: 1. Use attending skills to make sure you understand the situation and how it is understood by the client. 2. Encourage thinking about positive and negative consequences of a decision. 3. Provide the client with your data on the positive and negative consequences of a decision. 4. Summarize the positives and negatives. 5. Let the client decide what action to take.
Self-disclosure	Indicating your thoughts and feelings to a client constitutes self-disclosure, which necessitates the following: 1. Use personal pronouns ("I statements"). 2. Use a verb for content or feeling ("I feel . . . ," "I think . . . "). 3. Use an object coupled with adverb and adjective descriptors ("I feel happy about your being able to assert yourself . . . "). Self-disclosure tends to be most effective if it is genuine, timely, and phrased in the present tense.

(continued)

Box 11-3 (continued)

Feedback	Feedback entails providing accurate data on how the counselor or others view the client. Remember the following: 1. The client should be in charge. 2. Focus on strengths. 3. Be concrete and specific. 4. Be nonjudgmental. 5. Keep feedback lean and precise. 6. Check out how your feedback was received.
Interpretation/ reframing	This skill involves providing the client with an alternative frame of reference, using the following guidelines: 1. Attempt to use a reflection of meaning first to see if the client can make his or her own interpretation. 2. Provide your interpretation or reframing of the situation. 3. Check out how the information was received.
Influencing summary	This provides the client with a brief summary of what you have been saying or thinking over a session. Like other skills, it should be timely, be in words the client can understand, and include a check-out to determine how the summary was received.
Information/advice/ instruction/opinion/ suggestion	These skills call for passing on information and ideas of the interviewer to the client. The "1-2-3" pattern is again critical, and the information should be clear, concrete, and timely.

▲ Practice Exercises and Self-Assessment

Too many skills are mentioned in this chapter to expect early mastery of all. However, the more you practice the exercises, the more you can increase your understanding and mastery of these concepts.

Individual Practice in Observation of Competent Influencers

During the next week, observe conversations and meetings and note the frequency and effectiveness of influencing skills used by your friends and colleagues and by influential people you see in the media. Record your observations below:

_____

_____

_____

_____

_____

_____

_____

_____

_____

Systematic Group Practice

Small-group practice with the influencing skills requires practice with each skill. The general model of small-group work is suggested, but only one skill should be used at a time.

Step 1. Divide into practice groups.

Step 2. Select a leader of the group.

Step 3. Assign roles for each practice session.

▲ Role-played client
▲ Interviewer, who will begin by drawing out the client using listening skills, assess the client's developmental level, and then attempt one of the influencing skills
▲ Observer 1, who will observe the client and complete the CIS Rating Form (see Chapter 8), deciding how much of an impact the interviewer's influencing skills have made
▲ Observer 2, who will complete the Influencing Skills Feedback Sheet that follows

Step 4. Planning. In using influencing skills, the acid test of mastery is whether the client actually does what is expected (for example, does the client follow the direction given?) or responds to the feedback, self-disclosure, and so on in a positive way. For each skill, different topics are likely to be most useful. State goals you want to accomplish in each instance. Some ideas follow:

▲ *Directives.* The client may talk about a situation in which he or she was either insufficiently assertive or overly aggressive. The interviewer may first try a role-play to make the situation more specific and then may attempt one or more of the other directives to see how the client reacts. *Again, it is important to use listening skills to determine the key facts and feelings first, then assess the developmental level, so that the directive is more likely to be appropriate to the client.*

▲ *Logical consequences.* A member of the group may present a decision he or she is about to make. The counselor can explore the negative and positive consequences of that decision.

▲ *Self-disclosure.* A member of the group may present any personal issue. The task of the counselor is to share something personal that relates to the client's concern. Again, the check-out is important to obtain client feedback.

▲ *Feedback.* The most useful approach is for the interviewer to give direct feedback to another member of the group about his or her performance in the training sessions. Alternatively, the role-played client may talk about an issue for which the counselor will provide feedback, sharing his or her perceptions of the situation as objectively as possible. A check-out should be included.

▲ *Interpretation.* The role-played client may present an issue of interpersonal conflict. After using questions and reflective listening skills, the counselor may interpret, either from a personal point of view or from some theoretical orientation. The counselor may wish to try reframing at varying depth levels to determine their impact on and value to the client. This is a time to explore.

▲ *Influencing summary.* This skill may best be practiced in conjunction with other skills. At the end of the practice session, the counselor may summarize what he or she has been doing.

▲ *Information/advice/other.* The interviewer may give information about a particular theory or set of facts to the group. The group gives feedback on the ability of the information-giver to be clear, specific, interesting, and helpful. Psychological education may be used. Interviewing skills may be taught.

Step 5. Conduct a 5-minute practice session using the skill.   You will find it difficult to use each influencing skill frequently as they must be interspersed with attending skills to keep the interview going. Attempt to use the targeted skill at least twice during the practice session, however.

Step 6. Review the practice session and provide feedback for 10 to 12 minutes.   Remember to stop the tape to provide adequate feedback for the counselor.

Step 7. Rotate roles.

Influencing Skills Feedback Sheet

_____ (Date)

_____   _____
(Name of Interviewer)   (Name of Person Completing Form)

Instructions: Observer 1 will complete the CIS Rating Form in Chapter 8. Observer 2 will complete the
items below.

1. Did the interviewer use the BLS to draw out and clarify the client's concern? How effectively?

2. At what overall developmental level would you estimate the client to be?

_____ Level 1: Preoperational   _____ Level 3: Self-directed/formal operations

_____ Level 2: Concrete operations   _____ Level 4: Dialectic

3. Clients, regardless of general developmental level, often operate on their problems at different levels. At
what developmental level do you estimate this client is functioning on this _specific_ issue?

_____ Level 1   _____ Level 2   _____ Level 3   _____ Level 4

Summarize your observations of any developmental movement on the part of the client in the practice
session:

4. Provide nonjudgmental, factual, and specific feedback for the interviewer on the use of the specific skill.

5. Did the interviewer check out the client's reaction to the intervention?

Self-Assessment and Follow-Up

Seven skill areas are identified in this chapter. They are listed below with each level of mastery. Check off those areas for which you have demonstrated mastery. Demonstrated mastery, again, means evidence in written or taped form. Verification by an external observer competent in the skill is another form of validating mastery of a skill area. Remember the requirements for each level of mastery:

Identification.   Ability to write statements representing the skill in question and to identify and/or classify the skill when seen in an interview.

Basic mastery.   Demonstration of your ability to use the skill in a role-played interview.

Active mastery.   Demonstration of your ability to use the skill in interviews with specific impact and effects on clients. (Note functions of each skill at the beginning of the chapter.)

Teaching mastery.   Ability to teach the skill to others. In turn, the effectiveness of your teaching is demonstrated by their mastery level, as above.

Skill Area	Mastery Level				Brief Evidence of Mastery
	Identification	Basic	Active	Teaching	
Directives					
Logical consequences					
Self-disclosure					
Feedback					
Interpretation					
Influencing summary					
Information/advice/ instruction/opinion/ suggestion					

Given the complexity of this chapter and the many possible goals you might set for yourself, list below three specific goals you would like to attain in the use of influencing skills within the next month.

1. _____

2. _____

3. _____

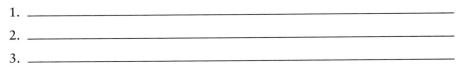

▲ References

Dreikurs, R., & Grey, L. (1968). *Logical consequences: A new approach to discipline.* New York: Dutton.

Ivey, A., & Authier, J. (1978). *Microcounseling.* Springfield, Ill.: Charles C Thomas.

Ivey, A., & Gluckstern, N. (1983). *Basic influencing skills.* No. Amherst, Mass.: Microtraining.

Ivey, A., & Litterer, J. (1979) *Face to face.* No. Amherst, Mass.: Amherst Consulting Group.

Ivey, A., Ivey, M., & Simek-Downing, L. (1987). *Counseling and psychotherapy* (2nd Ed.). Englewood Cliffs, N.J.: Prentice-Hall.

SECTION IV

Skill Integration

What is to be your own style of interviewing, counseling, or psychotherapy? This section provides a frame of reference within which to integrate the many skills and concepts of this book, so you can answer that question.

Chapter 12 presents an in-depth examination of a complete interview: you will see how to analyze an interview for skills and change in client developmental level. The chapter also contains information on how to plan for an interview, make case notes, and develop a long-term treatment plan. The final exercise in Chapter 12 is the most important one of this book, suggesting that you audio- or videorecord a full interview and develop a transcript of your work to analyze yourself and your own natural style.

Chapter 13 concludes this book; it points out how the several skills and concepts of the book may be used to examine other theories of helping. Special attention is given to assertiveness training as one additional specific-change method you will want to have available for certain clients.

By the time you have completed this book and this section in particular, you will have learned several culminating possibilities for mastery. You may aim to do the following:

1. Conduct an interview using three alternative theories:

▲ *Person-centered.* The ability to conduct an interview using only listening skills is a useful prerequisite for entering into and understanding this theory of helping.
▲ *Decisional counseling.* It has been suggested that decision making underlies most, perhaps all, counseling theory. The ability to conduct a basic decision-making interview is an important one for both decision making and understanding the methodological structure of other interviewing theories.
▲ *Behavioral counseling.* Assertiveness training is one important behavioral technique that can be used with many clients as an adjunct to several theories or by itself.

2. Examine and analyze your own behavior and thinking in the interview and discuss your specific impact on clients.
3. Define your ideas and intentions about the theory and methods you believe to be most important in counseling and interviewing.

These mastery goals are all important as you seek to develop your own culturally intentional, culturally appropriate interviewing style.

Finally, you may also want to examine the appendix of this book, which discusses how to use the teaching of interviewing skills as an adjunct to your interviewing practice. Furthermore, teaching other developing helpers and volunteers the skills of interviewing is an increasingly important aspect of a professional practice in interviewing and counseling.

12 Skill Integration: Putting It All Together

▲ Introduction

This chapter presents a detailed analysis of a single interview and shows how you can use a similar process to examine your own work. It is possible to take the many skills and concepts of this book and use them systematically in an entire interview. The basic objective of this chapter is to facilitate your examination of your own style. As you read this chapter, think ahead to how you will conduct your own interviews, develop your own plan for interviews, keep notes, and integrate your own ideas into a long-term treatment plan. The single practice exercise for this chapter will suggest that you audio- or videorecord an interview and use it as a basis to conduct a comprehensive analysis of your own style and its impact on the client.

▲ Instructional Reading

Decisional Counseling

Decisional counseling may be described as a practical model for counseling, interviewing, or psychotherapy that recognizes that decision making undergirds most—perhaps all—systems of counseling (Janis, 1983; Janis & Mann, 1977; Ivey, Ivey, & Simek-Downing, 1987). The basic point is simple: whether clients need to choose among vocations, decide whether or not to have an abortion or get married, *or* search for new ideas on how to live more effectively, *they are always making decisions.* Decisional counseling facilitates the process of decision making underlying life patterns.

Decisional counseling, then, argues that all theories of counseling and therapy—behavioral, person-centered, or even psychoanalytic—deal with decisions. The behavioral counseling process aims to teach clients how to make new decisions for assertive action or behavior control. The person-centered counselor seeks to enable clients to decide for themselves through self-examination and self-reflection. The psychoanalytic therapist is searching for the underlying factors leading to decisions. Thus decisional counseling is a basic framework useful in many settings.

The trait-and-factor legacy

Our goal in decisional counseling is to facilitate decisions and to consider the many *traits and factors* underlying any single decision. Trait-and-factor theory has a long history in the counseling field, dating back to Frank Parsons's development of the Boston Vocational Bureau in 1908. Parsons pointed out that in making a vocational decision the client needs to (1) consider personal traits, abilities, skills, and interests; (2) examine the environmental factors (opportunities, job availability, location, and so on); and (3) develop "true reasoning on the relations of these two groups of facts" (Parsons, 1909; 1967, p. 5). Trait-and-factor theory since that time has searched for the many dimensions that underlie "true reasoning" and decision making (Paterson & Darley, 1936; Williamson, 1939). Gradually trait-and-factor theory has been recognized as limited, and new decisional models have arisen (Brammer, 1985; Carkhuff, 1973; Janis & Mann, 1977; Ivey & Matthews, 1984). All of those models could be described as modern reformulations of the old trait-and-factor theory; however, they are based on more recent and sophisticated thinking and research.

Applications to the five-stage interview model

Decisional counseling concepts are basic to the five-stage model of the interview you have been working with. To help a client make an effective decision, you need to take the following five steps:

1. *Develop rapport and trust and help clients structure their problems.*
2. *Clarify the problem.* What are the key personal traits and environmental factors that need to be considered in making a decision? The positive asset search reveals client strengths that may facilitate decision making.
3. *Determine outcomes.* What does the client see as the ideal outcome of his or her decision? What are the traits and factors of a good decision or problem resolution?
4. *Generate alternatives.* This could be compared to Frank Parsons's "true reasoning" among the many traits and factors. It is here that you and the client will want to brainstorm and discover new alternatives for action. Then the client will want to decide what action to follow or what new way of thinking may be most helpful.

5. *Generalize.* Decisions made in the interview but not taken home for thought and action are not decisions. It is your responsibility to facilitate the client's action beyond the interview.

Thus, decisional counseling and decisional theory are inherent in the five-stage structure of the interview. The simplest decision model of all defines the problem, generates or brainstorms alternatives, and then decides from among the alternatives. The five-stage interview model given above is an expansion of that simple model, and you will find that all other decisional and trait-and-factor approaches use some variation on that theme.

Applications to counseling theories and settings

You will find it possible to integrate decisional concepts with many approaches to helping. Table 12-1 shows how many different theories and methods of helping can be described using the basic decisional model in the five-stage structure.

Table 12-1. Estimated time spent in stages of the decisional-model interview given different settings and approaches

	Decisional Counseling Interview	Psychoanalytic/ Psychotherapy	Assertiveness Training	Medical Diagnostic Interview	Rogerian Person-Centered Theory[3]	Manager Helping Subordinate Problem-Solve	Ineffective Welfare Interviewer
1. Rapport/structuring "Hello!"	Some	Little or none	Some	Little	Some	Some	Little or none
2. Gathering information/defining the problem and identifying assets "What's the problem?" "What are your strengths?"	Medium	Little or none	Great	Great	Great	Great	Some
3. Determining outcomes "What do you want to have happen?"	Medium	Little or none	Medium	Little or none	Little	Great	Little
4. Exploring alternatives/ confronting incongruities "What are we going to do about it?"	Medium	Great[1]	Medium	Some	Some	Medium	Great[4]
5. Generalization and transfer of learning "Will you do it?"	Great	Little or none	Medium	Little[2]	Little	Some	Some

[1]Psychoanalysis spends the bulk of its time exploring client issues.

[2]Most medical interviews are diagnostic and problem defining, with the physician telling the client what to do. Most physician directives are vague at Stage 5, which is a partial cause of low patient compliance with prescriptions.

[3]Person-centered counseling emphasizes rapport throughout. The major emphasis is on exploration and extensive discussion of the problem, which gradually merges with Stage 4, the generation of a solution.

[4]The ineffective welfare interviewer spends most of the time giving answers, with little attention to what the larger issues are.

Ivey, Ivey, and Simek-Downing (1987) provide extensive elaboration on how decisional models are implemented and used in many theories of helping. They illustrate in detail how 13 different theories may be related to the decisional model. If you are equipped with a solid base of skills and understanding gained from this book, you will find it possible to move rather rapidly into competence with seemingly widely diverse models of helping.

Let us now turn to an example interview.

▲ Example Interview: Plan, Interview, Analysis, and Further Treatment Plan

The five-stage structure of the interview will be useful to you in planning your own approach to the helping process: in developing an interview plan, conducting that interview, keeping notes on the session, and developing a long-term treatment plan; in other words, in every stage of professional concern.

Keep in mind as you read the example interview material that you will soon be analyzing your own interviewing style. You may want to organize your plan, transcript, and analysis in the same way.

Introductory client data

This initial interview illustrates that vocational counseling is closely related to personal counseling. Note how the relationship between job change and personal issues develops during the session.

The client is 36 years old and divorced, with two children. She has worked as a physical education teacher for a number of years. She stated in her information file completed before counseling that "I find myself bored and stymied in my present job as a PE teacher. I think it is time to look at something new. Possibly I should think about business. Sometimes I find myself a bit depressed by it all." The counselor will be attempting to illustrate several mastery goals of the interview in one demonstration session.

Planning the Goals of an Interview

Given the five-stage structure of the basic interview, it is possible to develop a plan for the interview before it takes place. If you don't know where you are heading, you are less likely to help the client. This does not mean you need to impose your view or concepts on the client; rather, you can think through what you want to do to help the client achieve his or her objectives.

You are about to read a transcript of an initial interview session. However, before the interview was held, the interviewer, Al, developed the interview plan presented in Box 12-1. This plan was developed from his study of a client file that consisted of a pre-interview questionnaire. As you will note, the interview plan is oriented to help the client develop her own unique vocational plan and to make possible a discussion of personal issues as well. The plan is considered a structure to help the client achieve her objectives and make her own decisions.

Box 12-1. First-Interview Plan and Objectives

	Before the first interview, study the client file and try to anticipate what issues you think will be important in the session and how you might handle them. (This plan is Al's assessment of his forthcoming interview with Jane.)
Rapport/structuring	*Special issues anticipated with regard to rapport development? What structure do you have for this interview? Do you plan to use a specific theory?* Jane appears to be a verbal and active person. I note she likes swimming and physical activity. I like to run . . . that may be a common bond. I think I'll be open about structure but keep the five stages in mind. It looks like she may want to look into vocational choice, and she may be unhappy with her present job. I should keep in mind her divorce, as this may also be a personal issue. I'll use the basic listening sequence to bring things out and probably work with a trait-and-factor decision-making model. She's probably a D-2 client: coaching helping style is needed.
Problem definition/ identification of assets	*What are the anticipated problems? Strengths? How do you plan to define the problem with the client? Will you emphasize behavior, thoughts, feelings, meanings?* Jane seems to be full of strengths. I tend too often to emphasize negatives. I should work on finding out what she *can do.* I'll use the basic listening sequence to bring out issues from her point of view. I'll be most interested in her thoughts about her job and her plans for the future; however, I should be flexible and watch for other issues. Jane may well bring up several issues. I'll summarize them toward the end of this phase, and we may have to list them and set priorities if they are many. Mainly, however, I expect an interview on vocational choice.
Defining outcomes	*What is the ideal outcome? How will you elicit the idealized self or world?* I'll ask her what her fantasies and ideas are for an ideal resolution and then follow up with the basic listening sequence. I'll end by confronting and summarizing the real and the ideal. It's worked for me in the past and probably will work again. As for outcome, I'd like to see Jane defining her own direction from a range of alternatives. Even if she stays in her present job, I hope we can find that it is the best alternative for her.
Exploring alternatives/ confronting incongruity	*What types of alternatives should be generated? What theories would you probably use here? What specific incongruities have you noted or do you anticipate in the client?* I hope to begin this stage by summarizing her positive strengths. Too early to say what are the best alternatives. However, I'd like to see several new possibilities considered. Counseling and business are indicated in her pre-interview form as two possibilities. They seem good. Are there other possibilities? The main incongruity will probably be between where she is and where she wants to go. I'll be interested in her personal life as well. How are things going since the divorce? What is it like to be a woman in a changing world? I expect to ask her questions and develop some concrete alternatives even in the first session . . . hopefully, she will act on some of them following our first session. I think vocational testing may be useful.
Generalization	*What specific plans, if any, do you have for transfer of training? What will enable you personally to feel that the interview was worthwhile?* Drawing from the above, I'll feel satisfied if we have generated some new possibilities and can do some exploration of vocational alternatives after the first session. We can plan from there. Hopefully, we can generate at least one thing she can do for homework before our second session.

Although it is, of course, sketchy, the plan does illustrate that it is possible to plan a session before it happens. As it turns out, Al's objectives were roughly realized in the session. However, if Jane had had different needs, the interview plan could have been scrapped at that time and more appropriate interventions used. Remember: an interview plan is only a plan; it is not a definitive roadmap.

Example Interview

Table 12-2 presents the interview as it actually happened, but structured to present the data according to the five-stage model. The counselor-and-client verbatim transcript is supplemented by a skill-and-focus analysis of the session. The "Comment" column analyzes the effectiveness of skills throughout the interview, with special attention given to the effect of confrontations ("C") on the client's developmental level.

Table 12-2. The Al-and-Jane five-stage interview

Skill Classifications				
Listening & Influencing	Focus	C[1]	Counselor and Client Statements	Comment
Open question	Client		**Stage 1. Rapport/structuring** 1. *Al:* Hi, Jane. How are you today?	As Jane walked in, Al saw her hesitate and sensed some awkwardness on her part. Note that she opens with two speech hesitations. Consequently, Al decides to take a little time to develop rapport and put Jane at ease in the interview. Note that he focused on a positive aspect of Jane's past. It is often useful to build on the client's strengths even this early in the session.
	Client, Interviewer		2. *Jane:* Ah . . . just fine . . . How are you?	
Information, paraphrase	Interviewer, Client		3. *Al:* Good, just fine. Nice to see you. . . . Hey, I was noting in the folder that you've done a lot of swimming.	
	Client, Main theme		4. *Jane:* Oh, yeah, (smiling) . . . I like swimming; I enjoy swimming a lot.	
Information, closed question	Main theme, Interviewer, Client		5. *Al:* With this hot weather, I've been getting out. Have you been able to?	The distinction between providing information and a self-disclosure is illustrated at *Al 5* and *Jane 6.* Al only comments that he's been getting out, whereas Janes gives information and personal feelings as well.
	Client		6. *Jane:* Yes, I enjoy the exercise. It's good relaxation.	

[1]This column will record the presence of a confrontation.

(continued)

Table 12-2 (continued)

Skill Classifications			Counselor and Client Statements	Comment
Listening & Influencing	Focus	C		
Paraphrase, reflection of feeling	Client		7. *Al:* I also saw you won quite a few awards along the way. (*Jane:* Um-humm.) . . . You must feel awfully good about that.	Jane's nonverbal behavior is now more relaxed. Client and counselor now have more body language symmetry.
	Client		8. *Jane:* I do. I do feel very good about that. It's been lots of fun.	
Information, closed question	Main theme		9. *Al:* Before we begin, I'd like to ask if I can tape-record this talk. I'll need your written permission, too. Do you mind?	Obtaining permission to tape-record interviews is essential. If the request is presented in a comfortable, easy way, most clients are glad to give permission. At times it may be useful to give the tapes to clients to take home and listen to again.
	Client		10. *Jane:* No, that's okay with me. (signs form permitting use of tape for *Intentional Interviewing and Counseling*)	
Open question	Client		**Stage 2. Gathering information/defining the problem** 11. **Al:** Could you tell me, Jane, what you'd like to talk about today?	In this series of leads you'll find that Al uses the basic listening sequence of open question, encourager, paraphrase, reflection of feeling, and summary, in order. Many interviewers in different settings will use the sequence or a variation to define the client's problem.
	Client, problem, others		12. *Jane:* Well . . . ah . . . I guess there's a lot that I'd like to talk about. You know, I went through . . . ah . . . a difficult divorce and it was hard on the kids and myself and . . . ah . . . we've done pretty well. We've pulled together. The kids are doing better in school and I'm	As many clients do, Jane starts the session with a "laundry list" of issues. Though the last thing in a laundry list is often what a client wants to talk about, the eye-contact break at mention of her "new friend" raises an issue that should be watched for in the interview.

(continued)

Table 12-2 (continued)

Skill Classifications				
Listening & Influencing	Focus	C	Counselor and Client Statements	Comment
			doing better. I've . . . ah . . . got a new friend. (breaks eye contact) But, you know, I've been teaching for 13 years and really feel kind of bored with it. It's the same old thing over and over every day; you know . . . parts of it are okay, but lots of it I'm bored with.	
Encourage	Client		13. *Al:* You say you're *bored* with it?	"I'm bored" is an important "I statement."
	Client, problem		14. *Jane:* Well, I'm bored, I guess . . . teaching field hockey and . . . ah . . . basketball and softball, certain of those team sports. There are certain things I like about it, though. You know, I like the dance, and you know, I like swimming—I like that. Ah . . . but . . . you know . . . I get tired of the same thing all the time. I guess I'd like to do some different things with my life.	Note that Jane elaborates in more detail on the word *bored*. Al used verbal underlining and gave emphasis to that word, and Jane did as most clients would: she elaborated on the meaning of the word to her. Many times short encouragers and restatements have the effect of encouraging client exploration of meaning and elaboration on a topic. "I'd like to do some different things" is a more positive "I statement."
Paraphrase	Client		15. *Al:* So, Jane, if I hear you correctly, sounds like change and variety are important instead of doing the same thing all the time.	Note that this paraphrase has some dimensions of an interpretation in that Jane did not use the words *change and variety*. These words are the opposite of boredom and doing "the same things all the time." This paraphrase takes a small risk and is slightly additive to Jane's understanding. It is an example of the positive asset search, in that it would have been possible to hear only the negative "bored." Working on the positive suggests what *can* be done. Note her response.

(continued)

Table 12-2 (continued)

Skill Classifications				
Listening & Influencing	Focus	C	Counselor and Client Statements	Comment
	Client, problem		16. *Jane:* Yeah . . . I'd like to be able to do something different. But, you know, ah . . . teaching's a very secure field, and I have tenure. You know, I'm the sole support of these two daughters, but I think, I don't know what else I can do exactly. Do you see what I'm saying?	Jane, being heard, is able to move to a deeper discussion of her issues. She has equated "something different" with a lack of security. As the interview progresses, you will note that she associates change with risk. It is these basic meaning constructs, already apparent in the interview, that undergird many of her issues.
Reflection of feeling	Client, problem	C	17. *Al:* Looks like the security of teaching makes you feel good, but it's the boredom you associate with that security that makes you feel uncomfortable. Is that correct?	This reflection of feeling contains elements of a confrontation as well, in that the good feelings of security are contrasted with the boredom associated with teaching. Note that Al matches Jane's visual system with "Looks like."
	Client, problem		18. *Jane:* Yeah, you know, it's that security. I feel good being . . . you know . . . having a steady income and I have a place to be, but it's boring at the same time. You know, ah . . . I wish I knew how to go about doing something else.	Note that Jane often responds with a "Yeah" to the reflections and paraphrases before going on. Here she is wrestling with confrontation of *Al 17.* She adds new data as well in the last sentence. On the CIS, this would be a Level-3 response.
Attending summary	Client, problem	C	19. *Al:* So, Jane, let me see if I can summarize what I've heard. Ah . . . it's been tough since the divorce, but you've gotten things together. You mentioned the kids are doing pretty well. You talked about a new relationship. *I heard you mention that.* (*Jane:* Yeah.) But the issue right now that you'd like to talk about is that . . . this feeling of boredom (*Jane:* Ummm . . .) on the job, and yet you like the security of it.	This summarization concludes the first attempt at problem definition in this brief interview. Al uses Jane's own words for the main things and attempts to distill what has been said thus far in a few words. The positive asset search has been used briefly in this section ("You've gotten things together . . . kids . . . doing well"). See also other leads in this section that emphasize client strength. Jane sits forward and nods with approval throughout this summary. The

(continued)

Table 12-2 (continued)

Skill Classifications				
Listening & Influencing	Focus	C	Counselor and Client Statements	Comment
			But maybe you'd like to try something new. Is that the essence of it?	confrontation of the old job with "maybe you'd like to try something new" concludes the summary. Note the check-out at the end of the summary to encourage Jane to react.
	Client, problem		20. *Jane:* That's right. That's it.	Jane again responds at Level 3 on the CIS.
Open question	Problem		**Stage 3: Determining outcomes** 21. *Al:* I think at this point it might be helpful if you could define for me what are some things that might represent a more ideal situation.	In Stage 3 the goal is to find where the client might want to go in a more ideal situation. You'll note that the basic listening sequence is present in this stage, but it does not follow in order, as in the preceding stage.
	Client, problem, others		22. *Jane:* Ummm. I'm not sure. There are some things I like about my job. I certainly like interacting with the other professional people on the staff. I enjoy working with the kids. I enjoy talking with the kids. That's kind of fun. You know, it's the stuff I have to teach I'm bored with. I have done some teaching of human sexuality and drug education.	Janes associates interacting with people as a positive aspect of her job. When she says "enjoy working with kids," her tone changes, suggesting that she doesn't enjoy it that much. But the spontaneous tone returns when she mentions "talking with them" and talks about teaching subjects other than team sports.
Paraphrase, open question	Client, problem		23. *Al:* So, would it be correct to say that some of the teaching, where you have worked with kids on content of interest to you, has been fun? What else have you enjoyed about your job?	The search here is for positive assets and things that Jane enjoys.
	Client, problem		24. *Jane:* Well, I must say I enjoy having summer vacations and the same vacation time that the kids have. That's a plus in the teaching field. (pause)	

(continued)

Table 12-2 (continued)

Skill Classifications				
Listening & Influencing	Focus	C	Counselor and Client Statements	Comment
Encourage			25. *Al:* Yeah . . .	Jane found only one plus in the job. Al probes for more data via an encourager. This type of encourager can't be classified in terms of focus.
	Client, others		26. *Jane:* You see, I like being able to . . . Oh, I know, one time I was able to do teaching of our own teachers and that was really . . . I really felt good being able to share some of my ideas with some people on the staff. I felt that was kind of neat, being able to teach other adults.	Jane brings out new data that support her earlier comment that she liked to teach when the content was of interest to her. The "I statements" here are more positive and the adjective descriptors indicate more self-assurance.
Closed question	Client, others		27. *Al:* Do you involve yourself very much in counseling with the students you have?	A closed question with a change of topic to explore other areas.
	Client, others		28. *Jane:* Well, the kids . . . you know, teaching them is a nice, comfortable environment, and kids stop in before class and after class and they talk about their boyfriends and the movies they go to and so on; I find I like that part of it too . . . about their concerns.	Jane responds to the word *counseling* again with discussion of interactions with people. It seems important to Jane that she have contact with others.
Attending summary, closed question	Client, problem, others		29. *Al:* So, as we've been reviewing your current job, it's the training, the drug education, some of the teaching you've done with kids on topics other than health and phys. ed. (*Jane:* That's right.) And getting out and doing training and other stuff with teachers . . . ah, sharing some of your expertise there. And the counseling relationships. (*Jane:* Ummmm.) Out of those things, are there fields you've thought of transferring to?	This summary attempts to bring out the main strands of the positive aspects of Jane's job. In an ongoing interview, a closed question on a relevant topic can be as facilitating as an open question. Note, however, that the interviewer still directs the flow with the closed question.

(continued)

Table 12-2 (continued)

| Skill Classifications | | | | |
Listening & Influencing	Focus	C	Counselor and Client Statements	Comment
	Client, problem		30. *Jane:* Well, a lot of people in physical education go into counseling. That seems like a natural second thing. Ah . . . of course, that would require some more going to school. Uhmm . . . I've also thought about doing some training for a business. Sometimes I think about moving into business . . . entirely away from education. Or even working in a college as opposed to working here in the high school. I've thought about those things, too. But I'm just not sure which one seems best for me.	Jane talks with only moderate enthusiasm about counseling. In discussing training and business, she appears more involved. Jane appears to have assets and abilities, has many positive "I statements," is aware of key incongruities in her life, and seems to be internally directed. She is most likely operating at client developmental Level D-3, but vocationally may be at Level D-2, where most clients are found. She is also preoperational, in that she is stuck and unable to act on this issue.
Paraphrase, closed question	Client, problem		31. *Al:* So the counseling field, the training field. You've thought about staying in schools and perhaps in management as well. (*Jane:* Um-hum, um-hum.) Anything else that occurs to you?	This brief paraphrase distills Jane's ideas in her own words.
	Problem		32. *Jane:* No, I think that seems about it.	
Attending summary, open question	Client, problem	C	33. *Al:* Before we go further, you've talked about teaching and the security it offers. But at the same time you talk about *boredom.* You talk with excitement about business and training. How do you put this together? What does it *mean* to you?	This summary includes confrontation and catches both content and feeling. The question at the end is directed toward issues of meaning. The word *boredom* was underlined with extra vocal emphasis.
	Client, others		34. *Jane:* Uhh . . . Ah . . . If I stay in the same place, it's just more of the same. I see older teachers, and I don't want to be like them. Oh, a few have fun; most seem just	Jane elaborates on the meaning and underlying structure of *why* she might want to avoid the occasional boredom of her job. When she talks about ending up like that, we see deeper meanings.

(continued)

Table 12-2 (continued)

| Skill Classifications | | | | |
Listening & Influencing	Focus	C	Counselor and Client Statements	Comment
			tired to me. I don't want to end up with that.	On the CIS, the client may again be rated as Level 3. While considerable depth of understanding and clarity is being developed, no change has really occurred. You will find that developmental movement often is slow and arduous. Nonetheless, each confrontation moves to more complete understanding.
Encourage	Client		35. *Al:* You don't want to end up with that.	
	Client		36. *Jane:* Yeah, I want to do something new, more exciting. Yet my life has been so confused in the past, and it is just settling down. I'm not sure I want to risk it.	Janes moves on to talk about what she wants, and a new element—risk—is introduced. Risk may be considered Jane's opposing construct to security.
Reflection of feeling	Client		37. *Al:* So, Jane, risk frightens you?	This reflection of feeling is tentative and said in a questioning tone. This provides an implied check-out and gives Jane room to accept it or suggest changes to clarify the feeling.
	Client, problem		38. *Jane:* Well, not really, but it does seem scary to give up all this security and stability just when I've started putting it together. It just feels strange. Yet I do want something new so that life doesn't seem so routine . . . and . . . ah . . . I think maybe I have more talent and ability than I used to think I did.	Jane uses many kinesthetic words. While visual descriptors are there as well, feeling and kinesthetic experience are more prominent. As meaning is explored, the interview moves toward deeper levels of experience. Jane maintains eye contact, but on close examination, she appears to be "in herself" and thinking inwardly rather than responding outwardly to Al. Her pupils are somewhat dilated in this internal frame of reference.
Reflection of meaning	Client, problem	C	39. *Al:* So you've felt the meaning in this possible job change as an opportunity to	This reflection of meaning also confronts underlying issues that impinge on Jane's decision. It

(continued)

Table 12-2 (continued)

Skill Classifications				
Listening & Influencing	Focus	C	Counselor and Client Statements	Comment
			use your *talent* and take risks in something new. This may be contrasted with the feelings of stability and certainty where you are now. But *now,* as you are, also means you may end up like some people you don't want to end up like. Am I reaching the sense of things? How does that grab you?	contains elements of the positive asset search or positive regard as Al verbally stresses the word *talent.* He is beginning to get a little closer to Jane's kinesthetic system in the check-out.
	Client, problem		40. *Jane:* Exactly! But I hadn't touched on it that way before. I do want stability and security, but not at the price of boredom and feeling down so much of the time as I have lately. Maybe I do have what it takes to risk more.	Jane is reinterpreting her situation from a more positive frame of reference. Al could have said the same thing via an interpretation, but reflection of meaning lets Jane come up with her own definition. This reinterpretation of Jane's represents a Level-5 response on the CIS. She has a new frame of reference with which to look at herself. But this newly integrated frame is *not* problem resolution; it is a *step* toward a new way of thinking and acting. After a Level-5 response, expect a client to move back to Level 3 or even Level 2. At this point, Al decides to move to Stage 4 of the interview. It would be possible to explore problem definition and ideal worlds in more detail. However, later interviews can take these matters up.
Feedback	Client		**Stage 4. Exploring alternatives/ confronting incongruity** 41. *Al:* Jane, from listening to you, I get the sense that you do have considerable ability. Specifically, you can be together in a warm, involved way with those you work	Al combines feedback on positive assets with some self-disclosure here and uses this lead as a transition to explore alternative actions. The emphasis here is on the positive side of Jane's past

(continued)

Table 12-2 (continued)

Skill Classifications				
Listening & Influencing	Focus	C	Counselor and Client Statements	Comment
			with. You can describe what is important to you. You come across to me as a thoughtful, able, sensitive person. (pause)	experience. Al's vocal tone communicates warmth, and he leans toward Jane in a genuine manner.
			42. *Jane:* Ummmm . . .	During the feedback, Jane at first shows signs of surprise. She sits up, then relaxes a bit, smiles and sits back in her chair as if to absorb what Al is saying more completely. There are elements of praise in Al's comment.
Directive, paraphrase, open question	Client, problem		43. *Al:* Other things for job ideas may develop as we talk . . . ah . . . I think it might be appropriate at this point to explore some alternatives you've talked about. (*Jane:* Um-huh.) The first thing you talked about was that what you liked teaching was drug education and sexuality. What else have you taught kids in that general area?	At this point, Al starts exploring alternatives in a little more depth. The systematic problem-solving model—define the problem, generate alternatives, and set priorities for solutions—is in his mind throughout this section. He begins with a mild directive.
	Client, problem		44. *Jane:* Let's see . . . The general areas I liked were human sexuality and drug education, and family life and family growth and those kinds of things. Ah . . . sometimes communication skills.	
Closed question	Problem		45. *Al:* Have you attended workshops on these types of things?	Closed questions can be helpful in determining specific background important in decision making.
	Client, problem, others		46. *Jane:* I've attended a few. I kind of enjoyed them. I've enjoyed them . . . I really did. You know, I've gone to	Note that virtually all counselor and client comments have focused on the client and the problem. It is important to consider

(continued)

Table 12-2 (continued)

Skill Classifications				
Listening & Influencing	Focus	C	Counselor and Client Statements	Comment
			the university and taken workshops in values clarification and communication skills. I liked the people I met.	the client in each of your responses; too heavy an emphasis on the problem may cause you to miss the unique person before you. At the same time, a broader focus might expand the issue and provide more understanding. Social work, for example, might emphasize the family and social context.
Information, reflection of feeling	Client, problem		47. *Al:* One of the roles that more and more teachers and pupil personnel people are getting into is psychological education and workshops . . . training in communication skills or values clarification. That's one aspect you would enjoy. Is that right?	Here, a brief piece of occupational information is being shared with Jane. It is followed by a reflection of feeling coupled with a check-out.
	Client, problem		48. *Jane:* I think I would enjoy that sort of thing. Um-hmmm . . . It sounds interesting.	
Paraphrase, open question	Client, problem		49. *Al:* Sounds like you have also given a good deal of thought to . . . ah . . . extending that to training in general. How aware are you of the business field as a place to train?	Jane's background and interest in a second alternative is explored.
	Client, problem, environmental context		50. *Jane:* I don't know that much about it. You know, I worked one summer in my Dad's office, so I do have an exposure to business. That's about it. They all have been saying that a lot of teachers are moving into the business field. Teaching is not too lucrative, and with all the	Jane talks in considerably greater depth and with more enthusiasm when she talks about business. The important descriptive words she has used with teaching include *boring, security,* and *interpersonal interactions,* while *interest* and *excitement* were used for training and teaching psychologically oriented subjects

(continued)

Table 12-2 (continued)

Skill Classifications				
Listening & Influencing	Focus	C	Counselor and Client Statements	Comment
			things happening with Proposition 13 here in California and all the cutbacks, business is a better possibility for teachers these days. It just seems like an intriguing possibility for me to investigate or look into. But I don't know much about it.	as opposed to physical education. Now she mentions cutbacks. Business has been described with more enthusiasm and as more lucrative. We may anticipate that she will eventually associate the potential excitement of business with the negative construct of risk and the lack of summer vacations and time to be with her children.
Paraphrase	Client, problem	C	51. *Al:* Mm-humm, . . . so you've thought about it . . . looking into business, but you've not done too much about it yet.	This paraphrase is somewhat subtractive. Jane did indicate that she had summer experience with her father. How much and how did she like it? Al missed that. The paraphrase involves a confrontation between what Jane says and her lack of doing anything extensive in terms of a search.
	Client		52. *Jane:* That's right. I've thought about it, but . . . ah . . . I've done very little about it. That's all . . .	Jane feels a little apologetic. She talks a bit more rapidly, breaks eye contact, and her body leans back a little. Jane's response is at Level 2 on the CIS. She is only partially able to work with the issues of the confrontation.
Interpretation	Problem		53. *Al:* And, finally, you mentioned that you have considered the counseling field as an alternative. Ah . . . what about that?	Al has missed the boat. More exploration of business should have followed. The confrontation of thinking but absence of action is probably appropriate, but it was brought in too early. If Al had focused on positive aspects of Jane's experience and learned more about her summer experience, the confrontation probably would have been received more easily. As this was a demonstration interview, Al sought to move through the stages perhaps a little too fast.

(continued)

Table 12-2 (continued)

Skill Classifications				
Listening & Influencing	Focus	C	Counselor and Client Statements	Comment
				Also, the counseling field is an alternative, but it seems to come more from Al than from Jane. An advantage of transcripts such as this is that one can see errors. Many of our errors arise from our own constructs and needs. This intended paraphrase is classified as an interpretation, as it comes more from Al's frame of reference than Jane's.
	Problem, others		54. *Jane:* Well, I've always been interested, like I said, in talking with people. People like to talk with me about all kinds of things. And *that* would be interesting . . . ah . . . I think, too.	Jane starts with some enthusiasm on this topic, but as she talks, her speech rate slows and she demonstrates less energy.
Encourage			55. *Al:* Um-hmmm.	
	Problem		56. *Jane:* You know, to explore that. (pause)	Said even more slowly.
Encourage			57. *Al:* Um-hmmm. (pause)	Al senses her change of enthusiasm, is a bit puzzled, and sits silently, encouraging her to *talk more.* When you have made an error and the client doesn't respond as you expect, return to attending skills.
	Problem		58. *Jane:* But . . . I'd have to take some *courses* . . . if I really wanted to get into it.	One reason for Jane's hesitation appears.
Interpretation	Client, problem		59. *Al:* So putting those three things together, it seems that you want people-oriented occupations. They are particularly interesting to you.	This is a mild interpretation, as it labels common elements in the three jobs. It could be classified also as a paraphrase.
	Client		60. *Jane:* Definitely . . . and that's where I am most happy.	Jane has returned to a Level 3 on the CIS.

(continued)

Table 12-2 (continued)

Skill Classifications				
Listening & Influencing	*Focus*	*C*	*Counselor and Client Statements*	*Comment*
Feedback	Client, problem	C	61. *Al:* And, Jane, as I talk I see you as . . . ah . . . coming across with a lot of enthusiasm and interest as we talk about these alternatives. I do feel you are a little less enthusiastic about returning to school. (*Jane:* Right!) I might contrast your enthusiasm about the possibilities of business and training with your feelings about education. There you talk a little more slowly and almost seem bored as you talk about it. You seem lively when you talk about business possibilities.	Al gives Jane specific and concrete feedback about how she comes across in the interview. There is a confrontation as he contrasts her behavior when discussing two topics. Confrontation—the presentation of discrepancies or incongruity—may appear with virtually all skills of the interview. It may be used to summarize past conversation and stimulate further discussion, leading toward a resolution of the incongruity.
	Client, problem		62. *Jane:* Well, they sound kind of exciting to me, Al. But I just don't know how to go about getting into those fields or what my next steps might be. They sound very exciting to me, and I think I may have some talents in those areas I haven't even discovered yet.	Jane talks rapidly, her face flushes slightly, and she gestures with enthusiasm. She meets the confrontation and seems to be willing to risk more intentionally. This, however, may still be considered a Level 3 on the CIS, although there may be movement ahead.
Feedback, information, logical consequences	Client, problem	C	63. *Al:* Um-hummm. Well, Jane, I can say one thing. Your enthusiasm and ability to be open and look at things is one part of your ability to do just that. As things get going in your search, you're going to find that helpful to you. Ah . . . at the same time, business and schools represent different types of lifestyles. I think I should give you a warning that if you go into the business area you're going to lose those summer vacations.	This statement combines mild feedback with logical consequences. A warning about the consequences of client action or inaction is spelled out. Jane is also confronted with some consequences of choice.

(continued)

Table 12-2 (continued)

Skill Classifications				
Listening & Influencing	Focus	C	Counselor and Client Statements	Comment
	Client, problem, others		64. *Jane:* Yeah, I know that . . . and you know, that special friend in my life—he's in education—I don't think he would like it if I was, you know, working all summer long. But business does pay a lot more, and it might have some interesting possibilities. (*Al:* Um-humm.) . . . It's a difficult situation.	Confrontations often result in clients presenting new concepts and facts important in life decisions that have not been discussed previously. A new problem has emerged that may need definition and exploration. Jane is still responding at Level 3 on the CIS, but Al is obtaining a more complete picture of the problem and of the client.
Encourage	Problem		65. *Al:* A difficult situation?	Again, the encourager is used to find deeper meanings and more information.
	Client, problem, others		66. *Jane:* Um-humm. I guess I'm saying that . . . I'm . . . ah . . . you know, my friend . . . I don't think he would approve or like the idea of my going to work in business and only having two weeks' vacation. (*Al:* Uh-huh.) He wants me to stay in some field where I have the same vacation time I have now so we can spend that time together.	Jane has more speech hesitations and difficulties in completing a sentence here than she has anywhere in the interview. This suggests that her relationship is important to her, and her friend's attitude may be important in the final vocational decision. Much vocational counseling involves personal issues as well as vocational choice. Both require resolution for true client satisfaction.
Paraphrase	Client		67. *Al:* I see; so that's an important issue in your decision as well. Is that correct?	
	Others		68. *Jane:* It really is . . . well, Bo's a special person . . .	Jane's eyes brighten.
Interpretation	Client, others		69. *Al:* And, I sense you have some reactions to his . . .	Al interrupts, perhaps unnecessarily. It might have been wise to allow Jane to talk about her positive feelings toward Bo.
	Client, problem		70. *Jane:* Yeah, I'd like to be able to explore some of my	Jane talks slowly and deliberately, with some sadness in her

(continued)

Table 12-2 (continued)

Listening & Influencing	Focus	C	Counselor and Client Statements	Comment
Skill Classifications				
			own potential without having those restraints put on me right from the beginning.	voice. Feelings are often expressed through intonation.
Interpretation	Client, problem, others	C	71. *Al:* Um-hmm . . . In a sense he's almost placing similar constraints on you that you feel in the job in physical education. There's certain things you have to do. Is that right?	This interpretation relates the construct of boredom and the implicit constraint of being held down with the constraints of Bo. The interpretation clearly comes from Al's frame of reference. With interpretations or helping leads from your frame of reference, the check-out of client reactions is even more important.
	Client, problem, others		72. *Jane:* Yes, probably so. He's putting some limits on me . . . setting limits on the fields I can explore and the job possibilities I can possibly have. Setting some limits so that my schedule matches his schedule.	Jane answers quickly. It seems the interpretation was relatively accurate and helpful. One measure of the function and value of a skill is what the client does with it. Jane changes the word *constraints* to the more powerful word *limits*. Jane remains at Level 3 on the CIS, as she is still expanding on aspects of the problem.
Open question	Client		73. *Al:* In response to that you feel . . .? (deliberate pause, waiting for Jane to supply the feeling)	Note that "pure" reflections of feeling almost always focus on the client.
	Client, problem		74. *Jane:* Ah . . . I feel I'm not at a point where I want to *limit things*. I want to see what's open, and I would like to keep things open and see what all the alternatives are. I don't want to shut off any possibility that might be really exciting for me. (*Al:* Um-humm.) A total lifetime of careers.	Jane determinedly emphasizes that she does not want limits.

(continued)

Table 12-2 (continued)

| Skill Classifications | | | | |
Listening & Influencing	Focus	C	Counselor and Client Statements	Comment
Reflection of feeling, paraphrase	Client, problem	C	75. *Al:* So you'd like to have a life of exciting opportunity, and you sense some limiting . . .	A brief, but important, confrontation of Bo versus career.
	Client, problem, others		76. *Jane:* He reminds me of my relationship with my first husband. You know, I think the reason that all fell apart was my going back to work. You know, assuming a more nontraditional role as a woman and exploring my potential as a woman rather than staying home with the children . . . ah . . . you know, sort of a similar thing happened there.	Again, the confrontation brings out important new data about Jane's present and past. Is she repeating old relationship patterns in this new relationship? The counselor should consider issues of cultural sexism as an environmental aspect of Jane's planning. This does not appear in this interview, but a broader focus on issues in the next session seems imperative. Other focus issues of possible importance include Jane's parental models, others in her life, a women's support group, the present economic climate, the attitudes of the counselor, and "we"—the immediate relationship of Jane and Al. Thus far he has assumed a typical Western "I" form of counseling, where the emphasis is on the client. Due to the development of new, more integrated data, this could be a Level-5 response on the CIS.
Paraphrase	Client, problem, others	C	77. *Al:* There really are a variety of issues that . . . you're looking at. One of these is the whole business of a job. Another is your relationship with Bo.	The interview time is waning, and Al must plan a smooth ending and plan for the next session. He catches here the confrontation that Jane faces between work and relationship.
			78. *Jane:* (slowly) Um-hmmm . . .	Jane looks down, relaxes, and seems to go into herself.
Reflection of feeling	Client		79. *Al:* You look a little sad as I say that.	This reflection of feeling comes from nonverbal observations.

(continued)

Table 12-2 (continued)

Skill Classifications				
Listening & Influencing	Focus	C	Counselor and Client Statements	Comment
	Problem		80. *Jane:* It would be nice if the two would mesh together, but it seems like it's kind of difficult to have both things fitting together nicely.	Jane here is describing her ideal resolution. Here the interview could recycle back to Stages 2 and 3, with more careful delineation of the problem between job and personal relationships and defining the ideal resolution more fully. "A problem only exists if there is a difference between what is actually happening and what you desire to be happening." This quote illustrates the importance of problem definition and goal setting. Jane's response to the confrontation is 5 on the CIS. We have an important new insight, but insight is not action. She also needs to act on this awareness.
Information, directive	Problem		81. *Al:* Well, that's something we can explore a little bit further. I see our time is about up now. But it might be useful if we can think of some actions we can take between now and the next time we get together.	Many clients bring up central issues just as the interview is about to end. Al makes the decision, difficult though it is, to stop for now and plan for more discussion later.
Influencing summary, open question	Client, problem		**Stage 5. Generalization/transfer of learning** 82. *Al:* We have come up so far with three things that seem to be logical: business, counseling, and training. I think it would be useful, though, if you were to take a set of vocational tests. (*Jane:* Mm-huh.) That will give us some additional things to check out to see if there are any additional alternatives for us to consider. How do you feel about taking tests?	Al continues his statement and moves to Stage 5. He summarizes the vocational alternatives generated thus far and raises the possibility of taking a test. Note that he provides a check-out to give Jane an opportunity to make her own decision about testing.

(continued)

Table 12-2 (continued)

Skill Classifications				
Listening & Influencing	Focus	C	Counselor and Client Statements	Comment
	Client, problem		83. *Jane:* I think that's a good idea. I'm at the stage where I want to check all alternatives. I don't want *anything* to be limited. I want to think about a lot of alternatives at this stage. And I think it would be good to take some tests.	Jane approves of testing and views this as a chance to open alternatives. She verbally emphasizes the word *anything,* which may be coupled with her desire to avoid limits to her potential. Many women would argue that a female counselor is needed at this stage. A male counselor may not be sufficiently aware of women's needs to grow. Al could unconsciously respond to Jane in the same ways she views Bo as responding to her.
Information	Client, problem		84. *Al:* Then another thing we can do . . . ah . . . is helpful. I have a friend at Jones Company who originally used to be a coach. He's moved into personnel and training at Jones. (*Jane:* Ummm.) I can arrange an appointment for you to see him. Would you like to go down and look at the possibilities there?	Al suggests another alternative action. Note that *he* is suggesting the alternatives. This may build dependency if continued over time and represents what is often done with a client at developmental level D-1. Fortunately, he provides a check-out to increase Jane's participation and uses coaching style and concrete operations to assist her move to action.
	Client, problem		85. *Jane:* Oh, I would like to do that. I'd get kind of a feel for what it's like being in a business world. I think talking with someone would be a good way to check it out.	Stated with enthusiasm. The proof of the helpfulness of the suggestion will be determined by whether or not she does indeed interview the friend at Jones and finds it helpful in her thinking.
Feedback, open question	Client, problem		86. *Al:* You're a person with a lot of assets. I don't have to tell you all the things that might be helpful. What other ideas do you think you might want to try during the week?	Al recognizes he may be taking charge too much. Especially as Jane is functioning vocationally at developmental level D-2, she needs to take more active direction, and Al should not set her limits. She'll set her own. A balance of attending and influencing is needed.

(continued)

Table 12-2 (continued)

Skill Classifications				
Listening & Influencing	Focus	C	Counselor and Client Statements	Comment
	Client, problem		87. *Jane:* What about checking into the university and ah . . . advanced degree programs? I have a bachelor's degree, but . . . maybe I should check into school and look into what it means to take more coursework.	Jane, on her own, decides to look into the university alternative. This is particularly important, as earlier indications were that she was not all that interested.
Paraphrase, influencing summary	Client, problem		88. *Al:* Okay, that's something else you could look into as well. (*Jane:* Uh-huh.) So let's arrange for you then to follow up on that. I'd like to see you doing that. (*Jane:* Um-hummmm.) And . . . ah . . . we can get together and talk again next week. You did express some concern about your relationship with your friend, Bo, ah . . . would you like to talk about that as well next week?	Al is preparing to terminate the interview.
	Client		89. *Jane:* I think so, they sort of all . . . one decision influences another. You know. It all sort of needs to be discussed.	An important insight at the end. Jane realizes her vocational issue is more complex than she originally believed. If you were Al's supervisor, would *you* recommend a primary emphasis on vocational counseling or on personal counseling in the next session? Or perhaps some combination of them both?
Self-disclosure	Client, interviewer		90. *Al:* Okay. I'll look forward to seeing you next week, then.	
			91. *Jane:* Thank you.	

This client may be described developmentally as concrete operational *and* self-directed/formal operational. She is able to work effectively in her environment and think about herself in that environment. Nonetheless, you will see that she remains preoperational in terms of her ability to act and do something about her situation. The developmental goal in this session, then, is to facilitate her examining her own career and then doing something about it. That action may be actually changing jobs, or it may be simply learning how to live more effectively with things as they are.

You will also note that this client responds primarily at Level 3 on the Confrontation Impact Scale. This means that she is understanding and expanding the complexity of her thinking, but in this session does not often reach response Levels 4 or 5. You will find that most clients move slowly toward decisions and new ways of thinking and acting. This is one of the reasons that the fifth stage of the interview—generalization—is particularly important. *The work that clients do after the interview is more important than what they do and think while you are physically present.* The transfer of ideas from the interview to daily life is the best evidence of the important movement from Levels 1, 2, and 3 to the change represented by Levels 4 and 5 of the Confrontation Impact Scale. Following the interview you will find a developmental analysis of the session.

Interview Analysis

Three commentaries on the interview will be presented: The first discusses taking notes on the session; the second reviews the skills used by the interviewer and their impact on the client; and the third examines the process of development in the client.

Notes

The interview plan in Box 12-1 described what the interviewer planned to do in the session. If you review the box, you will find that it closely approximates what happened in the session. While this indicates a well-thought-through decisional plan, it also indicates that other possibilities were not tested. If that plan had had different objectives, the interview would have been different—for example, if the interviewer had been oriented toward a Rogerian, person-centered style, the plan would have called for more client examination of self and feelings about self. Very different skills would have been used and the goal would have been phrased more in terms of self-understanding and self-actualization. It is important for counselors to realize that what they plan for the interview (and their own style and theory) has an impact on what actually happens.

The power of the counselor or interviewer to determine the session's direction cannot be denied. If you decide to do a vocational session, it usually turns out that this topic predominates. If you decide to help the person become more assertive, this too happens. And if you decide to "let the person talk and see what happens," it will occur of itself. Even though the interview may not completely follow your plan, it is your personal decision that mainly determines what happens. This is one reason why we need interview plans, examination of our own style, and notes. In this way, we can examine ourselves and at least be aware of the action and effect we have on others.

As you might anticipate, interview notes may be structured in a fashion similar to the five-stage plan. While not shown here, Al's notes might have summarized issues under rapport and structure, perhaps noting their good rapport and that they had decided to work on vocational issues. He should also have noted that his response to personal issues such as the relationship with Bo was limited. This was something that Al structured into the session. His rationale might have been "One can't talk about everything. I think Bo is important, but felt it more critical at this time to focus on vocational decisions." Structure notes such as this help to supervise and work with Al. Do you think he made the right decision? We can only really tell through examination of his interview plans, notes, and through talking with him. We do not often have verbatim transcripts of sessions.

Notes on the problem definition, Jane's goals, and the techniques and discussion of the fourth stage of the session would provide an understanding of the interview and its general function. Last but not least, notes on generalization plans should be made. You will find that you sometimes forget what happened with your clients; notes will facilitate planning for your next contact. Additionally, as we move toward increasing legal and professional accountability for our interviews, the importance of good notes cannot be overemphasized.

It may be helpful at this time if you develop a set of notes on this interview, using the five-stage model as a structure for your commentary.

Skills

Table 12-3 presents a skill summary of Al's interview with Jane. Note the different use of skills in each stage of this interview. Al used no influencing skills in Stages 2 or 3 (problem definition and determining outcomes) but a more balanced use of skills in the other stages. In Stage 4 Al used both influencing skills and confrontation of incongruity and discrepancies extensively. Stage 4 could be considered the "working" phase of the interview.

In terms of a total balance of skill usage, Al used a ratio of approximately two attending skills for every influencing skill. His focus remained primarily on the client, although the majority of his focus dimensions were dual, combining focus on Jane with focus on the problem or issue.

In examining this interview for mastery, we find that Al does manifest Level-1 mastery in that he is able to identify and classify the several skills and stages of the interview. He is able to identify some of the impact of his skills on the client.

Al also demonstrates Level 2, basic mastery, which calls for the ability to use the BLS to structure an interview in five simple stages, and to employ intentional interviewing skills in an actual interview.

Level 3, active mastery, is more difficult to assess. Let us examine this level in more detail. In terms of focus dimensions, as mentioned, Al focused primarily on Jane and her problem. Focus analysis is useful as it points out that he did not focus on others (Bo and Jane's children, for example), although some theorists might say others were the most important area of all. Furthermore, he did not use the cultural-environment-contextual focus, which might have stressed the

Table 12-3.   Skill summary of Al-and-Jane interview over five stages

	Attending summary	Enc./restatement	Paraphrase	Reflection feeling	Reflection meaning	Open question	Closed question	Client	Main theme/problem	Others	"We"/group/dyad	Interviewer	C-E-C situation	Feedback	Adv./info./expl.	Self-disclosure	Interpretation	Logical consequences	Directive	Infl. summary	Confrontation
		Attending							Focus						Influencing						C
Stage 1: Rapport/structuring (6 attending, 3 influencing skills)			2	1		1	2	9	3			2		3	1						
Stage 2: Problem definition (5 attending, 0 influencing, 2 confrontation)	1		1	2		1		9	7	1											2
Stage 3: Determining outcomes (14 attending, 0 influencing, 2 confrontation)	2	2	2	1	1	3	3	17	12	6											2
Stage 4: Explore alternatives/confront incongruities (18 attending, 13 influencing, 6 confrontation)		3	6	3		3	1	27	29	10			1	3	3			4	1	2	6
Stage 5: Generalization (3 attending, 5 influencing)			1			2		9	7			1		1	1	1				2	
Total: 45 attending, 20 influencing, 10 confrontation	3	5	13	7	1	11	6	71	58	17		3	1	4	7	2	3	1	2	2	10

world of work: Jane as a woman in a world coming to terms with sexism and job stereotyping for women. Thus, we have no real data on Al's mastery of two-thirds of the focus concepts; that would have to be demonstrated later.

But we should note that Al focused primarily on the client in the earlier phases of the interview and only in the latter portions increased his emphasis on the problem focus. Thus, he does seem to have mastered to some extent the ability to focus on the person and balance that effectively with problem focus. An ineffective interviewer might have focused early on the problem and missed the unique person completely.

In a general and perhaps more important sense, in each phase of the interview Al fulfilled the functions suggested for each stage. In the rapport stage he was able to use client observation skills to note that Jane was somewhat tense at the beginning and then to flex and select a rapport-building exchange that enabled the interview itself to be more comfortable. In the problem-definition stage Jane was able to identify a specific problem she wanted to resolve, which Al summarized at *Al 19.* In Stage 3 he again used the BLS to bring out some concrete goals (business, counseling), and through reflection of meaning *(Al 39)* he summarized some of the key aspects of Jane's thinking about the issue. In Stage 4 a number of incongruities were confronted, and with each confrontation Jane appeared to move a little deeper into some personal insights concerning her present and future. Note in particular *Al 63,* which led Jane into the important area of her personal life and relationship with Bo. The slightly inaccurate confrontation at *Al 71* fortunately included a check-out, and Jane was thus able to introduce her important construct, substituting the word *limits* for Al's *constraints.* In the final stage Jane appeared ready and willing to take action. However, the real proof of the value of the interview will have to wait until the next meeting, which will show whether the generalization plan was indeed followed through.

Examining specific skills, we might note that Al's open questions tended to encourage Jane to talk, that his paraphrases and reflections of feeling were often followed by Jane saying "Yes" or "Yeah." In the important reflection of meaning at *Al 39,* Jane responded with "Exactly! I hadn't touched on it that way before. . . . " In short, Al does seem to be able to use the skills to produce specific results with the client.

However, as noted earlier, Al's self-disclosures are not fully effective, and he did not demonstrate the full range of focusing that might have helped enlarge and round out the conception of Jane's problem. There is time for this, however, in ensuing interviews. The first interview is often a good time for general exploration. It might have been helpful if Al had used the newspaper framework (who, what, when, where, how, and why) to cover the bases more fully.

Has Al been able to produce predictable effects on Jane? "Predictable effects" refers to the functions of each of the skills and the functions of the five stages of the interview. Specifically, when an interviewer uses a particular skill or action, does the client *do* what is predicted by the defined function of the skill? Further, does the counselor actually accomplish the main goals of each stage of the session?

Another way to evaluate the effectiveness of an interview is in terms of the degree of freedom or choices available to Jane. In the words of a common counseling slogan, "If you don't have at least three possibilities, you don't have a choice." Jane appears to have achieved that objective in the interview, at least for the moment. In addition, the issue of her relationship with Bo has been unearthed, and this topic may open her to further counseling possibilities. Again, the question must be raised whether Al, as a man, is the most appropriate interviewer for Jane to see. Answers to that question will vary with your personal worldview. What are your evaluations? What would you do differently?

Developmental level

Jane's overall developmental level did not change in this session. She did appear to be clearer on the issue of what she wanted vocationally, and seemed ready to take action and follow up on the suggestions for vocational exploration. If she indeed came back the following week saying she had completed the homework, she would have moved toward greater intentionality and changed from the preoperational repetition-of-problem to doing something concrete. This "doing something different" is the best description of a Level-5 response to an entire interview or a confrontation statement.

With regard to issues of incongruity, note that Jane's verbal and nonverbal behavior gradually became more congruent and "together." Note her many speech hesitations and incongruous verbal behavior at *Jane 12* and how this changed during the session. Al's focus on Jane as a unique person helped elaborate the problem and made it possible for her to approach her issues more systematically. You will find that many of your clients are overwhelmed by the complexity of their problems. Through the careful listening and sorting skills typical of those involved in decisional counseling, you will produce considerable clarification of problems. The next step occurs with behavioral action taken on the decisional issue. This initial interview was probably aimed more at clarification than at action.

We can assume that Jane's negative "I statements" are likely to become more positive. It seems that she will probably do something to follow up on her homework assignment, but we can't know for sure until it happens. Certainly her confused emotions have been clarified through the process of the interview. Again, note *Jane 12*, then follow up and see how she becomes more congruent and integrated throughout the session. Jane also seems to move from an external locus of control to taking more responsibility for her own actions—the acid test of this, of course, is what happens after the interview is over.

In terms of the developmental theory, Jane must be considered preoperational in terms of acting on her vocational issue until she *does something*. Even though she is basically self-directed/formal operational, it seems clear that she needs the coaching/concrete operational style that the counselor uses to help her get moving. In terms of her relationship with Bo, Jane is also somewhat preoperational. She seems to be sitting on things, making no clear decision. The value of counseling in such situations often lies in sorting through issues. It may be anticipated that Jane will need a more formal operational, self- or client-directed approach from the counselor when she discusses her personal issues. As she thinks about things and makes a decision, she may need a more concrete/coaching style to help her act assertively on her decisions.

Again, the acid test of "client change beyond the interview" remains. Unless something happens as a result of this session, all the preceding analysis remains just that: analysis!

Planning for Further Interviews

Box 12-2 contains Al's interview plan for the second session. This plan derives from information gained in the first interview and organizes the central issues of the case, allowing for new input from Jane as the session progresses.

Box 12-2. Second-Interview Plan and Objectives

After reviewing the preceding session, identify issues you anticipate being important in the next session and plan how you might handle them. (This plan is Al's assessment of his forthcoming interview with Jane.)

Rapport/structuring

Special issues anticipated with regard to rapport development? What structure do you have for this interview? Do you plan to use a specific theory?
Jane and I seem to have reasonable rapport. As I look at the last session, I note I did not focus on Jane's context nor did I attend to other things that might be going on in her life. It may be helpful to plan some time for general exploration *after* I follow up on the testing and her interviews with people during the week. Jane indicated an interest in talking about Bo. Two issues need to be considered at this session in addition to general exploration of her present state. I'll introduce the tests and follow that with discussion of Bo. For Bo, I think a person-centered, Rogerian method emphasizing listening skills may be helpful.

Problem definition/ identification of assets

What are the anticipated problems? Strengths? How do you plan to define the problem with the client? Will you emphasize behavior, thoughts, feelings, meanings?

1. Check with Jane on her vocational plans and how she sees her career problem defined now. Use BLS.
2. Later in the interview, go back to the issue with Bo. Open it up with a question, then follow through with reflective listening skills. If she starts with Bo, save vocational issues until later.
3. Jane has many assets. She is bright, verbal, and successful in her job. She has good insight and is willing to take reasonable risks and explore new alternatives. These assets should be noted in our future interviews.

Defining outcomes

What is the ideal outcome? How will you bring out the idealized self or world?
This will not be too important in this interview. We already have her vocational goals, but they may need to be reconsidered in light of the tests, further discussion of Bo, and so on. It is possible that late in this interview or in a following session we may need to define a new outcome in which vocations and her relationships are both satisfied.

Exploring alternatives/ confronting incongruity

What types of alternatives should be generated? What theories would you probably use here? What specific incongruities have you noted or do you anticipate in the client?

1. Check on results of tests and report them to Jane.
2. Explore her reactions and consider alternative occupations.
3. Use person-centered, Rogerian counseling and explore her issues with Bo.
4. Relate vocations to Bo relationship. Give special attention to confronting the differences between her needs as a "person" and Bo's needs for her. Note and consider issue of women in a changing world. Does Jane need referral to a woman for additional guidance? Would assertiveness training be useful?

Generalization

What specific plans, if any, do you have for transfer of training? What will enable you personally to feel that the interview was worthwhile?
At the moment it seems clear that further exploration of vocations outside the interview is needed. We will have to explore the relationship with Bo and determine her objectives more precisely.

Box 12-3. Long-Term Treatment Plan (developed after three interviews)

Rapport/structuring	Jane seems to respond best when I am open. In the second interview she seemed to like and appreciate my self-disclosures, and it facilitated the assertiveness-training exercise. She responded well for a time when I tried Rogerian, person-centered methods but seemed to prefer more directiveness on my part. That may be me, or it may be her. We can talk about that during the next session. She does seem to like structured techniques more than unstructured.
Problem definition/ summary of assets	The following problems have been discussed thus far. Some have been touched on only briefly. In my opinion, the more important at the moment are as follows: 1. The relationship with Bo: shall she break up, or shall she stay with him? 2. Vocational choice: it now seems clear that she wants to leave the school setting, but it is quite unclear how she can handle it financially. 3. Finances are a problem we have explored only briefly. One of the attractions of the relationship with Bo is that it solves those problems. 4. Assertiveness: Jane has made a beginning but may profit from more training and practice. 5. Unpleasant dreams: Jane mentioned briefly that she had trouble sleeping this past week. I may need to explore the dream in some detail if she brings it up again. To the solution of these problems Jane brings a considerable number of assets. She is bright, attractive, verbal, and apparently has a large number of female friends. Her hobbies and leisure-time activities seem to interest her. She has worked through her divorce, and her children are doing well.
Defining outcomes	It seems safe to say the following: 1. Jane wants to make a decision one way or the other with Bo that makes it possible for her to be in a more satisfactory vocational setting. At the moment it appears that she wants to place her interests above Bo's. 2. She does want a satisfactory relationship with a man. 3. Financial planning may be necessary to help her handle her money more effectively. 4. Jane seeks to be more assertive and get her own way more often. 5. Dreams have been mentioned as a problem. 6. Further attention should be given to identifying other outcomes.
Routes toward problem resolution	1. Vocational decision will continue to be worked through with trait-and-factor decision-making counseling. 2. Explore relationship with Bo via person-centered counseling as in the past, but emphasize behavioral methods to help her act more decisively. 3. Financial advice via referral to the university may be helpful. 4. Gestalt or psychodynamic dream analysis should be kept on reserve if the dream topic comes up again. Alternatively, TA techniques may be employed. Involve Jane in this decision, as it may mean more long-term counseling than she wishes. Jane has enough assets to move forward easily on her own.
Generalization	Constantly keep in mind the array of generalization techniques available so that each problem or issue discussed gets worked on outside the interview.

In short-term counseling and interviewing, the interview plan serves as the treatment plan itself. As you move toward longer-term counseling, a more detailed treatment plan is important. There, the several problems and issues raised by the client may be outlined in much the same fashion as in the interview plan. However, problems and issues are listed at greater length, and priorities may be set. Similarly, an array of desired outcomes may be identified. For exploring alternatives and incongruity, several alternative interview plans and theoretical methods may be employed. A wide variety of generalization plans may be needed. Box 12-3 presents a sample treatment plan for Jane, assuming that she wishes to continue counseling over a longer period, such as 20 sessions.

Within the profession there is disagreement on the need for an interviewing plan and treatment plan. The more structured counseling theories, such as behavioral and strategic/structural, strongly urge interview and treatment plans with specific goals developed for each. Their interview and treatment plans are often more specific than those presented here. Less structured counseling theories (Gestalt, psychodynamic, Rogerian) tend not to have treatment plans, preferring to work in the moment with the client. The interview and treatment plan forms suggested here represent a midpoint that you may find helpful in thinking through your own opinion on this important issue.

Box 12-4. Key Points

Decisional counseling	Decisional counseling, a modern reformulation of trait-and-factor theory, assumes that most—perhaps all—clients are involved in making decisions. By considering the many traits of the person and factors in the environment, it is possible to arrive at a more rational and emotionally satisfying decision.
Decisional structure and alternative theories	The five-stage structure of the interview can be considered a basic decisional model underlying other theories of counseling and therapy. Once you have mastered the skills and strategies of intentional interviewing and the five-stage model, you will find that you can more easily master other theories of helping.
Interview analysis	Using the constructs of this book, it is possible to examine your own interviewing style and that of others for microskill usage, focus, structure of the interview, and the resultant effect on a client's developmental level.
Interview plan and notetaking	It is possible to use the five-stage interview structure to plan your interview before you actually meet with a client. This same five-stage structure can be used as an outline for note-taking after the interview is completed.
Treatment plan	A treatment plan is a long-term plan for conducting a course of interviews or counseling sessions. Using the same five-stage interview structure, it is possible to consider issues of rapport and alternative structures over time. Furthermore, one may list and prioritize key client problems and assets and list client goals to be achieved. Several alternative strategies for change may be summarized in an overall treatment plan. Finally, it is critical to develop specific plans for treatment to be generalized to daily life.

▲ Practice Exercise and Self-Assessment

Attending behavior, the first concept of this book, has served as the foundation for each successively more complex skill. By now you have experienced an array of skills and concepts. Can you integrate them into a successful interview?

This chapter presents one major practice exercise: prepare a paper in which you demonstrate your interviewing style, classify your behavior, and comment on your own skill development as an interviewer. (Following this exercise you will find a final self-assessment form.)

The steps below are suggested for this major presentation of your interviewing style.

1. Plan to conduct an interview with a member of your group, a friend, or an actual client. This interview should last at least 15 minutes (although most prefer a longer time) and should follow the basic five-stage structure. It should be an interview you are satisfied to present to others. Before you conduct the interview, be sure you have your role-played client's permission to record the session.
2. Before this interview is actually held, fill in an Interview Plan Form (Box 12-5) for the session.
3. Audiorecord or videorecord the interview.
4. Develop a transcript of the session. Place the transcript in a format similar to Table 12-4. Leave space for comments on the form.
5. Classify your interviewing leads by skill and focus; classify the client's focus as well.
6. Identify the specific stages of the interview as you move through them. Note that you may not always follow the order sequentially: indicate clearly that you have returned to Stage 2 from Stage 4 if that occurs.
7. Make comments on the transcript. Use your own impressions plus the descriptive ideas and conceptual frames of this book.
8. Develop interview notes on your session using the five-stage structure of the interview.
9. Develop an interview plan for the next session (Box 12-5).
10. Develop a long-term treatment plan (see Box 12-6).

Box 12-5. Interview Plan and Objectives Form

	After studying the client file before the first session or after reviewing the preceding session, complete this form indicating issues you anticipate being important in the session and how you plan to handle them.
Rapport/structuring	Special issues anticipated with regard to rapport development? What structure do you have for this interview? Do you plan to use a specific theory? Skill sequence?
Problem definition and identification of assets	What are the anticipated problems for this client? Strengths? How do you plan to define the problem with the client? Will you emphasize behavior, thoughts, feelings, meanings? In what areas do you anticipate working on problems?
Defining outcomes	Where do you believe this client would like to go? How will you elicit the idealized self or world? What would you like to see as the outcome?
Exploring alternatives/ confronting incongruity	What types of alternatives would be generated? What theories would you probably use here? What specific incongruities have you noted or do you anticipate in the client? What skills are you likely to use? Skill sequences?
Generalization	What specific plans, if any, do you have for transfer of training? What will enable you personally to feel that the interview was worthwhile?

Box 12-6.   Long-Term Treatment Plan

Rapport/structuring	How does this client develop rapport? What issues are of most comfort/discomfort? How does the client respond to structuring? At what place will structuring be most helpful?
Problem definition/ summary of assets	List below, in order of importance, the several problem areas of the client. Include a list of the client's strengths and assets for coping with these issues.
Defining outcomes	What are your and the client's ideal outcomes for these and other issues?
Exploring alternatives/ confronting incongruity	What are the client's main alternatives? What are your treatment alternatives? What are the main items of client incongruity? How might they best be confronted?
Generalization	What are your specific plans for generalization of learning from the interview?

Table 12-4. Form for recording transcript of an interviewing session (indicate stages of the interview as they occur)

Skill Classification			Counselor and client statements	Comment
Listening and influencing	Focus	C²		

²C = confrontation

Self-Assessment and Follow-Up

After you have completed the practice exercise for this chapter, go back to your interview completed in Chapter 1, and note how your style has changed and evolved since then. What particular strengths do you note in your own work?

_____

_____

_____

_____

_____

_____

_____

_____

_____

_____

_____

_____

_____

▲ References

Brammer, L. (1985). *The helping relationship*. Englewood Cliffs, NJ: Prentice-Hall.

Carkhuff, R. (1973). *The art of problem solving*. Amherst, Mass.: Human Resource Development.

Ivey, A., Ivey, M., & Simek-Downing, L. (1987). *Counseling and psychotherapy: Integrating skills, theory, and practice*. Englewood Cliffs, N.J.: Prentice-Hall.

Ivey, A., & Matthews, W. (1984). A meta-model for structuring the clinical interview. *Journal of Counseling and Development, 63*, 237–243.

Janis, I. (1983). *Short-term counseling*. New Haven, Conn.: Yale University Press.

Janis, I., & Mann, L. (1977). *Decision making: A psychological analysis of conflict, choice, and commitment*. New York: Free Press.

Parsons, F. (1909; 1967). *Choosing a vocation*. New York: Agathon.

Paterson, D., & Darley, J. (1936). *Men, women, and jobs*. Minneapolis: University of Minnesota Press.

Williamson, E. (1939). *How to counsel students*. New York: McGraw-Hill.

CHAPTER

13

Determining Personal Style and Theory: Life Is Not a Straight Line

---

How can determining your own personal style and theory help you and your clients?

Major function

You are an individual just as your client is an individual. While we may have many similarities and shared interests and develop many skills in common, the uniqueness remains. You can be most effective as an interviewer and counselor if you take your own natural being, combine it with information from this book and from other sources, and gradually evolve your own formulation of the helping process.

Your client will benefit from this as well. If you are comfortable with your approach and it fits *you*, the client is likely to benefit from your genuineness and authenticity. At the same time, it is hoped that you will be able to change and shift your style to meet the needs of your complex, ever-changing clients. At this point, no one theory seems able to meet the needs of our diverse clientele.

Secondary functions

Developing your own personal style and theory may be expected to result in the following:

▲ A greater awareness that interviewing and counseling are not simple, but rather incredibly complex processes requiring movement, change, and constant development
▲ An awareness of the rich array of theories and concepts available to you and your clients that may be used to facilitate the development of both

---

▲ Introduction

Developing your own personal approach to counseling and therapy involves a number of factors. It is *not* "doing your own thing" in the narcissistic sense once exemplified by those who overused Fritz Perls's concepts. Rather, it is doing your own thing in synchrony with another person doing his or her own thing. Developing your own personal style requires an audience—the client—who can appreciate and participate in your performance, just as you can appreciate and develop your own self *with* the client's help.

Some counselors and therapists have developed individual styles of helping that require their clients to join them in their orientation to the world. Such individuals have found the one "true and correct" formula for counseling and therapy; clients who have difficulty with that formula are often termed "resistant" and "not ready" for counseling. While these counselors have their own

313

style, their methods tend to be rigid and dogmatic. Such counselors and therapists can and do produce effective change, but they may be unable to serve many client populations. Missing from their orientation is an understanding of the complexity of humanity and the helping process.

Thus, as you develop your own personal style and theory of helping, try to expand the number of individuals of varying developmental levels, special populations, and cultures with whom you can work. Culture in this book has been defined rather broadly as ethnic, religious, lifestyle, sex, handicap, and more traditional cultural differences usually described as racial and geopolitical in origin.

This chapter seeks some structure for your evolving identification of your own personal style. To that end, the microskills hierarchy will be reviewed, but this time as a complex matrix for decision making on your part. The purpose now is to remind you just how many skills and concepts have been presented in this book. A brief map showing how those skills and concepts play themselves out in different modes of counseling and therapy should aid you in the search for your personal style.

One new concept is introduced in this chapter: assertiveness training will be presented as one systematic approach to change. It is hoped that it will be a useful addition to your array of tools and techniques.

▲ Instructional Reading

The Microskills Hierarchy: A Summary

You have thus far been presented with 12 chapters of reading containing 28 major concepts and skill categories. Within those major divisions are somewhat more than 100 specific stages, steps, levels, and dimensions. Ideally, you should

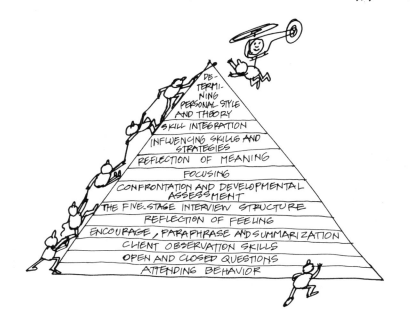

commit them all to memory and be able to draw on them immediately in practice to facilitate your clients' development and progress in the interview.

And these items are primarily skills, concepts, and understandings that are but a beginning. This book has not considered details of personality development, testing, and the over 250 theories of counseling and therapy available. While it has shown that these skills and training concepts are used in fields as varied as medicine, management, social work, and parent education—and with many cultural groups—only a brief introduction to the multitude of applications has been given.

How can you manage to retain all of this book's concepts? Most likely, you cannot at this point. However, as you develop as an interviewer, counselor, or therapist, you will find the ideas expressed here to become increasingly clarified, as your mastery of skills and theories will likewise continually increase.

In addition, retaining and mastering the concepts of the microskills hierarchy may be facilitated by what is termed *chunking*. We do not learn information just in bits and pieces; we organize it into patterns. The microskills hierarchy is a pattern that can be visualized and experienced. For example, at this moment you can probably immediately recall that attending behavior has certain major concepts "chunked" under it (culturally and individually appropriate eye contact, body language, vocal qualities, and verbal tracking). You can probably also recall the purpose of open questions and perhaps which questions lead to what likely outcome (for example, how questions lead to process and feelings).

With periodic review and experience, the many concepts will become increasingly familiar to you. If you complete a transcript examining and classifying your own interviewing style similar to the one presented in Chapter 12, the ideas of this book will become especially clear. As you must have noticed, those skills you have practiced instead of just reading about are the ones you understand best and that have most relevance for you. Reading is a useful introduction to counseling and interviewing, but the results of practice and experience will stick with you far into the future.

Table 13-1 summarizes the major concepts of the book; take some time to review your own mastery levels in each of the 28 major areas and enter the results on the table. Can you do the following?

1. *Identify and describe the concept?* If it is present in an interview, can you label it? These concepts provide a vocabulary and communication tool with which to understand and analyze your interviewing and counseling behavior and that of others. The ability to identify concepts means most likely that you have "chunked" most of the major points of the skill together in your mind. You may not immediately recall the six types of focus, but when you see an interview in progress you will probably recall which one is being used.

2. *Demonstrate basic mastery?* Basic mastery simply means that you have practiced the construct and have been able to recall it enough to use it. Such mastery facilitates retention and eventual active mastery. You may claim basic mastery of all the skills you have practiced.

3. *Demonstrate active mastery?* Skilled interviewers, counselors, and therapists can use the microskills and the concepts of this book to produce specific,

concrete effects with their clients. If you reflect feelings, do clients actually talk more about their emotions? If you provide an interpretation, do your clients see their situation from a new perspective? If you work through some variation of the positive asset search, do your clients actually view the situation more hopefully? If you conduct a well-formed, five-stage interview, do clients change their self-concept and/or developmental level? Do they change their behavior and thinking?

Active mastery shows not in your use of the skills and concepts, but rather in what your client does. To demonstrate active mastery, you must be able to produce *results* due to your efforts in helping.

4. *Demonstrate teaching mastery?* The concept of teaching skills to others has always remained in the background of this book. Psychoeducation—teaching clients and colleagues what you know about skills—is a vital role of the intentional interviewer, counselor, or therapist. Teaching requires the ability to reflect on the skills and concepts and on those with whom you would share them. (In entering your mastery levels on Table 13-1, check the teaching box only if you have actually taught the skill or concept to clients or some other group.)

Teaching these skills as communication units may be considered a treatment alternative in its own right. For further discussion of teaching skills as a therapeutic alternative, see Ivey (1973), Ivey, Ivey, and Simek-Downing (1987), and Larson (1984).

You will note that two additional major concepts appear in the table, based on new material covered later in this chapter: (1) assertiveness training and (2) defining your own system of helping.

Table 13-1. Mastery level self-assessment summary

Skill or Concept	Identification	Basic mastery	Active mastery	Teaching mastery	Evidence of Achieving Mastery Level
1. Attending behavior					
2. Questioning					
3. Client observation					
4. Encouraging					
5. Paraphrasing					
6. Summarizing					

(continued)

Table 13-1 (continued)

Skill or Concept	Identification	Basic mastery	Active mastery	Teaching mastery	Evidence of Achieving Mastery Level
7. Reflecting feelings					
8. Basic listening sequence					
9. Positive asset search					
10. Empathy					
11. Five stages of the interview					
12. Confrontation					
13. Assessment of developmental level					
14. Assessment of counseling style					
15. Focusing					
16. Reflection of meaning					
17. Directives					
18. Logical consequences					
19. Self-disclosure					
20. Feedback					
21. Interpretation					
22. Influencing summary					
23. Information/advice/instruction/ opinion/suggestion					
24. Interviewing plans					
25. Vocational/decisional counseling					
26. Person-centered counseling					
27. Assertiveness training					
28. Defining personal style and theory					

A developmental theory of skills

The four mastery levels just listed bear a rough correspondence to the four developmental levels presented in Chapter 8. Many beginners enter interviewing and counseling training as D-1, preoperational; they may be initially confused about what helping is and how it works.

Through the identification of skills and concepts, they find that those bits and pieces of helping can be organized into meaningful units to produce change. But at the identification level, they may still be preoperational. Identification does not mean one is able to operate concretely in the fields of counseling and therapy or to conduct an interview.

The transformation to concrete operations and skillful interviewing is made through practicing the microskills and interviewing structure. Basic mastery may be considered the beginning level of concrete operational interviewing and counseling, where counseling trainees can demonstrate the ability to engage in a skill. But they still have not demonstrated the ability to be relevant to or have an impact on the client; that remains to be seen in the late concrete operations level, in which they predictably use a skill with a measurable result. Active mastery is achieved when they can concretely operate in the environment, when they can use skills with predictable benefit to the client.

But what of the self-directed/formal operations D-3 level? Formal operational thought is characterized by thinking about oneself and one's behavior. At the end of each chapter, you were requested to conduct a self-assessment. In particular, you were constantly asked to think about the skill, its relevance to you, and how you might want to use it. You were asked to establish goals for the further use of that skill. Through your personal integration of skills with self-reflection, you have been moving toward the formal operations level.

Thus, as you fill in Table 13-1, reflect on each concept and how it relates to you personally. This self-reflection is an important part of defining your own space, your own method of helping.

The dialectical or mutual D-4 level is entered when you are no longer just deciding what your favorite mode of helping is to be, but how it is relevant to your client as well. You will find as you work with clients that you learn from them, just as they will learn from you. You may engage in constant change and development through your interaction with them, and your style of counseling will undoubtedly shift and change in response to their needs. If you remain solely at the self-directed/formal operational level, you may crudely impose your mode of helping on others without consideration for individual and cultural differences. The most effective helper is often willing to change and learn as a result of contact with clients. There is always something more to learn in counseling and psychotherapy.

The written word, unfortunately, tends to stand still. This makes dialectical, interactive dialogue with you, the reader, difficult. However, methods such as requesting that you examine each skill carefully and make your own determination about it help to create a dialogue with you. The concepts in this book have changed over the years due to interaction with others and with readers and

co-participants in the process of learning. Please take time to fill out the questionnaire at the end of this book and return it to the publisher so that this book will continue to change and develop.

And so it is: we are humans co-developing, co-evolving together. Counseling and therapy are about development. If you find these ideas interesting, you may want to read *Developmental Therapy: Theory into Practice* (Ivey, 1986); in it, the developmental concepts are integrated with the ideas of Piaget and philosopher Plato, with many suggestions for facilitating developmental movement and progress in the client. Let us now turn to how specific theories manifest themselves in the helping interview.

Alternative Theories of Helping

If you are equipped with a solid understanding of the foundation skills of attending and observing, the BLS, the five-stage structure of the interview, confrontation, and some of the influencing skills, you have a base that will enable you to engage in many widely different theories of helping. At this point, you may wish to return to Table 1-1 and note the following:

1. Different theories use different patterns of microskills.
2. Each theory focuses on a somewhat different definition of what is the main theme or problem to be addressed. For example, decisional vocational counseling focuses on future plans, Rogerian person-centered therapy on feeling and meanings, and behavioral counseling on directly observable behavior.

Also important is Table 13-2, which illustrates that all theories may be understood via the five-stage interviewing structure. With just this limited information, you can obtain a broad sense of how different theories relate to one another. The purpose of this section is to further illustrate how theories relate and how you can use the skills you have mastered to learn new theoretical patterns, integrating them more easily with your own conceptions.

Table 13-2.   Three major approaches to counseling and the five-stage interview structure

Decisional Vocational Counseling	*Person-Centered Helping*	*Behavioral Assertiveness Training*
Stage 1: Rapport/Structuring		
All three orientations suggest the need to establish rapport with your client in an easy, natural style.		
Will describe purpose of interview as examining the decisional process. May even outline the five stages of the interview at this point.	Tends not to discuss structure and purpose of session with client. Will tend to move immediately to discussion of current issues of the client. As the issues come up, stress may be on pointing out the importance of the client directing the session.	Will emphasize client participation in the process and state the importance of client's defining the problem and the goals of counseling. May point out that emphasis in interview will be on specific, behavioral problem solving.

(continued)

Table 13-2 (continued)

Decisional Vocational Counseling	Person-Centered Helping	Behavioral Assertiveness Training

Stage 2: Defining the Problem/Identifying Positive Assets

BLS used to draw out the facts, feelings, and organization of the client's vocational decision problem or other decisional issues.	BLS used to draw out client concerns. Focus will vary, but most basic focus will be on the client's facts and feelings about self. The developmental issue is self-reflection, a Level-3 concern. In some orientations, questioning is considered inappropriate. Good reflective listening skills can accomplish the same thing as questions *if* you have a high-developmental-level, verbal client. Reflection of feeling and meaning are important skills here and throughout session.	BLS emphasis is on behavior and facts, with secondary emphasis on feelings. Focus will tend to be more comprehensive and aware of contextual-environmental issues than other theories.
Specific BLS emphasis on past strengths and successes of the client via positive asset search. Focus will tend to be on the problem and others.		Positive asset search uses BLS to find positive behaviors and strengths in person and in the environmental support system.
	Constant emphasis on positive asset search, positive regard, and positive reframing of client experience.	Role-play of a specific problem example of client usually found at this stage. The role-play is reviewed for behavioral specifics, self-talk, some emphasis on feelings.

Stage 3: Defining Goals

BLS used to draw out client's ideal vocational and decisional goals.	BLS used to draw out person's *ideal self,* which can be contrasted with the *real self* identified in Stage 2. Reflection of meaning may be especially important here.	BLS facilitates the client's determining goals for behavioral change. Major emphasis is on defining very accurately the desired behavioral change.

In all three theories, the counselor or therapist may use feedback, interpretive, or advice skills to add to the client's goal statement. The decisional counselor and the behavioral counselor are somewhat more willing to use these skills than is the person-centered counselor.

Stage 4: Confronting Incongruity/Generating Alternatives

Basic confrontation is between the present decisional problem and the ideal goal.	Basic confrontation is between the person's real self and ideal self.	Basic confrontation is between present behavior and goal behavior.
May use vocational tests, occupational or decisional information, role-playing of job interviews, or careful weighing of pros and cons of each possible decision.	Major emphasis is on helping the client explore life patterns more fully and gain a sense of self. Relatively little emphasis on specific decisions and actions.	Repeats the role-play again and again until client can demonstrate the behavioral goals to both the client's and the counselor's satisfaction. There will be a discussion of the many factors in the client's environmental context that tend to work for or against the maintenance of the newly learned behavior.
Will tend to move to more extensive use of influencing skills such as directives, feedback, and logical consequences to help client become more aware of the future impact of decisions.	The BLS (with the possible exception of questions) continues to be central in this basically listening form of helping. Feedback and self-disclosure tend to be important. As issues become more complex, reflection of meaning may become central.	
Ultimate focus is on helping the client to select one or more decisional possibilities and then to *act* on the decision.	Ultimate focus is on the person finding a unique sense of self and	Directives, feedback, and logical consequences are important skills at this phase of behavioral assertiveness training. The counselor is willing to influence the client, but

(continued)

Table 13-2 (continued)

Decisional Vocational Counseling	Person-Centered Helping	Behavioral Assertiveness Training
	the integration of the real and ideal self.	always toward the client's goal. Ultimate focus is on the client being able to demonstrate new behavior and to plan its transfer to the "real world."
Stage 5: Generalization Some type of homework or follow-up on decisions after the interview is considered essential. Behavioral-type role-plays may be used to facilitate generalization—or person-centered methods to help the client examine the self in relation to the decision.	Relatively little emphasis on generalization unless the client brings up the issue. As the goal is self-reflection rather than action, one may expect some generalization of thinking processes, but not necessarily behavioral change. If one has a solid sense of personal life meaning and values, however, many aspects of life may change.	Major emphasis is on generalization. Often uses written contracts or the systematic framework of relapse prevention. Behavioral counseling has taken the lead in demonstrating the importance of planning generalization of learnings from counseling and therapy. Change that is not carried beyond the laboratory of the interview to the real world is not change.

To illustrate this point, let us take the case study of Jane from the preceding chapter. Let us assume that Jane comes to us with the vocational problem presented at *Jane 12*. You have seen how the vocational decisional counselor, Al, used the BLS to draw out client facts and feelings and then summarized them at *Al 19*. The problem focus was on vocational decisional issues. If Jane were to see a person-centered counselor or behavioral counselor, similar listening skills would be used, but the focus would be quite different.

Person-centered theory

A person-centered counselor is most often interested in focusing on the meaning and feelings of the client; the actual facts of the problem are considered less important. The goal is self-actualization, helping clients realize themselves more fully. Decisions may be made, but it is how the client feels about himself or herself that is most important. Therefore, the focus is much more on the person and much less on the problem. Questions are considered intrusive and generally to be avoided in this orientation.

Person-centered theory is considered most appropriate for developmental Level D-3 self-directed/formal operational clients who are best able to think through their own direction, although the concepts may be helpful with many other clients as well.

The person-centered counselor may be expected to wait for Jane to initiate the conversational topic. After a moment's pause, Jane begins:

Jane: Well . . . ah . . . I guess there's a lot of things that I'd like to talk about. You know, I went through a difficult divorce and it was hard on the kids and myself and . . . ah . . . we've done pretty well. We've pulled together. The kids are doing better in school and I'm doing better. I've . . . ah . . . got a new friend (breaks eye contact). But, you know, I've been teaching for 13 years and I'm really kind of bored with it. It's the same old thing over and over every day; you know . . . parts of it are okay, but lots of it I'm bored with.

Counselor: Sounds as if *you* feel rather good about *yourself* and pulling it together, yet there are parts of *you* that feel bored and incomplete.

(This reflection of feeling includes a strong dimension of recognition and confrontation of mixed feelings. Person-centered counselors often give attention to the word *you* and emphasize it through verbal underlining—See Chapter 2— thus personalizing the interview.)

Jane: Yes, sometimes I feel confused. I know I've done well, but where do I go next? Something seems to be missing. Here I am, 36, yet alone and feeling stalemated. What does it all mean?

Counselor: Jane, you say something is missing; you feel alone and stalemated when *you* look at *yourself* from a deeper level. There's something *missing* for you . . . (pause) . . . there's something missing that's *meaningful.*

(This is basically a reflection of meaning. The counselor is searching for Jane's underlying values and meanings in the belief that if she finds her true self, she will self-actualize and solve many issues spontaneously. Here you see the client-directed/formal operational style that expects clients to be able to solve their own dilemmas.)

Jane: Yes. . . . (pause) . . . (starts quietly crying) . . . I feel so alone. I've had several menfriends, but none ever seem to work out. It's been so hard over these years. . . . Where am I? What should I do?

Counselor: You've felt alone at the deepest level. You've had the strength and wisdom to work through many difficulties, but somehow, somewhere, something meaningful is missing for *you.* . . .

(This is a complex statement, typical of those who adopt the person-centered style. Note the reflection of feeling at the beginning, followed by feedback that points out positive assets of the client; this is characteristic of the Rogerian concept of positive regard. The final portion of the statement orients itself again to meaning: the underlying, deeply felt issues that impel us to action, often without our awareness.)

Perhaps you can see the value and effectiveness of this Style-3 client-directed approach to helping. It provides Jane with the opportunity to reflect on herself and her state of being. Vocational and personal decisional issues may resolve themselves over time. On the other hand, it may be wise to alternate between such personal reflections and the decisional model. Moreover, the behavioral approach may provide a helpful supplement.

Behavioral theory

The behaviorally oriented counselor might compliment the counselor above for empathy and sensitivity but would point to research suggesting that interpersonal change occurs more quickly and directly through counseling oriented toward observable behavior. Let us assume Jane begins the interview in the same way. The behavioral counselor would tend to respond differently and search for directly observable things that might be identified and changed. The behavioral counselor tends to assume a Style-2, coaching approach and is concerned with action and *doing*, helping clients concretely operate in their environment.

Counselor: You say you are *bored*, even though you sound very busy and active. What is going on, what are *you doing* when you are bored? What's going on?

(The behavioral counselor is interested in knowing the concrete specifics of what is happening behaviorally in the person and in the surrounding environment. What can the client, Jane, see, hear, and observe directly?)

Jane: Well, so many things are happening, between the job and the kids, that I never get time to stop and think. Something is happening all the time. I just keep going. There is always someone demanding something from me. . . . It's very frustrating not being able to *ever* have a minute.

Counselor: I see; never a minute for yourself. What are some objectives you have for yourself here today?

(The counselor is aware that the session could go in many possible directions. As is typical of behavioral counselors, there is an emphasis on having Jane *participate* in that direction and goal selection. Whereas the person-centered counselor does not aim to direct the client, the behavioral counselor usually seeks to have specific objectives in mind.)

Jane: Well, I heard that you were good at helping people become more assertive, expressing themselves more . . . maybe through that I can find myself more clearly.

Counselor: That sounds like a reasonable objective, Jane. If I hear you correctly, you feel pretty overwhelmed by life and are tired of living without time for yourself. You're hoping assertiveness training can be part of that process. Is that right?

In this brief excerpt, you'll have noticed an emphasis on *doing* and on *observable behavior.* You probably observed that the vocational counselor in Chapter 12, the person-centered counselor, and the behavioral counselor all used basic listening skills to draw out the problem, of which you are now quite aware. Yet you may also have noticed that they *attended* to different things and that the interview was very different in each case. Hopefully, you can see the potential value in each of the three very different theories of helping. Jane could profit from a clearer vocational choice; she could also benefit from becoming more self-directed and aware of herself; and, in addition, she certainly could become more assertive in expressing her point of view. The assertiveness-training interview is pursued in more detail later in this chapter.

Personal implications for your theory

What does this imply for you, the individual developing his or her own theory of counseling? Several things. First, you probably found that you preferred one of these three theoretical organizations to the others. Which did you prefer?

Perhaps you have other approaches that you personally feel might be more useful than any of these. A useful step in developing your own style is to examine other styles and compare them to your own. What do you value? What makes sense to you? With what skills and strategies are you most comfortable? You may want to go back to transcripts or tapes of interviews you conducted when you first began reading this book, or to past case notes on your work in interviewing or counseling.

Through completing Chapter 12's important exercise, which asked that you make a transcript of a complete interview of your own and analyze your own behavior, you took important action to define your own style and theory. This self-examination and analysis could be described as the *heart* of finding one's own personal style and orientation to interviewing and counseling.

A second step in determining your own theory is to plan to develop a broader awareness of the theoretical and methodological alternatives available to you to supplement your own basic style. If you have mastered the basic listening skills, you now know that you can use the BLS to draw out client behavior *or* to help clients talk about their feelings and meanings *or* to learn about vocational problems *and so on* through the many orientations to helping. All interviewing methods use microskills; however, they use them very differently. Just as the microskills vary in quantity and style of usage among different theories, remember that the five stages of the interview are used differently in different theories (see Table 12-1).

Thus, the two main dimensions of developing your own personal style of helping are (1) analyzing and understanding your own approach to helping through self-analysis; and (2) examining other approaches to the helping field and selecting those most compatible with your own natural style of being. Through that decisional process, it is possible that you may choose to make a specific theoretical commitment. There is much to learn and use in all theories; full mastery of even one of them can take years. A good argument can be made for the effective helper not trying to master the theories all at once, but rather selecting one or two established theories and mastering those before attempting more.

Table 13-2 (page 320) presents three alternative methods of helping. The first is a Rogerian person-centered orientation, the second is a decisional vocational session, and the third is a model behavioral assertiveness training interview. You may use the outline in Box 13-2 as a guide for practice of these theories. An abbreviated assertiveness training transcript will be in the following section.

Assertiveness Training

Assertiveness training is an important technique to master and have available for some of your clients; it was developed by behavioral psychologists (Alberti & Emmons, 1970), but has come to be one of the more widely accepted techniques for assisting clients regardless of theoretical orientations. For example, many feminist-oriented helpers use this method to help women become more direct and achieve their own goals. You will find that assertiveness training will often be used as part of rational-emotive therapy, that it is often needed to help

vocational counseling clients communicate better at work or conduct better job interviews, and that even psychoanalysis may refer clients to a behavioral specialist to learn the skills of life management via assertiveness training.

Assertiveness training requires that you use a coaching, concrete operations style in which both attending and listening skills help the client reach his or her goals. In some cases, like a good coach, you may suggest goals for the client, but you will not want to impose them.

In the preceding section, you saw Jane work toward assertiveness training in her interview with a behavioral therapist. Let us continue examining how the technique might be conducted with Jane. Using the same client helps us see that very different styles of counseling can benefit her, although the methods and goals may vary considerably.

Stage 1: Rapport/structuring

The initial part of the interview will not differ from other types of counseling, since the behavioral counselor or assertiveness-training specialist also cares about people. Rapport will be established with the client, because unless there is a caring, relaxed atmosphere, change and development are virtually impossible.

Thus, the beginning part of the assertiveness-training interview would look very much like the start of the decisional counseling session in Chapter 12. Once rapport is established, the structure of the interview may be outlined so that the client knows what to expect. In this stage of the interview, the counselor might say something like this:

"Jane, you've been referred to me for work on assertiveness training. As you know, this system is often helpful in enabling us to speak up more effectively and to obtain our goals—without overruling or overrunning other people. We'll discuss your situation and then role-play some ideas that may help you work through some of the issues. Is that okay?"

This comment would most likely immediately precede the introduction of Stage 2. Jane would be involved in the decisional process as much as necessary. Structuring of assertiveness training or any other style of counseling and interviewing helps the client understand what is going on and may even enable the client to work with the therapist in a more mutual fashion.

Behavioral counseling, once assumed to be an imposition on the client, over time has become one of the most sophisticated methods of helping, and works actively to ensure that the interview is "person-centered" in the best sense of that term.

Stage 2: Gathering information/defining the problem/identifying assets

(Jane has stated her general problem as never having a minute for herself and as desiring to speak for herself more clearly. The interview has set some general objectives, but the counselor wants more behavioral, observable specifics. The interview continues.)

Jane: Yes, that's right, everyone seems to run over me. I can't say no.

Counselor: Could you give me a specific, recent example of a time when you didn't say no? What happened? What did you do?

Jane: Well, I was talking to the principal today. He wants me to take on advising still another club. I'm coach of two sports now and advising the Tri-Hi-Y's. Every activity I do makes me stay after school and I get home late. And when I get home late the kids want even more from me . . . and then Bo seems to want more too! I can't say no to any of them.

Counselor: You can't say no to any of them. I can see your frustration and how you are trying. Must be difficult. Let's take just one of these and examine it more closely. Which one?

(Jane clearly has a repeating pattern of behavior and thought in which she consistently allows others to direct her life. She could benefit from a person-centered approach, which would help her understand the pattern, but the issue here is concrete behavior and action, not self-directed personal reflection.)

Jane: The principal . . . he just walks all over me. If I could start with him, maybe I could learn what to do with the others . . . maybe even Bo.

Counselor: (interrupts) Okay. Rather than talk about it and analyze it to death, I'd like to see what really happens when you have to engage in a decision like that. You know, role-playing. . . . I'm going to be your principal and ask you to take on that activity. You play yourself and react to me just as you did earlier today. Okay? (Jane nods in agreement.) I'm the principal now. Jane . . . thanks for coming in. It's good to see you. You've done a great job with the swim team and the field hockey team this year. We like what we see.

Jane: (smiles) Thanks.

Counselor: Jane, we've got a problem. The community is asking us to do more about drugs, and a group of parents have assembled a committee and want school participation. You have really good relations with the kids and have done a few workshops on the problems of drugs. I want you to join that committee.

Jane: (smiles, but a little weakly) Uhh . . . I'd sure like to do it. I'm beginning to see some real problems in some of my classes. But I'm simply overloaded with the teams, and my kids are getting older and need me to drive them places. I don't see how I could. . . . (hesitates, eyes downcast).

Counselor: I'm glad you're interested. . . . It's only one night a week. The group wants to work with us in developing a curriculum and I want to be sure our point of view is represented. I'll call and tell them you'll do it.

Jane: (somewhat desperately, but weakly) Harry, I don't see how I can do it. . . . Sure, I'd like to help, but. . . .

Counselor: And you *are* a help. I'll meet with you during the week to give you additional support. I want to keep in touch with this.

Jane: (weakly) Okay.

Counselor: (leaving role of principal) Is that how it is? You give in that easily?

Jane: I'm afraid so. . . . It happens all the time. I'm just so anxious to please others.

Counselor: I can understand that. Jane, what did you *do* in that role-play that got in your way? What *specifically* were you *doing* that allowed the principal to run over you?

 (Note the search for concreteness and specificity typical of the Style-2 coaching/concrete operational counselor.)

Jane: Well, I certainly give in easily. I noted that I let him do most of the talking. He didn't listen to me. I felt pretty uncomfortable.

Counselor: And, Jane, your eyes were looking down; you hesitated; your voice sounded weak.

Jane: In situations like that, I *feel* very weak. And I suppose I smiled a lot. I do that when I feel cornered. Somehow that is a symptom of my wanting to help others and please them.

 (Note that a person-centered counselor might be tempted to follow up on this behavior pattern and move to Style-3 helping. For example, "In difficult situations, you seem to seek to please others, almost as if it is your only way of being.")

Counselor: So, Jane, if you are going to be more assertive, you're going to have to take charge. We've noted several specific things that you *do:* first, you smile, even though you don't mean it, thus weakening your position. Then you look down, speak weakly and softly, and certainly don't say what is important to you. You let the other person carry the topic.

 (You will note that much, perhaps most, of assertiveness training involves altering some aspect of the client's four basic dimensions of attention. Almost inevitably, your client will benefit from learning new patterns of eye contact, body language, vocal qualities, and verbal tracking. These dimensions, well known to you, underlie many goals and aspects of assertiveness training—but there is more, of course.)

Jane: It makes me very discouraged and tired.

Counselor: (ignores emotions) But, Jane, let us not forget that you are doing several things right. What are they?

Jane: It all seems pretty bad to me.

Counselor: First, the principal said you were doing a good job at school . . . you've apparently done a lot there. He wouldn't have selected you for this job if you weren't effective. And, you couldn't do those things so well if parts of you weren't assertive. Right?

 (Here we see elements of the positive asset search. Clients grow from strengths, and Jane has obvious abilities. If your clients know that you respect what they *can* do, they have a greater strength and potential for attacking their problems.)

Jane: (brightens up, smiles more hopefully) I hadn't thought of it that way. I guess I can do *some* things.

Stage 3: Determining outcomes

(A concrete example of Jane's problem has been presented, with behavioral specifics that can be seen directly and even measured. Armed with an awareness of her strengths, she is now able to set up some specific goals for change.)

Counselor: Given what's going on, Jane, what are some specific goals and behaviors you might want to change the next time we try that role-play?

Jane: Well, I'd like to smile less and talk more.

Counselor: And what about more direct eye contact and a louder, stronger voice?

(The interview continues, and Jane and the counselor work out specific goals for change in her interview with the principal. They focus on some dimensions of her attending behavior mentioned above—less smiling, for example—and Jane assertively saying no.)

Stage 4: Exploring alternatives/confronting incongruity

Counselor: To summarize where we are, Jane, in the past and in this interview with the principal, you gave in—and giving in is represented by smiling, looking down, and letting the other person take charge of the topic. On the other hand, your goal is to change these behaviors and take more control of your daily life. Does that sum it up?

(This is the classic confrontation statement, useful at the beginning of the fourth stage of the interview. The client's problem or past behavior is contrasted with the goal behavior. The discrepancy between the two is the issue to be resolved in this stage. At this point, the counselor is demonstrating Level-4 empathy—see Chapter 7—in that he has summarized the client's problem clearly for her—something that had not been done before and that hence may be termed additive empathy. In terms of the Confrontation Impact Scale, the goal for Jane will probably be a Level-5 resolution response: the creation of something new, change, and development.)

Jane: Yeah, that seems to sum it up. What next?

Counselor: Well, what we do next is another practice role-play, and we continue that until you demonstrate assertiveness with me in the situation. . . . That may take several practice sessions or it might be accomplished today. Regardless, what you take home to the school, and to your kids and Bo, is far more important than what happens here. We'll work together until you master these skills and are getting what you want. Okay, let's try another role-play. (The role-play starts.) Jane, I'd like you to take over the new drug program. The parents want your involvement.

Jane: Harry, that sounds great. I wish I could, but I have got so many things going right now, and the kids need me to drive them places. (Her vocal qualities are strong, but her eye contact is still poor.)

Counselor: I can understand that. It's the ones who are busiest that you always ask. You can do it . . . you've done great workshops on drugs, and it fits with your good work in physical education.

Jane: (more weakly) No, I don't think I can. I don't want to . . . Nuts! There, you can see what I do!

Counselor: Well, Jane, it was better. You did speak up stronger, and I liked the way you came up with reasons. We'll continue practicing.

(Jane and the counselor continue to practice via role-play and discussion. Gradually, Jane gets stronger and demonstrates an assertive no. This represents resolution of the discrepancy between where she was when she started—the "problem"—and where she wanted to go—"the goal or outcome." She has reached a full Level-5 response on the CIS. There are some "buts" to this rating, however, as you will see in Stage 5.)

Stage 5: Generalization and transfer of learning

Learning in the laboratory of the interview may appear to result in developmental change; however, real change only occurs in life, after the interview. Many of your clients will show considerable promise for change in the interview and then continue to behave and think in old patterns after the interview is over. Homework, planned transfer, and prevention of relapse (Marlatt & Gordon, 1985; Marx, 1982) are critical parts of effective change. In the following exchange, the counselor introduces Jane to relapse prevention, a systematic framework to help prevent loss of learning from the counseling session.

If you fail to include generalization and transfer of learning from your helping sessions, regardless of your theoretical decisions you will find that much of your work in helping is of little avail.

Counselor: Well, this is the time, Jane, that is perhaps most important in our interview. You've certainly demonstrated that you can be more assertive and say no. The big question is whether or not you can generalize this to your principal and start taking charge of your own life.

Jane: Yes, and I want to do it with my kids, with some of my students, and with Bo. Everyone is running all over me.

Counselor: Generally speaking, it is best to focus on one behavioral change at a time. After you have succeeded with one, you'll find the others will follow. Now, I'd like to go over the Relapse Prevention Worksheet with you. This is a way to give you some homework to ensure that you will continue to be more assertive.

The counselor hands Jane the worksheet (see Box 13-1). They work through it together, giving special emphasis to things that may come up to prevent Jane from being assertive. Research and clinical experience in counseling both reveal that this may be the most important thing you can do with clients: help them ensure that they actually do *do* something different as a result of their experience in the interview. The interview closes . . .

Counselor: Well, Jane, we've made good progress today. You've demonstrated that you can be assertive with a little practice. The big test will come tomorrow, with Harry. I'm sure you will maintain strong eye contact and vocal tone and will remember your very good reasons for saying no. We'll meet next week to see how it went.

Box 13-1. Relapse Prevention Worksheet: Self-Management Strategies for Skill Retention[1]

I. Choosing an appropriate behavior to retain

Describe in detail the behavior you intend to retain:

_____

_____

How often will you use it? _____

How will you know when a slip occurs? _____

_____

II. Relapse prevention strategies

A. Strategies to help you anticipate and monitor potential difficulties: regulating stimuli.

Strategy	Assessing Your Situation
1. Do you understand the relapse process? What is it?	_____
2. What are the differences between learning the behavioral skill or thought and using it in a difficult situation?	_____
3. Support network? Who can help you maintain the skill?	_____
4. High-risk situations? What kind of people, places, or things will make retention especially difficult?	_____

B. Strategies to increase rational thinking: regulating thoughts and feelings.

5. What might be an unreasonable emotional response to a temporary slip or relapse?	_____
6. What can you do to think more effectively in tempting situations or after a relapse?	_____

C. Strategies to diagnose and practice related support skills: regulating behaviors.

7. What additional support skills do you need to retain the skill? Assertiveness? Relaxation? Microskills?	_____

(continued)

Box 13-1 (continued)

D. Strategies to provide appropriate outcomes for behaviors: regulating consequences.

8. Can you identify some probable outcomes of succeeding with your new behavior?

9. How can you reward yourself for a job well done? Generate specific rewards and satisfactions.

_____

_____

_____

_____

_____

Predicting the circumstance of the first lapse

Describe the details of how the first lapse might occur, including people, places, times, and emotional states. This will be helpful to you in coping with the relapse when and if it comes.

---

[1]Permission to use this adaptation of the Relapse Prevention Worksheet was given by Robert Marx.

▲ Summary

Assertiveness training is simply one of many behavioral techniques that you may find useful for your clients. Remember: there are more theories available in the marketplace for you to consider. The earlier sessions and the assertiveness-training section have now offered you three basic approaches to helping others make decisions, find their own direction, and live their lives more in accordance with their own wishes. If you have attempted to work with the ideas in Table 13-2 and with other key practice exercises before that, you can now (1) take your clients through a complete interview using only listening skills; (2) conduct a basic decision-making interview; and (3) provide your clients with assertiveness skills to help them act on their own decisions. It is hoped that you will use these experiences as you continue to expand and develop your own conceptions of helping in the future.

▲ Exercises Leading toward the Future

This chapter has already presented you with exercises and experiences to help you bring together the concepts of this book and to suggest paths leading to the future. Particularly important exercises from this book are the following:

1. Summarizing your own mastery of the 28 major concepts of this book (Table 13-1)
2. Participating in working through a vocational decisional interview (Table 12-3)
3. Completing a session using only listening skills (Chapter 7)
4. Conducting an assertiveness-training session including completing a Relapse Prevention Worksheet
5. Writing your own plans for development and generating your own formulations of counseling theory and practice (Box 13-3)

The apex, the top of the microskills hierarchy, has been achieved. However, it is *you* who must be on top of things and make your own decisions about your favored style and theory. Box 13-3, which ends this book, provides you with an opportunity to further search for your own concepts of helping.

▲ References

Alberti, R., & Emmons, M. (1970). *Your perfect right.* San Luis Obispo, Calif.: Impact.

Ivey, A. (1986). *Developmental therapy: Theory into practice.* San Francisco: Jossey-Bass.

Ivey, A. (1973). Media therapy: Educational change planning for psychiatric patients. *Journal of Counseling Psychology, 20,* 338–343.

Ivey, A., Ivey, M., & Simek-Downing, L. (1987). *Counseling and psychotherapy: Integrating skills, theory, and practice.* Englewood Cliffs, N.J.: Prentice-Hall.

Larson, D. (Ed.). (1984). *Teaching psychological skills: Models for giving psychology away.* (1984). Monterey, Calif.: Brooks/Cole.

Marlatt, A., & Gordon, J. (Eds.). (1985). *Relapse prevention: Maintenance strategies in the treatment of addictive behaviors.* New York: Guilford.

Marx, R. (1982). Relapse prevention for managerial training: A model for maintenance of behavior change. *Academy of Management Review, 7,* 433–441.

Perls, F. (1969). *Gestalt therapy verbatim.* Moab, Utah: Real People Press.

Box 13-2.   Key Points

Personal style and awareness of the client	Your arrival at the top of the microskills hierarchy means it's time to reflect, examine your own style, consider your own unique methods and strategies for working with clients, and think about your future development as an interviewer, counselor, or therapist. This closing chapter suggests that you spend considerable time determining your own natural style. However, clients also have a natural style of being; you will want to assess and respect their styles as well. You may decide to operate from a single theoretical orientation or you may decide to offer your clients an array of skills, strategies, and theories. It is critical that you be aware of and respect both yourself and your clients as you develop a natural, integrated style of helping.
Mastery of the microskills hierarchy	See Table 13-1 for a summary of the many skills and concepts of this book. It is hoped that you will complete this table as part of your developing awareness of your skills and knowledge. Furthermore, the table can provide helpful insights into where you might want to go next in your development of skill mastery.
Alternative theories of helping	This book is designed to equip you to complete three types of interviews, derived from Rogerian or person-centered, decisional, and behavioral theories. If you complete the practice exercises in interviewing, you will be able to conduct an interview using only listening skills (person-centered), a basic decisional model, and assertiveness training (behavioral). Furthermore, with an understanding of skills and the decisional structure, you will be able to engage other theories more directly and analyze how they function for client benefit. This chapter has also specifically shown how the BLS might be used differently with the same client, depending on the theoretical orientation of the counselor.
Assertiveness training	One of the most effective coaching/concrete operational modes of assisting your client to develop is that of assertiveness training. A transcript of an assertiveness-training interview was presented in this chapter. It is suggested you use Table 13-2 as a set of guidelines for practicing assertiveness training.

Box 13-3.   Steps toward Determining Your Own Theory of Helping

	You will find it helpful to write your answers to the following questions as you develop your unique approach to interviewing, counseling, or therapy.
Goals	What do you want to happen to and for your clients as a result of their working with you? What would you *desire* for them?
Skills and strategies	What skills and strategies do you feel you have to offer clients who come to you? Which would you like to develop in the near future?
Cultural intentionality	With what cultural groups and special populations do you feel capable of working? What knowledge do you need to gain in the future? Are you able to observe and sense the ever-present possibility of cultural and individual differences and continue to learn in this area?
Counseling and interviewing style	Four broad types of interviewing style were presented in Chapter 8. Which style feels most compatible with you and your life experience? Given that your basic style may not match the developmental needs of all your possible clients, can you work in other styles of helping as well?
Theory	The next step in putting together a fully integrated position is becoming aware of theory, which informs and guides your practice. A theory provides a rationale for your behavior in the interview. It can serve as a guide when things get difficult and provide you with ideas to help many different types of people. This book has discussed several theories informally, although it is not a theory text. At the same time, it may be considered meta-theoretical, or a broad, general theory about other theories, since the concepts here underlie many. Given what you have learned from this book, your past experience, and what you have heard from others, what theory and/or theories appeal to you most and where would you like to head next?
	The next step is yours—good luck!

Teaching Interviewing Skills

How can teaching interviewing skills help you and your clients?

The skills of intentional interviewing apply in many settings:

Counseling	Corrections	Communication in general
Interviewing	Social work	Parenting
Psychotherapy	Police work	Patient/client training
Management	Community agencies	Family education
Medicine	Teaching	Social skills training
Nursing	Administration	Individual communication

Teaching interviewing skills to others serves many functions:

Major functions

▲ To share important dimensions of interviewing with other interviewing trainees
▲ To share important dimensions of communication with clients and people in general

Secondary functions

▲ To help you learn how to manage workshops, short training programs, and longer courses of training
▲ To increase your understanding of the microskills and interviewing process through teaching others specific skills
▲ To give you experience and confidence in a newly developing role of professional interviewers—that of psychological educator, teaching basic skills to clients and groups

---

▲ Introduction

All professional groups—from accountants to park service workers to physicians—use the basic interviewing skills of this book in some fashion. However, the skills of interviewing are too important to be kept within strictly professional boundaries. *A critical present and future role of the intentional interviewer is to impart the skills of interviewing to other people.*

Interviewers and counselors are becoming *psychological educators.* Psychological educators teach skills and concepts of effective communication, values clarification, self-development, career planning, and other life skills to a wide variety of client populations (Dinkmeyer & McKay, 1976; Goldstein, 1973; Gordon, 1970; Guerney, 1977; Ivey & Alschuler, 1973). Perhaps the clearest and most definitive statement about the role of psychological education, or *psychoeducation,* is the following:

The psychoeducational model, therefore, views the role of the psychological practitioner not in terms of abnormality (or illness) → diagnosis → prescription → therapy → cure; but rather, in terms of client dissatisfaction (or ambition) → goal-setting → skill teaching → satisfaction (or goal achievement). Likewise, the client is viewed as a pupil rather than as a patient. [Authier et al., 1975, p. 15]

Thus, two roles for you as an interviewer are suggested: (1) teaching what you are learning and have learned to others interested in interviewing, and (2) sharing those skills with your clients and with people in general. When you teach professional and lay groups interviewing skills, you will want to use methods similar to those used in this book. The same principles hold for working with clients, but you will require individual adaptations for your clients' immediate needs.

▲ Instructional Reading

Where to Start in Teaching Interviewing Skills

Mastery in teaching interviewing skills is best developed through the following sequence:

1. Teaching one person. Teach a classmate, a family member, or another interested and willing person what you have learned in your own way. For example, perhaps you have found the use of open questions interesting and helpful. Simply tell the other person what you have learned in your own words and then conduct a brief practice session in which you serve as the role-played client and the other person serves as the interviewer. This informal approach seems to work best as a starting point. You use your own natural teaching skills, you start from a point of interest to you, and you are not confined to any special process. Later, you will find that this method is often the best way to apply teaching skills to your own clients in the interview.

2. Teaching a small group. After you have taught one or more persons several skills, you may want to test your ability to teach a small practice group of three to eight members. At this point you'll find the basic teaching model outlined in the next section helpful: (1) warm-up and introduction to the skill; (2) example of the skill in operation; (3) reading; (4) practice; and (5) self-assessment and generalization.

3. Teaching larger groups. As you gain experience, you can teach these skills to larger groups—up to 200 people. In large workshops and courses it is important to design time schedules, space arrangements, and equipment especially carefully.

4. Teaching clients. The methods for teaching clients are the same as those for teaching other nonprofessional and professional interviewers. If you find a client who can profit from one or more interviewing skills in the course of your sessions (for example, a client who might need more effective questioning and self-disclosure skills for a job interview), use the same informal procedures as are suggested for teaching one person. You'll also find client groups who can profit from regular, systematic practice in interviewing skills (for instance, a group of high school students taking a speech development course, or a group of psychiatric outpatients). With such groups the procedures used in this book have been found effective. However, interviewing skills are redefined as communication skills, and only those skills that meet the needs of the particular group are used. For example, most such groups find attending behavior, questions, and the other skills of the basic listening sequence particularly helpful. Skills such as reflection of meaning, interpretation, and logical consequences generally are less relevant.

The Basic Microskills Teaching Model

The model you have experienced in this book has been developed and tested over 22 years of clinical work and research and has been found to be most effective. However, each teacher of skills must redefine the model to meet personal beliefs and needs, both for self-satisfaction and for varying trainee interests. It is your responsibility to shape and adapt the basic model. Use the model as a guideline, but add your own variations! Here are the five steps of the model:

Step 1. Warm-up and introduction to the skill.   If you are teaching attending behavior, for example, introduce the concept briefly and provide a personalized exercise that produces involvement and demonstrates the need for the skill. What can learning this skill do for your trainee(s)?

Step 2. Example of the skill in action.   It is best if you present video, audio, or live demonstrations of the skill. A second choice is to ask your trainee(s) to read the appropriate transcript in this book and then to follow the reading with a discussion. You'll find trainee involvement and interest higher with a live or video model of the skill.

Step 3. Reading.   Each skill chapter ends with a "Key Points" box outlining the most important aspects of each skill. People have different learning styles. It is helpful to ask your trainees to read these short sections in the training sessions, as they provide clear examples and descriptions of what is being taught. It also provides them with "alone time" to reflect on their learning.

Step 4. Practice.   The most important part of the entire microskills training framework is practicing the skill. Use the seven steps for practice outlined in "Systematic Group Practice" in each chapter. It is possible to "walk through" skill practice and not have demonstrated real mastery. The levels of identification, basic and active mastery, will provide you with clues to how much more practice your trainees need. Teaching mastery will be helpful for those who wish to share these skills with clients and others.

Step 5. Self-assessment and generalization.   If your trainees have mastered a skill to a sufficient level, work with them to plan for generalization beyond the practice session role-play. If a trainee has not yet mastered the skill, return to Step 1. You may wish to use individual practice exercises and self-assessment concepts to facilitate generalization of the skills you have taught. You also may want to use the feedback form at the end of this Appendix to obtain information from your trainees on your own work as teacher.

Again, this is the basic instructional model; you must shape and adapt it to meet the needs of your particular individual or group. Following are some general planning considerations for most skill-teaching situations.

Planning for Teaching Skills

Teaching interviewing skills can be facilitated by considering ahead of time a few basic dimensions of effective workshop development. Keep the following important issues in mind as you plan, and outline a plan of action and time schedule for your program *before* you start.

Consider your trainee(s).   How experienced is the individual or group? If you are working with beginners, simple, direct language is most effective. You might think that the concepts of the early part of the book are too simple for more experienced people. However, if the mastery goals are emphasized clearly, even highly experienced professionals find themselves engaged and highly involved in the training. It is also important to provide examples relevant to each group. In working with correctional officers, for example, be sure that the demonstration, discussion of the skill, and practice sessions fit their interests and needs; a school counseling practice session would be irrelevant to them. Develop your training program considering the place and needs of the group.

Setting.   The location should be attractive, clean, and relatively organized. Movable chairs and a comfortable rug can make a workshop or training session much more pleasant.

Practice space.   Ideally, seek to have separate practice rooms for each group of four people. As this is not usually practical when working with larger groups, you should plan to provide as much room and privacy as possible. On the other hand, there is some benefit from the excitement and general noise of a larger group working in a comfortable, large room.

Equipment.   In the ideal training session you will have a closed-circuit video system for each group. As a second option, each group of four should have access to an audiorecorder. For practice outside the group, it is strongly urged that each trainee have a recorder. However, it is possible to run workshops without any equipment and to rely on Observers 1 and 2 alone.

Breaks.   As a trainer and teacher of skills, you'll find the workshop and training energizing. Remember, however, that your group often finds the new concepts and methods difficult and tiring. Provide adequate break time and refreshments insofar as possible.

Group size and timing.   With one person you'll find that a training plan can be flexible and meet the needs of the individual. With larger groups a carefully planned schedule will save time, avoid confusion, and enable you to teach more with more trainee satisfaction. *As groups get larger, you cannot overplan!*

Getting acquainted.   As a group starts, be sure that you have provided some information or formal way for people to get to know one another and feel more comfortable in the group. This can take the form of name games and group exercises, or it can be as simple as having each person introduce himself or herself. Taking time early in the meeting to let the group know the location of telephones and bathrooms, and the schedule can save you all time later on. Allow an opportunity for the group to raise any questions about the program before you start. Those questions will come out later if they are not answered at the beginning. Starting with them will indicate to the group your interest and willingness to explore their needs.

Eliciting group expectations.   Many training sessions go down in flames because the trainer did not ask the group what their special needs and interests were. Begin a course or workshop by dividing into groups of four or six and asking the trainees to brainstorm their special needs, wishes, expectations, and desires for the training. These expectations can be shared in the group, and you as leader can respond to them. It is useful to post them on a chalkboard or on newsprint on the wall and refer to the group's needs periodically throughout the training.

Reading material.   It is helpful to have a copy of the interview skill training book for each trainee. This provides them with feedback forms, the reading material, and the individual practice exercises. You'll also find the systematic steps for group practice helpful.

Practice sessions.   Before groups break up into small groups for practice, go through the seven steps for systematic practice carefully. The steps seem clear, but most groups get lost at first. Take extra time here!

Resistance.   In most training sessions you'll run into one or more individuals who clearly resist training and the ideas you are trying to share. A basic rule is "Go with the resistance!" Do not fight or argue with the person challenging you or the concept. Point out that this is simply one alternative for teaching the structure of the interview, and not everyone will find it the most comfortable option. A useful method many effective trainers use when resistance appears is to step forward, smile, and lean toward the person, saying "That's an interesting and important point." Follow this by a direct answer in a nondefensive manner. After you have answered the challenge, *do not* look at the person who asked the question; look at the group. Looking at the person who asked the question often prompts further questions and may leave the rest of the group bored and uninterested.

Questions from the group.   This is an extension of the above point. As a group develops, you'll find that certain individuals gradually dominate. If you observe the others carefully, you'll note that they gradually lose interest when the dominating people ask questions. Again, *do not* look at the person asking the question; look to the group while answering. This involves the rest of the group more fully. If necessary, set up a rule that any one individual may ask only two questions per session. This is important for the well-being and satisfaction of your group.

Cultural differences.   The concepts of this book are drawn from typical White, middle-class helping patterns *and* from extensive work in other cultures. Experience has revealed that the microskills are highly workable in cultures as diverse as Eskimo and Inuit populations in the Arctic, aboriginal Australians, Swedish migrant populations, German management officials, and Native American and Black groups in this country. The models and examples (and skills, in some cases) must be adapted to meet the needs and practices of the particular cultural group. One useful exercise is to involve your group in developing training materials that are culturally relevant to their needs. Start with the basic model and encourage them in practice sessions to adapt the concepts for their own setting.

Ethics.   General rules of effective interviewing and counseling ethics should apply. With groups that are going to move into extensive discussion of personal issues, spend time at the beginning with the ethical statements of the American Association of Counseling and Development and the American Psychological Association. When taping an interview, always begin the interview with the question "Do you mind if I tape this session?" If the real or role-played client wishes the tape to stop, immediately turn off the machine. If clients wish the tape to be erased, let them observe the erasure.

Sensible limits of confidentiality are suggested. There are no real legal protections for confidentiality in this type of training, and the group needs to be reminded of this fact. Nevertheless, what goes on in the group belongs to the group and not to the public. A professional helper should be available for support and consultation should referral become necessary. One good approach is to start longer periods of training with a discussion of general ethics. The group can develop their own safeguards and a systematic list of agreed-on standards before they begin training.

At the same time, too much emphasis on possible problems can produce the very problems you are trying to prevent. Among thousands of individuals trained with this program, only an extremely small minority has had any problems with the framework. Those trainees who seem to require more caution can either leave the training or role-play standard roles. If you are relaxed and expect cooperation and ethical standards, you'll receive what you expect. If you are anxious and waver, anticipate difficulty! This is one reason you are urged to begin your training of others with only one other person.

Designing a training session, workshop, or course.   Once again, change the suggestions here to fit your and the group's needs!

Mastery Levels

Four levels of mastery are used in this book:

Level 1: Identification.   You will be able to identify the skill and the impact of the skill on the client.

Level 2: Basic mastery.   You will be able to use the skill in the role-played interview.

Level 3: Active mastery.   You will be able to use the skill with specific impact on the client.

Level 4: Teaching mastery.   You will be able to teach the skill to clients and other trainees.

Experience has shown that too many people going through interviewing training stop at the basic mastery level. This level demands that the interviewer simply use the skill (paraphrase, question, interpretation, and so on) in the interview. The use can be of relatively low quality or high quality, but little attention may be given to its impact on the client.

Active mastery demands the intentional ability to use the skill for client benefit and to change client conversational flow at will. Active mastery takes time and more practice than is available in the teaching sessions discussed here. In basic mastery the emphasis is on the interviewer, and goals can be easily accomplished. In active mastery, by contrast, the emphasis is on the client—what does the counselor or interviewer do to produce specific effects on client conversational flow? Special attention must be given to ensure that full mastery of the concepts occurs. Suggestions for encouraging active mastery are to be found in the Instructor's Manual accompanying this book.

The teaching sessions presented here aim for basic mastery, though some competent trainees will be able to develop active-mastery levels. For one person, simply asking an open question is an accomplishment. For another, the higher mastery required to use open and closed questions to speed and to slow the pace of an interview will be a more interesting and challenging assignment. Use the self-assessment forms at the end of each chapter to verify what levels of mastery your trainees have actually achieved.

Teaching Interviewing Skills Feedback Sheet

_____ (Date)

_____   _____
(Name of Interviewer)   (Name of Person Completing Form)

Instructions: Provide your trainer with feedback on the effectiveness of her or his teaching procedures. Be
as specific as possible.

1. What are you able to do differently or more effectively as a result of the training you just went through?
The most important outcome of effective interviewing training is development of your own skills.

2. Rate the following dimensions commonly included in training. Rate, numerically, the phase most helpful
to you, the next most helpful, and so on.

_____ Warm-up and general introduction to the skill or concept
_____ Audiotape/reading of interview transcript/videotape/film
_____ Instructional reading about skill or concept
_____ Practice with the skill
_____ Exercises in generalization of the skill to new settings, and self-assessment

3. Name one specific thing the trainer did that was significant to your learning. Describe it clearly.

4. Name one specific thing the trainer could have added that would have been helpful to your learning.
Describe it clearly.

5. Provide other comments you may have.

▲ References

Authier, J., Gustafson, K., Guerney, B., Jr., & Kasdorf, J. (1975). The psychological practitioner as a teacher: A theoretical-historical and practical review. *The Counseling Psychologist, 5,* 31–50.

Dinkmeyer, D., & McKay, G. (1976). *Systematic training for effective parenting (STEP).* Circle Pines, Minn.: American Guidance Service.

Goldstein, A. (1973). *Structured learning therapy: Toward a psychotherapy for the poor.* New York: Academic Press.

Gordon, T. (1970) *Parent effectiveness training.* New York: Wyden.

Guerney, B., Jr. (1977). *Relationship enhancement: Skill training programs for therapy, problem prevention, and enrichment.* San Francisco: Jossey-Bass.

Ivey, A., & Alschuler, A. (Eds.) (1973). Psychological education. Special issue of *Personnel and Guidance Journal, 51.*

Name Index

Subject Index

To the owner of this book:

I hope that you have enjoyed *Intentional Interviewing and Counseling* (Second Edition) as much as I enjoyed writing it. I'd like to know as much about your experiences with the book as you care to offer. Only through your comments and the comments of others can I learn how to make this a better book for future readers.

Your School: _____

Your Instructor's Name: _____

1. What did you like *most* about *Intentional Interviewing and Counseling?* _____

_____

_____

2. What did you like *least* about the book? _____

_____

3. Were all of the chapters of the book assigned for you to read? _____

4. What material do you think could be omitted in future editions? _____

_____

_____

5. In the space below or in a separate letter, please let me know any other comments about the book you'd like to make. (For example, were any chapters or concepts particularly difficult?) Please recommend specific changes you'd like to see in future editions. I'd be delighted to hear from you!

Optional

Your name: _____ Date: _____

May Brooks/Cole quote you, either in promotion for *Intentional Interviewing and Counseling* or in future publishing ventures? Yes _____ No _____

Sincerely,

Allen Ivey

CUT OUT PAGE AND FOLD HERE

NO POSTAGE
NECESSARY
IF MAILED
IN THE
UNITED STATES

BUSINESS REPLY MAIL

FIRST CLASS   PERMIT NO. 358   PACIFIC GROVE, CA

POSTAGE WILL BE PAID BY ADDRESSEE

ATT: *Allen Ivey*

Brooks/Cole Publishing Company
511 Forest Lodge Road
Pacific Grove, California 93950-9968

FOLD HERE